the home gu
DECORATING

the home guide to
DECORATING

Vinny Lee

Projects devised and written by Jane Davies

Photography by Ray Main and Graeme Ainscough

bay books

Contents

c o n t e n t s

Introduction

This book is an informative and illustrated guide to all aspects of decorating your home, introducing the basics, such as planning your decorative scheme, explaining the main techniques that you may need, and providing you with ideas and inspiration for every room. Armed with this book and a little imagination, you can create the interior that you have always longed for.

A changing world

Interest in decorating has become increasingly popular recently, due to changes in both the approach to our home lives and in our response to personal environments. Where colors were once dictated by what was available in the local stores or by a limited palette of standard shades produced by a few commercial paint manufacturers, it seems now that the sky is the limit. For example, paint colors can be blended to match fabrics exactly and created à la carte to suit your whims and wishes.

Available to all

Inspired by TV programs and magazine features, the increasing home-improvement market has brought the once secretive world of the professional decorator, painter, carpenter, and other specialists out into the open. Large supermarket-style stores offer everything, from light fixtures to kitchen sinks, and from wallpaper borders to bed throws, direct to the public. Items that were once bought through trade stores, or had to be specially made to measure, are now available instantly.

As decorating has become such a readily accessible activity there is a growing need for good, basic information about how to create a decorating scheme, on elementary techniques, and tips of the trade, so that the enthusiastic layperson can get to grips with the terminology and practical aspects of decorating. Because technology and advancements in paints and other finishes mean that there is an increasingly wide range of products to choose from, it can be difficult to know where to start, so a little guidance is useful when making your selection.

Using this book

It is important to get the basics right, to do the groundwork, and to accumulate some knowledge about what is involved and how to go about a project. In this book,

Above: It is important to think about how functional and decorative objects will work together in an overall scheme as you plan.

Opposite: This contemporary interior has white walls, but set against them are strong accent colors used in the sofa and accessories, such as cushions and even paintings. The wooden floor also adds a touch of warmth.

we look at the basics of decorating the home before moving on to the dressing and styling of each room. This is accompanied by a variety of inspiring projects to recreate. These vary in difficulty and size so that there is something for everyone to tackle, from the cautious starter to the more confident, advanced decorator. Written in an easy-to-follow manner, they incorporate clear, step-by-step photographs. We also look at where to find inspiration and how to build up sample boards. Building up a scheme should be an exciting and creative experience and an opportunity to learn how to focus your taste and what suits your lifestyle.

This book is aimed at all enthusiasts, for those in permanent or temporary accommodation, in large or small homes, and in urban or rural settings. It is a practical and informative guide to making the most of your own space as well as an inspirational book that will show you how to create your own style.

Creating your own
environment

Tailoring your surroundings to suit the layout, style, and shape of the building, as well as your personal tastes, is what makes a house into a home. Home is a fixed residence, a place where you return to—it is familiar, and should be designed to accommodate your needs and requirements.

Finding your own style

Because of the increasing choice of materials available to us it is now easier to tailor our environment to our own individual taste. As such, your home and the way it is decorated says a lot about you. Some may decorate in an aspirational classic period style, some may opt for a look that is practical and easy to live with, while others may choose to follow a fashion or trend.

The most important thing is to create a space that you are comfortable living in. There are strong, fashionable trends that hit the headlines and make the pages of leading interior magazines, which may have an influence on the interiors market for a time, but they may not be right for you. Although a particular look may appeal, you may have to dilute or adapt it to suit your lifestyle.

For example, the minimalist style of the work of the architect

Claudio Silvestrin, a master of the spiritually clean environment, is a purist's dream. His interiors are almost monastic, made up mainly of white and linear spaces, but Silvestrin happily admits that his look is not for everyone—you have to be disciplined to live with it and appreciate the thought that goes in to achieving the balance of space and light.

But you can admire the perfection of Silvestrin's work without having to follow it slavishly. Start

with the principal features—the clean lines and beautiful shapes—and then make use of ample storage space, editing down your possessions. In time, you may find you are throwing out more and buying less, slowly becoming a follower of the minimalist regime.

You might find yourself inspired by a photograph of a fantastic house in a glossy book or magazine. The room shown would have cost a great deal of money and taken many months or even years of dedicated work to achieve—that may be way beyond your means and inclination. The key here is to think practically, analyze the photographs, and extract the elements that really appeal to you.

Ask yourself what it is that draws you to that particular room. Is it the color of the walls? The style and arrangement of the furniture? The floor covering or the aspect of the room? Once you have worked out exactly what it is, then think through whether it is a practical style for you. Will it work in your room and suit your lifestyle? Most importantly, is it just a fad that you will tire of?

Personalizing your space

French designer extraordinaire Philippe Starck once said, "It is important to inject love into the place where you live. It is not healthy to rent an interior designer to create a home for you, because it is not good to live in another person's fantasy. People should select for themselves and stamp their own identity on a place. They should mix and match everything to make their own cocktail."

When embarking on decorating your home, think about your lifestyle and how and where you live. Do you have a room in a shared house? Are there communal living areas shared by others? You might be a student with a room in a rented house, a teenage child in a family home, or own your own apartment.

The degree of personalization of a space may vary. For example, your own room may be the place where you can truly express yourself, but a shared area, such as a sitting room or dining area, may need to be a compromise scheme that works around the likes and dislikes of others who are using the space too.

In a shared room, a neutral décor may suit best, with simple wall and floor coverings that can be enlivened by accessories. In a shared kitchen or bathroom, the priority is most likely to be practicality—hardwearing easily cleaned surfaces.

Above: Glass can be used to create the illusion of space, as it is in this stunning contemporary stairwell.

Opposite: Your home should be an expression of your own style. Here, dark colors are twinned with bold accessories to create a dramatic look.

Color and
texture

Color and texture are important ingredients in the overall appearance of a room. Color helps to define the mood and ambience, and can be used to disguise or accentuate features. Texture will add highlights and interest, not just to wall surfaces, but also to furniture and accessories.

Above: This yellow vase is shown against an orange wall. Yellow and orange are compatible colors within the same "family."

Opposite top: A tone-on-tone scheme of pale yellow and white creates a subtle effect.

Opposite bottom: This heavy-texture rug provides contrast in a room that has lots of smooth surfaces.

Finding inspiration

Bringing together a color palette for a room's overall scheme will depend on the style or type of decoration that you opt for, and the key to deciding this is inspiration. You may start by finding a curtain fabric that you like, and the colors in the pattern will lead you into a scheme, or it might be a painting, a piece of furniture, or a handmade piece of craftwork that triggers your ideas.

Inspiration now comes from all over the globe. Film, television, and increased accessibility to world travel mean that the look of the sunwashed walls of an Italian villa can be recreated in a kitchen in London, and the subtle gray-blues and greens of a traditional Scandinavian home can be found in a New York apartment.

Color theory

When it comes to planning a color scheme there are various options —including choosing colors that are part of the same family (have a similar base color), colors that are opposites or tonal colors. The easiest way to see these choices is to look at a color wheel. The color wheel is like the rainbow, but the colors are laid around in a circle, rather than laterally in an arc. The primary colors—red, yellow, and blue—are the main spokes, and between them you get colors that are made up from a mix of them. This means that between red and yellow you will find a red with a hint of yellow, then a true orange, followed by yellow with a hint of red. Between yellow and blue the colors are yellow with a hint of blue, true green, and blue with a hint of yellow.

Colors that belong to the same family are these mixed ones, so red, yellow, and orange are of the same family as red, purple, and blue. Opposite or contrasting colors are those diametrically facing on the wheel, so red and green, orange and blue, yellow and violet are opposites. Tonal schemes select a single color such as red and use darker and lighter shades of it, rather than mixing with other colors.

Choosing your colors

Choosing color is very personal, and people react differently to various shades. You should, above all, choose colors that you and your family feel comfortable with.

Neutral colors have long been popular—the universally favored painter's finish, magnolia, is a standard, as are beige, soft yellows, and off-whites because they are all easy to live with and make a room look light and bright.

There is a standard decorating guideline that says that dark colors make surfaces advance and that light colors make them recede, but there are exceptions to the rule. Dark colors can be effective in making a ceiling seem farther away. Dark colors can

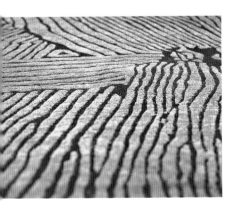

also be used to camouflage uneven surfaces.

For impact and drama, bold colors are the best. It may take time to get accustomed to rich, dark shades, so you can take it step by step. Paint one wall in a strong shade and live with it for a few weeks, or start with a base coat of a paler shade and add a top layer of the darker color later.

Tone-on-tone schemes

You could use the interior designers' trick of tone-on-tone schemes —this involves using a variety of different shades of the same color. For example, if you paint your walls in a mid-coffee brown and put a paler, light brown carpet on the floor, you can use a patterned upholstery fabric that contains

both those shades and perhaps add a deeper tone of furniture to make a stronger statement. However, take care the scheme does not look dull by using plenty of patterns and textures.

Texture

The type of finish that you choose for the walls will also influence the overall effect. A flat, chalky surface will make a dark tone seem duskier. It will absorb light making the effect a little darker. A shiny gloss surface will emphasize the depth of color and can double the impact of natural or artificial lighting.

Texture is important in the mix of materials that you use—a room full of smooth surfaces will look flat, but a few cushion covers in a knobbly chenille will add variety.

Mood boards

Mood boards are put together by professional decorators to show their clients a selection of materials, paint colors, wallpapers, trimmings, and floor coverings, so that the textures and colors can be seen together. Mood boards are a way of showing all the ingredients of the recipe before it is prepared.

A mood board is a way of gathering together elements of decorating materials so that you can see and touch them, and mix and match until you find your perfect scheme. Trying to explain to someone verbally, or imagine in your mind's eye, how colors and textures work together is almost impossible. One person will say that they are looking at a cream color, while someone else may describe it as yellow or golden. The word "fringe" can be used to describe a million different trimmings and finishes, but only one will be the right one for your lampshade or valance, so it is important to see an actual sample.

The mood board also gives you the chance to play around with various samples and see how they relate. For example, if you like a warm cream paint and have found a fabric with a similar color, then you can try them with different highlighting colors such as red or green, to see which works best for an overall palette.

Making a mood board

To construct a mood board, you need a large sheet of thick white cardboard. Start by tacking small swatches and samples to it. As you update or modify the board, remove and discard the older or replaced pieces. When you have arrived at a final selection, glue them in place so that that there is no danger of pieces falling off or being lost.

Although the board is primarily a visual guide, make sure that you keep the references of items that you attach to it, so that you have a record of the manufacturers' details.

The board is also a useful way of seeing how the colors and fabrics react in different lights. You can take it to a window and see if the colors look good together in daylight, then at night try them under an electric light to see if they are still compatible, and if any tonal alterations occur.

You should make a separate board for each room in the house—don't try and cram two or three schemes onto one board, or it will become a confusing muddle. It can also be helpful to take the board with you when you go to choose furnishing, floor covering, or other finishes, as it will give both you and the supplier or store owner a point of reference.

Items for mood boards

Some items on the board can just be temporary—for example, you may find a leaf or a candy wrapper that is just the right color for a paint or fabric you want. Keep the wrapper or leaf, and pin it to the board until you can find the paint color to match. You may also come across inspirational pictures or postcards that show a room, setting, or piece of furniture that has the right features or is an interesting shape—you can tack these to your boards to remind you of what you are looking for. Remember, inspiration is all around you.

Above: A mood board encapsulates your ideas for a decorative scheme, including your chosen colors, textures, patterns, and fabrics.

Opposite: When you have created your mood board, you can recreate the ideas for real in your home.

Style and
period

You can create your own unique style by mixing antique and modern schemes, or old and new furniture. You may choose a period design that is appropriate to the age of your home, or one you admire. Whatever elements you decide on, try to use a cohesive color and fabric scheme.

Finding your style

The past, future, or current trends can influence your decorating scheme. The building you live in may be of a certain period or style that relates to a range of colors and a certain type of furniture, and this may inspire you to echo those elements in your décor. For example, a 1950s- or

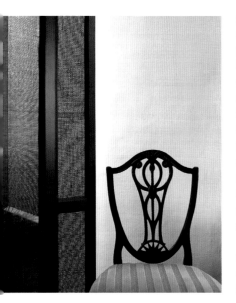

1960s-built apartment block would be the perfect setting for collectable, retro-style furniture with geometric print fabrics. An early 20th-century house may still have original features, such as plaster details and marble or plaster fireplaces—these may take you in the direction of a more classic collection of furniture and fabrics.

Even if the building in which your home is located doesn't have a tangible style, there may be periods of history or eras that you have a nostalgic feeling for or enjoy. For example, you may favor Art Deco and the Jazz Age, with its angular, boxlike furniture, champagne-tinted mirrors, and feeling of opulence and decadence. Or perhaps the Shaker style is more to your taste—restrained and wholesome, with an emphasis on craftsmanship and utility.

Oriental influences in interior style tend to be cyclical—black-and-red lacquer furnishings and Zen-style simplicity are both

currently fashionable, but during the early 1900s a more ornate Oriental style was in vogue—the fashion was for chinoiserie and richly embroidered silks, ornately painted and inlaid furniture, and large vases and painted bowls. So although the inspiration was derived from the same source, the Orient, this influence was interpreted in different ways.

Recreating period style

Tastes in style and period living vary widely too. There are those who choose to ignore totally the style of the building or apartment in which they live, and cover over cove details and block out door panels so that they are left with a blank canvas on which they can create their own individual look. Others spend a great deal of time and money trying to put back elements of the original décor of their home, searching through markets and specialist clearance warehouses to find just

Right: Timeless pieces, such as this chrome and wood table, will fit into any scheme.

Opposite page: This shieldback chair is a classic period feature.

the right period fireplace, and employ master craftspeople to copy back old plaster details.

Whichever path you choose to follow, it is important to be 100 percent behind it. If you are going to restore a place to its original period style, then do your research into the colors and fabrics that were available. For example, there is no point in using obviously synthetic fabrics, such as shiny nylon curtains, in a turn-of-the-century room, because nylon was not invented until the 1930s. Large pictorial printed fabrics featuring Chinese urns and cranes will look equally odd in a 1960s-inspired apartment.

All decorative elements, from the curtains to the carpets, wall colors, and furnishings, should be harmonious—they don't have to be from the same year, but they should have a common theme.

When recreating a certain period, start with the basics, such as paint. There are now many paint companies that specialize in historically accurate paint colors and finishes, so it should be easy

to find a period paint color. Some companies even emulate the old flat and chalk effects within their paints.

With the revival of interest in wallpaper, it is also easier to find geometric 1950s and 1960s-style prints, many of which have had a 21st-century adaptation in coloring. Today, some designers have used 1960s-style shapes in their collection of wallpapers, but using subtle, rather than garish tones—and for more fun you can find some delightful ranges that show a variety of nostalgic floral prints and mid-century cowboy designs.

An eclectic mix

For those who opt for a more eclectic and easygoing style, it is, however, simple enough to mix the old and the new together. You do not have to stick rigidly to every decorating rule in order to create a successful interior, so feel free to experiment with what you already have.

Many people inherit pieces of furniture from family and friends, or build up a collection over the years from different homes. Not all the pieces will necessarily be of the same period or style, and the background elements play an important role in bringing all these pieces together.

Seasonal living

Seasons and cycles of time bring different needs and requirements. For example, we often long to be cool in the height of summer and warm in the depths of winter—our surroundings should be arranged so that they are adaptable enough to make us comfortable with these extremes.

After the long, dark days of winter, spring is a welcome change, bringing buds, brightness, and a feeling of freshness and renewal. This is a good time to fling open windows and blow away the hibernal cobwebs. As spring turns into summer and the weather warms, flowers are abundant and succulent fruits come into season, which can add zesty freshness and color to your rooms.

Fall is a rich time of harvest and changing colors, when russet reds, bronze, and copper colors abound. As winter comes around again, we settle down to rest in our cosy homes and await the arrival of the next burst of spring.

Seasonal fabrics

In recent times the trend for replacing the summer surface dressings of a room with winter ones has become popular. This may be because soft furnishings have become less expensive and easier to buy, so there is huge choice and availability. Also, having two sets of covers spreads the wear and tear on the materials, and leaves one change free for repairs, cleaning, or washing.

If you want to change significantly the appearance of a room,

Left: Yellow is an adaptable color. It can be strong, warm, and sunny, or pale and refreshing.

start with the windows. Take down dark-colored, heavyweight winter curtains and replace them with fine pale or white cotton voiles or sheers for spring and summer. Then swap the covers on scatter cushions, from richly textured, jewel tones and ornate patterns to crisp cotton, linen, and slubbed silk in pastel shades, and light checks or prints. Finally, replace wool throws and blankets with waffle or textured cotton. You aren't changing the furnishings, just the dressings, but you will feel a really noticeable difference in your surroundings inside as the seasons change outside.

Tabard covers for bedheads and highback dining chairs are simple ways of ringing seasonal changes. Purchase rich, warm-colored covers for the winter and fall, and fresh, zesty ones for the spring and summer. Tabards also help to preserve the fitted covers underneath, and are easily removed for washing if they become stained or marked.

Seasonal changes can also give a cosmetic lift to your surroundings, creating a welcome change that echoes the cycles of nature and the landscape outside. It can also be beneficial to your health and outlook. For example, you probably change your bedding from a winterweight feather or down duvet to a light, waffle cotton blanket between winter and summer, so why not change to a linen sheet or cover during the hot months?

Reversible fabrics are useful for seasonal changes. For example, curtains with a dark side and a light side could be used with the pale side to the front in the summer and the more colorful side to the fore in the winter.

Seasonal mood changes

Removable covers also give you the opportunity to change the pace or style of your home—for example, one set of covers and soft furnishings could be classic or neutral, and the other modern or bright, so that it is not only a seasonal change but also a mood or style change as well.

Variety is the spice of life, so changing the emphasis of color and/or pattern in your home will alleviate any staleness or boredom with your surroundings. The changes don't have to be radical to have an effect.

By linking color and pattern, subtle but impressive changes can be made. Take, for example, a room with pale to mid-blue walls. For the winter, use accessories from the darker end of the spectrum, such as navy and midnight blue. Then inject warmth with mulberry and burgundy, which have a blue base note but also a warm red element. In the spring and summer, the blue could be made cooler with the addition of silver-gray, white, and icy blue accessories, to enhance the color's coldish trait.

A neutral room with white, pale cream, or beige walls offers a whole range of opportunities when it comes to seasonal accessorizing. For example, spring and summer could be a time for vivid, zesty colors such as orange, green, and lemon, but in the winter you could add the mellow tones of mink, mouse, toffee, and coffee for a snug, relaxing, and cosy environment.

Fabrics

Fabrics are either made up of natural or synthetic fibers and come in plain, self-patterned, textured, printed, or woven designs in a wide variety of weights and finishes. When choosing material for a scheme, try to visualize the overall effect it will have. If the room is otherwise plain, you can afford to indulge in a pattern at the window or on the sofa and armchairs, but if the room is full of pattern, then keep it simple and plain. Some fabrics are better for upholstery than others, so make sure that you choose a fabric of a specific upholstery weight. Cost will be another factor in your choice of fabrics. If you have large windows and you want to dress them from floor to ceiling with generously gathered curtains, then you will need to buy a large amount of fabric. This may mean that you choose a cheaper fabric. If you fall in love with an expensive fabric, limit its use to smaller areas. A little can be made to go a long way if used well—for example, you could place the fabric on a couple of scatter cushions that are strategically placed on a sofa.

Clockwise from top left:

Long-pile fabrics look luxurious but are more suitable for cushions and small areas, rather than larger upholstery requirements.

Trimmings and braids can lift and embellish a plain cushion or curtain—these small glass beads add to the opulence of the shiny cushion cover.

The fabrics that you choose will have a lasting effect on the overall feel of a room. This sheer devoré velvet will add a sense of romance wherever it is placed.

Sheer voile is an effective window dressing because it lets plenty of light into the room.

A blanket does not need to be monochrome—here, the blanket is a rich mix of blue, brown, and cream colors.

For curtains and shades, choose materials that are soft and drape well. A stiff or rigid fabric will hang awkwardly in lumps and ridges, rather than soft furls and pleats.

Try using rich velvets and chenilles on throws and cushions to add a feeling of luxury to a room.

Vivid colors and geometric patterns can be used on rugs to create a truly dramatic floor area.

Thick chenille like this is well-suited to all general upholstery needs.

Fun fur is often made from synthetic fibers, and should carry a flame-retardant label to make sure of its safe use.

Loose-weave fabrics, like this open configuration in mohair, is decorative rather than practical and may be used as a throw over the back of a chair or sofa, or as a wall hanging.

Intricately woven, patterned fabrics with no surface pile or loops are good for upholstery and curtains.

Light, colorful materials with fresh, summery prints can help to lift a dark room where natural light is restricted.

Classic patterns, such as this check, never seem to decline in popularity.

Planning your home

Before you start work on a new property or alterations to an existing home, take time to plan and discuss your aims. Ask yourself what you want, and how best this can be achieved—it is easier and less costly to spend more time and effort on planning, than to rush in and make errors that will need to be fixed later.

Above: Your plan can showcase items of special interest.

Opposite: Before decoration, draw a plan featuring built-in items, such as fireplaces and alcoves, and furniture, such as tables and chairs.

Drawing out your plan

The first thing to do when planning decoration is to look at the overall layout of your home. Write down a list of functions that take place in each room—if it is a studio apartment or includes a home office-cum-spare room, you will need to combine several functions in one place and devise a scheme that will work around the various activities. If you have a larger home, there will be rooms that have only a single purpose, and the decoration can be focused on that single activity.

Once you have made a list of functions, work out the allocation of space. Even within a sole-purpose room you will need to define areas for storage and larger pieces of furniture. Draw a room plan to scale on squared paper with a pencil, and put in the features and immovable objects, such as windows, doors, fireplaces, and chimney breasts.

When you are happy with the plan, ink in the outline with a permanent marker or pen.

Once the room plan is finished, make small, scaled cutouts of the larger, movable pieces of furniture, such as bookcases, sofas, and beds. Place these on the floor plan of the room and move them around until you think you have the right configuration. It is much easier to move small pieces of paper around than to lift and shift heavy furniture in situ.

Planning each room

There is a logical procedure for laying out furniture. Think of the way the room is used—imagine walking into it and carrying out the activity appropriate to the space, such as working, bathing, or cooking. For example, in a study area the desk should be near the phone and light receptacles, and by a window to use natural light.

In a bedroom, try to keep electrical appliances to a minimum, and avoid keeping computers and work items here. If you have a studio apartment, place a screen or mobile wall in front of the work area to create a barrier between the sleeping and working parts of the room.

Kitchens and bathrooms are usually located according to the layout of waste and water pipes, which will be placed so that they connect with main sewers and drains. In some homes, these rooms become dual-purpose due to their size. For example, if you have a small kitchen and a large bathroom, consider putting the clothes washer in the bathroom. If the bathroom is small but drying space is needed, place a retractable drying line over the tub.

In a large bathroom, you may want to keep a yoga or exercise mat and light weights or a tape and player so that you can do keep-fit or exercise routines. If so, storage for these items will also have to be allotted in your plan.

The kitchen is increasingly becoming the main living area of the home, with open-plan dining and seating areas joining up with the cooking space. When planning an area like this, keep certain constraints in mind. The kitchen sink or main section of worktop is best placed by a window so that most of the natural light will be focused on one of the primary working areas.

Include a barrier between the kitchen and dining areas—this is especially useful in households where there are young children. A breakfast bar or similar mid-height divide will enable someone in the kitchen to keep an eye on small children playing nearby, but can also form a protective barrier that will make it easier to confine children to a safe distance away from the heat and dangers of the kitchen (see box, page 293).

Decoration of the utility areas, such as bathrooms and kitchens, usually centers on the need for durable and waterproof materials. Both rooms require good ventilation, but the surfaces and materials used within the space should also be easy to clean. Ceramic tiles have long been the favored surface behind sinks, but now tempered glass, stainless steel, and cement are often used.

Bathrooms, shower stalls, wet rooms, and separate toilets are sometimes windowless, dark, and boxlike, so a decorative scheme should counteract this by making the place appear light, colorful, and spacious.

Making the most of natural light

According to Oriental traditions, you should wake facing the sunrise and go to sleep in the direction of the sunset. Orientating your home on this axis has many practical elements in that you start the day and spend the morning in rooms that make the most of the natural daylight, but as the light fades, your activities move to other rooms where light is not as readily available, but may not be as necessary. You may find that by removing or opening up interior walls, you get a better and more effective flow of light from one side of the building to the other.

Opposite: Plan the link between rooms, and make sure that adjacent areas are decorated in a complementary fashion.

Basic
techniques

Getting
started

Before you start the decoration, take time out for research and preparation. Do some research into the materials so that you can choose the right finish for the right area. Next, do any preparatory work. The more preparation you put in, the better the end result will be. All that filling and sanding, washing, and stripping will seem worthwhile when you see the final, smooth-painted ceiling or papered wall. Once this is done, you can start to decorate—this chapter explores the basic techniques, from painting to wallpapering, tiling to flooring, and also looks at ways of using architectural features to their best advantage.

Above: Preparation is the key to a successful finish—here, a wooden floor is sanded before a finish is applied.

Opposite: Any cracks and holes in walls will need filling in before you can paint.

This chapter will provide you with a thorough grounding in all the basic decoration techniques. After a brief introduction to each method of decoration, the book focuses on the range of materials available, and recommended tools and applicators. The practical step-by-step sections take you through all essential groundwork (such as filling holes or stripping wallpaper), as well as covering more complex techniques (such as laying a tongue-and-groove wood floor or making a fire surround).

For competent enthusiasts, this information is a good way of refreshing the memory, whereas for the beginner it is aimed to be instructive as well as helpful. Even if you are not going to be tackling the decoration yourself, this will help you in planning a timescale and enable you to check on the progress of the work.

Preparing a room

To prepare a room for decoration, you should empty it as much as possible. Take out all the furniture, pictures, fabrics, and fixtures that you can. Anything that has to stay behind and is not being decorated should be protected against any splashes or spills. Good wooden floors should be protected with a copious amount of old newspaper or a large, heavy-duty polyethylene sheet, which can be bought at most hardware stores.

Very large pieces of furniture may need to be moved to the center of the room and protected with drop cloths or old bed sheets. You can buy roller bases, extendable metal brackets with rollers at each end, which make it easier to maneuver large cupboards and chests around the room.

Be very careful when moving furniture—don't do it single-handed, but get a couple of friends round to help.

Order of work

Unsightly features may need to be camouflaged, and this is the time to plan how and where it will be done. Water pipes, telephone cables, and other domestic wiring are best boxed or hidden behind a window seat or some other piece of built-in furniture. In some cases, wiring can be laid under floorboards or put under the edge of a carpet.

If you are going for a radical redecoration, this is the time to have wiring set into the walls. If you have contemplated radiant heating, this is also the time to install it, when carpets and furniture are out of the way and you have easy access to the uncovered floor surface or boards. Try to think from the underneath out, so that all the work is carried out in logical stages before the paint or paper is put in place.

Stripping varnish or paint finishes off a wooden floor should be done well before any paint can is opened. The microfine dust generated by an electric sander and even handheld abrasive paper will take time to settle, and will only be thoroughly removed after a couple of wipes over with a damp cloth. Even lifting a carpet will cause dust to rise, so mats, rugs, and carpets should be removed before walls and paintwork are wiped down.

Don't be tempted to start jobs in the wrong order. For example, sanding down the window frames while the wall paint is drying elsewhere in the room is not a good idea, because the dust from the frames will stick to the wet wall paint and damage the surface and finish of the wall. Always think through the order of your jobs before starting them.

Preparing the surfaces

Unless you are moving into a recently completed renovation or a new-built home, you will have to prepare the walls and ceiling before any decoration takes place.

Wearing suitable clothing

When tackling any project, make sure that you are properly dressed for it. Even for furniture-moving you should wear good, stout shoes or boots that will protect your feet, ankles, and toes. If you are doing a messy job such as sanding, rubbing down, or using a caustic paint remover or similar chemical-based product, you should leave windows and doors open for good ventilation. It is also vital that you wear a mask over your mouth as well as protective glasses.

Even in new-built homes you may need to rake out and fill in cracks—fresh plaster will shrink as it dries, and if it dries quickly in a room where a heating system is in use, fine, hairline cracks will appear where the plaster has been used over joints in plasterboard or in corners. There is also a certain amount of what is known in the trade as settling, as bricks and boards adjust to their resting places.

In an older building or room that has been previously decorated, you will most likely need to strip the existing paper. This is a laborious task, but you can rent industrial steamers from most commercial rental stores, which will make the job much easier.

It is well worth spending time on preparation, even filling in small holes where picture nails have been, because the effort put into the groundwork will make sure that the final finish is good. It is pointless sticking sheets of expensive wallpaper over a badly prepared surface, because they won't adhere properly and when the paper dries, the surface will be lumpy and uneven. Plain-painted surfaces also need to be well prepared, because any blemish or mark will be all the more noticeable, as there is no pattern to distract the eye.

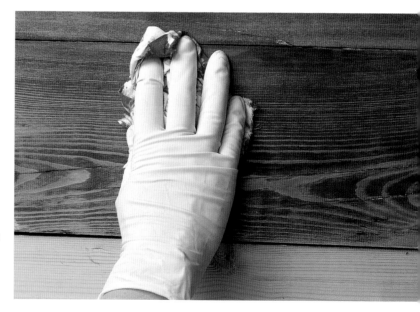

Right: Before you start to decorate your home, make sure that you have all the necessary protective clothing, such as these gloves, which protect your hands when you are applying woodstain.

Choosing your paint

Paint is one of the most versatile and easy finishes to apply—it can look plain, smooth, and flat, or rough and textured. Patterns can be painted over a base coat, block-printed, or stenciled. Paints can also be used to create a faux or trompe l'oeil effect that makes the wall look like marble or wood.

History of paint

Paint is usually a liquid, made up of a pigment that is dissolved in water or oil. Many centuries ago, pigments used to come from natural sources (see box, page 31). These early paints were expensive because they took time and trouble to prepare, and the basic ingredients had to be imported from far away. Therefore wall paints tended to be confined to the homes of wealthy city dwellers, and would be mixed on site by master craftsmen.

The Industrial Revolution had an effect on paint—carbon or gas black was a by-product of the incomplete combustion of natural gas. Some discoveries are relatively recent—the earliest synthetic dye, mauve, was obtained in the late 19th century, while the vivid greens, like forest and emerald, were not developed until 1938.

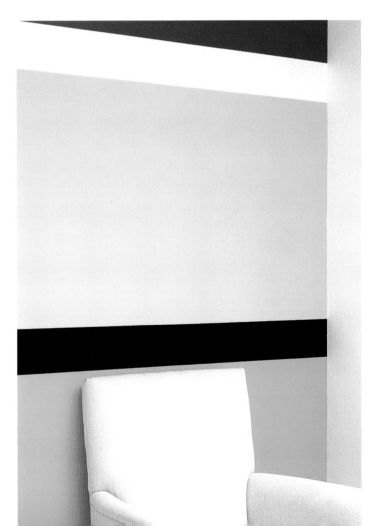

Right: Consider applying bands of different colors to a single wall to create a striking look.

Even though the dyes and pigments themselves have advanced, there are many who look to the past for inspiration. There is an increasing interest, not only in traditional colors but also in old techniques, such as limewashing and distemper, which, with some modifications, can be a more stable and long-lasting finish than they were when originally in use.

Choosing a color

The best way to get an idea of the range of colors available is to get hold of some sample cards. These are strips of a whole range of shades of one color, and are available from most paint and hardware stores. Take some strips home and see how they look next to furniture and fabrics. Isolate one or two of the tones that you feel comfortable with, and then buy sample pots. These are small tester quantities of paint, which give you the scope to try out the colors in situ without buying a lot of paint. You can either paint the color directly onto a patch of wall, or use a piece of lining paper or cardboard that can be tacked or temporarily stuck up on the wall.

This trial patch will give you a chance to see a volume of color and to study it in different lights. Look at the paint patch during the day in natural light, and then again in the evening in artificial illumination, as colors can vary. What appears to be a muted ocher yellow in daylight may look sad and sludgy by electric light.

When building up a wall color from a pale base, you may well be advised by the paint manufacturer to choose a colored base coat that complements the final paint color. A colored base coat will help build up the depth of color. Conversely, if you are going to use a lighter color over a dark base, put down a base coat of white or beige first to block out the strong tones as

completely as possible, before applying the top coat.

There are now a number of "one-coat" paints on the market too, which claim that they will cover walls in one single application, on a prepared wall without base coat. This does work well if you are applying a color with a similar strength of tone as the color already on the wall. However, when it comes to painting a much lighter color over a dark base color, you may still have to use two coats of this paint.

There is a huge range of paint effects available (see pages 48–9) and these can look good in moderation, if skilfully carried out. In a period setting, they can be used to create panels of interest in a long corridor, or to mimic the effect of expensive wallpapers or woods. But the fashion for paint effects has also spread to wallpapers, and you can now buy papers printed with rag-rolled effects, for example, which may be a simpler alternative.

The paint finish that you choose will also affect lighting. Dark, flat surfaces absorb light, while light and shiny paint surfaces reflect it more. Textured surfaces are also more light-absorbent than smooth finishes.

Early paint sources

In early times pigments came from natural sources such as earth—for example, the color sienna is named after the red Tuscan earth from which it was made. Plants, leaves, and mosses were frequently used to obtain green colorings, and red was often made using animal blood or crushed insects. Blue used to be extracted from the woad plant, which is a member of the mustard family, and indigo, most commonly known as the color of denim jeans, came from the *Indigofera* plant and was introduced into the Western world from the East in the 16th century.

Opposite: Dark, flat paint colors, such as this deep blue decorative scheme, tend to absorb light and work well in rooms that have ample natural lighting.

Above left: Sample boards allow you to see how colors will combine together.

Types of paint

Paint is one of the cheapest, most effective ways to finish and seal a surface. It protects against wear and tear as well as adding color and disguising any surface imperfections. To achieve a durable finish it is important to choose the correct formulation for the surface. Paint manufacturers are responding to consumer demands for paint that is odor free, pleasant to use, and easy to clean up. As such, the range now available is vast.

Common paint types

There are many types of paint to choose from, and each gives a slightly different finish. The most common is latex (acrylic).

Latex (acrylic) paint

This water-based paint formulation is commonly used on interior walls and ceilings. It is available in different finishes, such as flat, satin, and vinyl. Flat finish has no sheen, while satin and eggshell (semigloss) finishes have a slight gloss, and vinyl is formulated to cope with moisture and heat in bathrooms and kitchens. Vinyl may also be used in busy hallways, because it dries to a wipeable finish so that marks can be sponged off easily.

Flat finish This type of paint has a flat, matte finish, which is suitable for use in most areas in the house—it will mark and show fingerprints, but can be carefully wiped down with a damp sponge. There are a great many

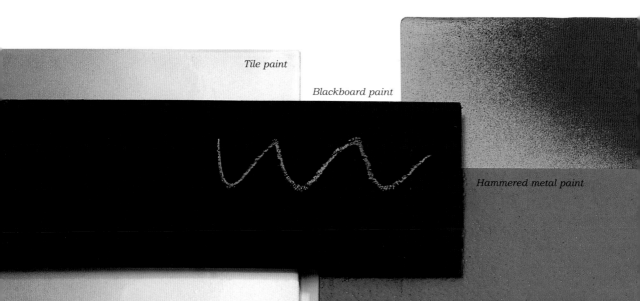

Tile paint

Blackboard paint

Hammered metal paint

"heritage" ranges available on the market, which claim an extra-flat finish with less acrylic than standard paint ranges. Heritage paints have been formulated to appeal to period property owners who want to achieve a dead flat, non-reflective finish that is reminiscent of the traditional distemper finish.

Eggshell (semigloss) finish

Eggshell is a traditional paint that gives a hard, semi-flat finish and is available in water- and oil-based formulations. It can be used for walls and woodwork.

Satin finish More recently, people have taken to using satin finishes rather than eggshell (semigloss),

on some wood surfaces, to give a soft, mellow appearance.

Soft-sheen finish This paint has a more robust finish with a slight sheen, making it more suitable for heavy-wear areas such as hallways. Its higher acrylic content makes it easily wipeable. It is also suitable for use in kitchens and bathrooms. Many varieties also claim one-coat coverage.

Kitchen and bathroom paint

This latex (acrylic) paint has been specially formulated for use in areas that are prone to condensation and steam. It has added fungicides to prevent the development of mold and mildew, which can be a problem in areas

Paint maintenance

Many types of durable paint have been developed in recent years—tough, acrylic-based formulations are available for use on interior wood and metalwork, while oil-based formulations are essential for exterior paintwork to withstand changes of temperature and harsh weather conditions. However, painted finishes that are subject to wear and tear should be maintained periodically. A light sanding and recoating of interior and exterior paintwork every couple of years will prevent time-consuming stripping and refinishing.

Metal primer

Satinwood

Oil-based eggshell/ semi-gloss

Gloss paint

Woodwash floor paint

Preparing gloss paint surfaces

Gloss surfaces such as window sills, baseboards, and doors will need to be rubbed down with a piece of abrasive paper before a new coat of paint can be applied. The gloss of the old surface has to be taken back to a smooth, matte finish so that the new gloss paint can be applied to a surface to which it can grip or adhere. When using gloss, remember to put just a little amount of paint on the brush, and then to work it in really well. By applying heavy brushfuls you will only end up with a dribbled and untidy finish.

with high moisture levels, such as bathrooms or kitchens.

Multi-surface paint

This is a fairly recent development in paint technology—a mid-sheen formulation that can be used on walls, ceilings, woodwork, and metal. Although it tends not to be as durable as an oil-based gloss or satinwood paint, this will still give a perfectly good finish. It is relatively odor-free, and so is particularly good for use in children's rooms. It is also ideal for people with allergies like asthma, who may be adversely affected by paint fumes.

Gloss enamel paint

This tough, oil-based formulation is ideal for interior and exterior wood and metalwork. It is traditionally used on wood surfaces such as built-in bookcases, window sills, and baseboards. Gloss is very durable and easy to clean, with a high-shine finish. It is available in quick-drying and one-coat formulations, which make it practical to use.

Recently, gloss enamel has also appeared on walls, creating a lacquer-like surface, and is particularly effective in the darker, richer tones of Malachite Green, Eating Room Red, Chocolate Brown, and even Midnight Black.

Satinwood

This mid-sheen paint is an alternative to gloss for interior wood and metalwork, and is gaining in popularity, as it is available in both acrylic- and oil-based formulations.

Specialized paints

These paints are formulated to solve specific problems.

Radiator paint

This paint formulation for use on radiators withstands temperature change—standard gloss enamel or satinwood paint has a tendency to yellow slightly when it is exposed to high temperatures. It is available in white as well as a range of other colors.

Tile paint

This is a tough, enamel formulation that can be cleaned like normal tiles when applied to ceramic surfaces.

Floor enamel paint

There are various formulations that are available for different types of flooring, including wooden floorboards, vinyl flooring, tiled floors, and concrete floors. These types of paint are very durable, and in most cases do not require an additional coat of varnish.

Woodcare brushes for applying woodcare products

Masonry brush

Metal paint kettle

Brushes for applying latex (acrylic) and gloss enamel paint

Laminate paint

This is a paint formulated to adhere to shiny, non-porous, laminated surfaces such as kitchen cabinets, knockdown, and built-in furniture.

Metal paint

This tough enamel paint inhibits rust on interior or exterior metal-work, and is available in a smooth or hammered finish. It comes in a wide range of colors.

Preparation

When applying a painted finish, it is often necessary to apply a base coat or primer. This pre-pares the surface and reduces the absorption of the final coat. It is important to check the com-patibility of the base coat with your chosen finish. Oil-based top coats require oil-based primers, and acrylic-based top coats need acrylic primers.

Multi-surface primer

This primer is suitable for use on most sound surfaces including wood, metal, and laminate.

Oil-based primer and base coat

This has been specially formulat-ed to reduce lengthy preparation time for gloss finishes on bare woodwork. It is a simple one-step preparation for unfinished wood.

Acrylic primer and base coat

This primer is a quick-drying formulation and should be applied to bare wood before applying the top coat.

Metal primers

There are a variety of different metal primers available for ferrous and non-ferrous metals—some are specially formulated so that they will prevent rust. They all provide a key for the paint to adhere to.

Tile primer

This primer provides a key so that paint adheres to all types of glossy ceramic surfaces.

Laminate primer

This type of primer provides a key for paint to adhere to this shiny, non-porous material.

Paint applicators

There are various methods of applying paint, including paintbrushes, rollers, and paint pads. At the end of the day, it comes down to personal preference which method you choose to use.

Paintbrushes

A huge number of different paintbrushes are available in a variety of sizes. The best-quality professional brushes are more expensive but produce the best results—the bristles remain flexible, hold a large amount of paint, and do not shed. Cheaper brushes can ruin a paint finish as the bristles can fall out.

Choose a large brush for big areas and a smaller brush for cutting in or painting around the edges of a ceiling or wall, and painting woodwork. Generally, synthetic bristles perform better when painting with gloss paints, while natural bristles are more absorbent with latex paints.

Specialized brushes are also available for creating particular types of paint effects—they tend to be fairly expensive because they are made of animal hair, but if they are well looked after, they will last a lifetime.

Paint rollers

A variety of different removable roller sleeves are available for different types of paint.

Rollers tend to be the quickest method of applying paint and can be attached to extending poles, which are good for painting difficult areas such as ceilings.

Sponge rollers should be used for applying gloss and satinwood paint to areas such as doors, because they provide smooth, even coverage without brush marks. Shaggy rollers should be used to paint textured surfaces such as exposed brickwork, textured wallpaper, and textured paint as the long hairs carry more paint, which can be worked into the crevices. Mini rollers with long handles are also available for painting particularly tricky areas such as behind radiators.

Painting pads

These foam pads are a relatively recent invention—the absorbent, spongy pads are held on plastic or wooden handles. They are available in a variety of different shapes and sizes that will suit different areas.

Care and maintenance of equipment

Paintbrushes

Professional painters recommend soaking brand-new brushes overnight—this loosens any bristles that will otherwise be shed while you are painting.

Paintbrushes should always be cleaned immediately after use—

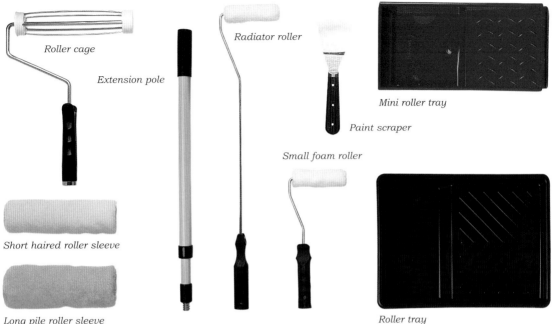

Roller cage

Extension pole

Radiator roller

Mini roller tray

Paint scraper

Small foam roller

Short haired roller sleeve

Long pile roller sleeve

Roller tray

acrylic- or water-based paint should be removed with water and a little detergent if required. Oil-based paint should be removed with mineral spirits or a brush-cleaning solvent.

Concentrate on the area of the brush where the bristles meet the handle, where paint gets lodged. Never allow paintbrushes to soak for too long unsupported because you will end up with bent bristles.

Some paintbrushes are sold with holes through the handles—this allows them to be threaded onto a thin length of doweling or wire and then suspended in water

or mineral spirits over a paint bucket without ruining their bristles. Some paint buckets are sold with plastic clips around the edges that suspend the brushes in the liquid.

Rollers

Paint rollers are a great way of covering a large wall area quickly. They are, however, difficult to clean because of their absorbency. To do this successfully, soak them in running water and then work a little detergent into the pile until the water runs clear. Make sure that all the air bubbles are

squeezed out from the roller after washing, otherwise, the next time you use it, you will get a mottled effect on your paint surface.

For really stubborn paint, you can buy an attachment for a power drill, onto which you attach the roller. This is then spun in a high-sided bucket, and the paint is gradually removed using centrifugal force.

Paint pads

These pads can be cleaned by being immersed in a bucket or bowl of warm water with a little mild detergent.

Painting techniques

The most important thing you can do when you decide to paint is to prepare the surfaces well. Assess the quality of your walls honestly before you begin to use any paint at all, identify the current finish, and try to discover any problems that may lie beneath it before you begin. This may result in you needing to fill holes or cracks in plasterwork or around pipes, but the effort you put in right at the start will make all the difference.

When do you need to strip wallpaper?

If the room you intend to paint is papered in pale wallpaper that is in good condition, it is possible to paint directly over it. This will actually provide a good smooth surface for the paint finish to be painted onto.

Strong-colored wallpaper, vinyl wallpaper, textured wallpaper, or wallpaper in a bad condition should, however, be removed before painting. Some vinyl wallpapers are designed to peel cleanly off the walls to leave a backing paper in place that can then simply be painted in a similar way to lining paper.

If you do not have any backing paper, you should line the walls before painting. This will also prevent a build-up of paint on plaster, which becomes difficult to remove after several coats have been applied to it.

Preparation methods

If you want to achieve a professional-looking finish there is no escaping preparation—getting a surface ready for paint can take longer than the painting itself, but the results will be worth it. Take your time—it can be tempting to rush through the preparation so that you can start painting, but the overall finish will be affected if you don't do a thorough job.

Stripping wallpaper

Wallpaper should be stripped using a sponge and warm water or an electric steamer. For the perfect finish, line the walls.

Tools and materials

Implement to score wallpaper
(or homemade scorer)

Electric steamer

Metal taping knife or wire brush

Sponge and warm water

1 Use the taping knife or wire brush to make slits all over the surface of the existing wallpaper.

Use a wire brush to cut slits into the existing wallpaper.

2 Fill the electric steamer with water to the level that is indicated on it, and then switch the power on.

3 Hold the plate of the electric steamer carefully over one section of the papered surface until you can see that it is beginning to blister and bubble.

Once it is hot, hold the electric steamer plate over the wallpaper.

4 Slide the taping knife underneath the bubbling paper. Then carefully remove the paper in strips—it should come away easily by this stage.

Remove the bubbling wallpaper with a taping knife.

5 Finish the stripping by removing any residue that is left on the wall by soaking a sponge in warm water and wiping the surface down.

Filling small holes or cracks in plaster walls

Tools and materials

Scraper

Multi-purpose or masonry filler

Putty knife

Fine-grit abrasive paper and block or flexible sanding block

1 Before you begin this process remove any loose rubble and dust from the hole or crack in your wall with a scraper and then cut the crack or hole back to form a V-shaped groove, which will give the filler a stronger surface to adhere to.

First remove any dust and debris from the hole or crack.

2 Apply filler with a putty knife so that it sits above the hole in the wall. It is important to do this, because the filler will eventually shrink back slightly as it dries.

Use a putty knife to apply the filler, working out from the center.

3 Once the filler has dried (after about 20 minutes), completely sand the surface smooth by using fine-grit abrasive paper wrapped around a sanding block.

Use a sanding block to smooth the surface flush with the wall.

4 Deep holes, such as those that will be left when wall plugs are removed, can be plugged using crumpled newspaper before filling.

Filling large holes in plaster or around pipe work

Tools and materials

Spray gun and water

Expandable foam filler

Safety gloves

Sharp knife

Filler

Fine-grit abrasive paper and block or flexible sanding block

1 Brush away any remnants of loose and crumbling plaster, and wet the area by spraying it with water from a spray gun.

Use a spray gun to apply plenty of water to the crumbling plaster.

2 Wearing safety gloves apply the expandable foam to the hole. You will only need to half fill the hole, as the foam will expand when it comes in contact with the water.

Hollow walls

Hollow or stud partition walls are made up of a sandwich of studs or joists between plasterboard panels, and are the most common types of interior wall in modern houses. The studs run vertically from ceiling to floor at regular intervals (usually every 1ft/30cm). Plasterboard or drywall walls are not as robust as brick-built walls, and can be easily damaged (often by furniture legs).

Half fill the hole with expanding foam filler.

3 Spray water on the repair as you work. The foam will expand to fill the hole. Allow to dry.

4 Use a sharp knife to trim any excess filler, until it is level

with the surface of the wall. Sand to a smooth finish with a flexible sanding block.

Remove any excess filler by trimming it carefully with a sharp knife.

Filling small holes in plasterboard

Tools and materials

Small knife

Pair of scissors

Self-adhesive wallboard tape (fiberglass)

Putty knife

Filler

Fine-grit abrasive paper and sanding block

1 If you are filling a small-sized hole in drywall or plaster-board, such as that caused by a hammer slipping off a nail, begin by using a sharp knife to cut away any loose areas of plaster that are crumbling.

Use a small knife to cut away the loose areas of plaster.

2 Use the scissors to cut the wallboard tape into a number of small pieces. Then apply the wallboard tape in overlapping layers so that they completely cover the hole.

3 Apply filler over the repair tape, using a filling knife and working from the center of the hole outwards. Allow to dry, then sand smooth.

Use a putty knife to apply the filler, working out from the center.

Repairing large holes in plasterboard walls

Although large holes in hollow plasterboard walls can look daunting, they are relatively easy to repair.

Tools and materials

Utility knife
Scrap plasterboard
Plasterboard nails and hammer
Self-adhesive wallboard tape
Finishing plaster
Plasterer's trowel

1 Use a sharp utility knife to cut out a neat, regular-shape piece of plasterboard around the damaged area, back to the nearest studs. You need to cut the plasterboard back until it slightly overlaps the stud, which will give you an

Use a utility knife to cut a neat shape around the damaged area.

anchor so you can firmly attach your repair patch.

2 Cut a repair patch of new plasterboard, using the damaged piece as a guide to the required shape and size.

Cut out a new piece of plasterboard, using the old as a guide.

3 Position the repair patch and nail it along the studs, using galvanized drywall nails at regular intervals.

Hammer the new piece of plaster-board into place.

4 Use a strip of self-adhesive wallboard tape to cover the joints completely.

Apply self-adhesive wallboard tape over the joints.

5 Mix the finishing plaster and apply it in a sweeping movement, using the trowel to work it into the edges. When the plaster is almost dry, smooth the surface with the trowel, and apply another layer if required, again smoothing over carefully.

Apply plaster to the whole repaired area, using the trowel.

Filling gaps around casing and baseboards

The areas where woodwork meets plaster are prone to gaps because of the way the different materials expand and contract. Large gaps are ugly and allow heat to escape from the house. Tackle them before decoration.

Tools and materials

Utility knife

Decorator's caulk

Caulk gun

Damp cloth

1 Use a utility knife to cut the plastic nozzle off the top of the decorator's caulking. Load the canister onto the caulk gun. Use a slow, squeezing movement to apply the caulking in a long bead along the baseboard or casing.

Apply the caulking along the length of the baseboard.

2 Wrap the damp cloth around your finger and smooth it along the bead, forcing it into the gap.

Use the damp cloth to force the caulking into the gap.

Painting ceilings

Once you have completed the preparation, you are ready to start painting.

Order of work

Rooms should be painted from the top down to avoid spoiling areas you have just painted. Start with the ceiling, followed by the walls, then the woodwork, which will take longer to dry, and finally the floor if painting it. If you are sanding floorboards, do this after painting the walls, but before painting the baseboards, as they are likely to get scuffed in the process.

For perfect, professional results, bare plaster ceilings should be papered before painting. If you prefer not to, then the bare plaster should be sealed with a suitable general-purpose primer, which is used to seal the porous surface and prevent the bare plaster or paper from absorbing excess paint. Specialized primers and paints are available for problem areas, for example, damp, nicotine, or water stains. Flexible ceiling paint is also available for use on ceilings prone to fine, hairline cracks often caused by movement in rooms above—its acrylic formulation flexes with the ceiling. It is also possible to buy non-drip paints, which are less messy to use than are standard latex (acrylic) paints.

Most people prefer to paint their ceilings a light color. This is a matter of personal preference, but ceilings that are lighter than the surrounding walls tend to give the illusion of height and reflect a lot of light back into the room. Dark-painted ceilings can look dramatic, but do give the illusion of a lower ceiling.

Dealing with previously painted ceilings

If painting a previously painted ceiling wipe it down first with a solution of degreasant, using a sponge or long-handled mop. Seal stubborn stains with primer.

Tools and materials

Drop cloths

Painter's tape

Paintbrushes and paint

Small screwdriver (optional)

Rollers

Roller trays

Roller extension pole

Suitable ladder/work platform (optional)

1 If possible, clear the room of all its furniture and protect the floor with a fabric or polethylene drop cloth. If necessary, tape this to the baseboard with painter's tape to prevent it from moving. Begin by cutting in with a small paintbrush. If you have cove, do not worry if you overpaint the edges slightly, because coving is usually finished in satinwood or gloss enamel paint, so this will be painted over later anyway. If you have an unpainted plaster cornice, you can protect it with painter's tape.

2 Mask off pendant light fixtures and paint around them. If you are having difficulties painting close to the ceiling rose, switch the power supply off at the fuse box and then remove the plastic rose with a small screwdriver, which will expose the box and the wiring.

Mask off your light fixtures and then paint around them.

You can paint your ceiling in a darker shade of the predominant color in your scheme. Remember, however, that painting a ceiling dark can make it look lower.

3 When cutting in is complete, fill in the remaining ceiling area with a roller or a large brush. Attach an extension pole to a standard roller cage, in order to reach high ceilings, or use a stepladder. Allow the first coat to dry before applying a second coat.

Use a roller on an extension pole to paint the majority of the ceiling area.

Painting walls

Walls should be carefully prepared before repainting (see page 38). Flaws and imperfections should be filled and sanded, and ideally bare plaster should be sized and papered. If you prefer to paint directly onto new plaster, then seal it first with a multi-surface primer to prevent it from absorbing excess paint.

Previously painted surfaces should be wiped down with degreasant solution to remove dirt and grease, and any rough patches or holes should be filled and sanded. Strong, dark paint colors and very patterned wallpapers are particularly difficult to cover with lighter paint colors. It is advisable to paint a coat of white multi-purpose primer before applying the new color in such cases.

Painting rooms in different color combinations is a very popular look. Many people like picking out feature walls, for example chimney breasts or alcoves, in different colors. Inside corners, where two colors meet, can be difficult to paint neatly, particularly if the walls are not completely perpendicular. It is best to wait for one color to dry, then mask it off with low-tack painter's tape, and paint the second color.

Tools and materials

Degreasant solution and sponge

Paintbrushes and paint

Paint bucket (optional)

Painter's tape

Rollers

Roller trays

1 Prepare previously painted walls by washing them down with degreasant solution.

Always wash down previously painted surfaces with degreasant.

2 Load a small paintbrush by dipping the bristles about halfway into the paint, and then wipe off the excess paint on the edge of the can. Cut in around the edges of the room. Treat each wall as a panel, working the color into the corners. Mask off the top of the baseboards if you are not confident about painting to the edge. Use painter's tape around obstacles such as wall switches to protect them.

Paint each wall, using painter's tape to protect baseboards.

3 Use a roller or large brush to fill in, painting one wall at a time. It is easiest if you work from the top to the bottom and start in the top right-hand corner, which will prevent you brushing against areas you have just painted (reverse this if you are left-handed). Allow paint to dry, then apply a second coat using the same method.

Bright colors, such as this yellow, will require at least two coats of paint.

Painting baseboards (and woodwork)

Tools and materials

Flexible sanding pad
Damp cloth
Polyethylene sheet and tape
Piece of cardboard
Brushes and gloss or satinwood

1 Prepare previously painted baseboards by rubbing down with a flexible sanding pad—this will key the surface, giving the new

paint something to adhere to. Use a damp cloth to wipe away dust before applying new paint.

Use a roller to paint over each wall expanse.

Sand the baseboard before you paint it.

Hints and tips

You may find that the first coat of paint highlights blemishes in the wall surface that you missed at preparation stage. It is not too late to remedy these. Simply apply filler, allow to dry, and then sand back as usual before applying two coats to the surface.

When you are applying filler you should always over-fill the area slightly. This is because as the filler dries it contracts, and so what looked like a level, filled hole will eventually become a concave one.

Right: Baseboards should be painted in colors that complement the wall and floor.

2 Protect the floor with a polyethylene sheet taped to the floor just below the baseboard (if the room is carpeted, slip a piece of stiff cardboard between the carpet and baseboard). Hold a piece of cardboard against the wall while you paint the baseboard using a small paintbrush.

Hold some cardboard against the wall to protect it while painting.

Painting radiators

Radiators are awkward to paint, and they also make it difficult to paint the wall behind them. This is a case when having the right equipment for the job will make the task easier.

Painting behind a radiator

The quickest way to paint behind a radiator is to use a mini roller on a special long-handled roller cage—this allows you to reach down the back of the radiator.

Use a long-handled roller brush to get to hard-to-reach areas behind radiators.

Spray painting a radiator

Radiators must be painted with special heat-resistant enamel paint. If you use standard gloss paint, the heat from the radiator will make it yellow with time.

Tools and materials

Polyethylene sheet and tape

Degreasant solution

Flexible sanding block

Spray paint for radiators or radiator enamel

1 Remember to turn the radiator off and allow it to cool down first. Mask off the area behind the radiator by taping a polyethylene sheet to the wall. Clean the radiator thoroughly with degreasant solution to remove any grease, then sand lightly to key the surface.

2 Shake the can thoroughly, then, holding the can upright. apply paint in even sweeps from a distance of approximately 12in (32cm). Allow the first coat to dry thoroughly before applying a second coat of the spray paint by using the same method as before.

Hold the can upright and apply the paint in even sprays.

Using a paintbrush to paint a radiator

Alternatively, you can paint a radiator by using a special brush with an angled head to help you to reach the awkward areas. If you are painting an old-fashioned radiator with separate sections then you should begin painting on the inside and then outwards. A standard modern panel radiator can be painted with a brush or a foam roller as usual but be sure to use radiator paint.

Types of paint effects

There are a huge variety of paint effects to try out, which allow you to create all sorts of finishes within your home. Some involve manipulating glaze, while others create a textured surface. There is something out there for everyone. If you are attempting a paint effect for the first time, however, it would be a good idea to practice on a piece of masonite—this will allow you to get a feel for the materials and experiment with color before committing your effect to the walls.

Paint effects

The various types of paint effects available today are described in detail in the following pages (pages 52–9).

Broken-color finishes

These techniques are generally applied onto large, flat surfaces, and are ideal for walls. They involve the manipulation of glaze, which is a translucent veil of color that is applied over an opaque base coat, and then removed by various means so as to expose the base coat in places.

Effects such as colorwashing, dragging, rag rolling, stippling, and sponging all fall into this category. Many paint effects have their roots in earlier centuries and seem to come in and out of fashion fairly rapidly. They provide

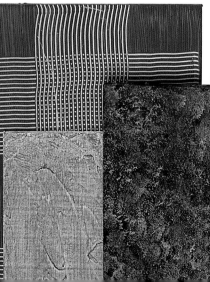

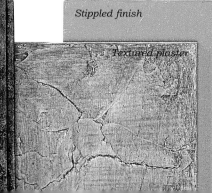

Combing

Pewter metallic effect

Stippled finish

Textured plaster

Faux stone finish

Solid metallic finish

quick cover for less than perfect plastering, or can distract the eye from textured surfaces that would be costly to remove. Most paint effects can appear new and fresh if interpreted in a more subtle way, using fresh, contemporary colors.

Faux finishes

These finishes were historically used to mimic expensive materials such as marble, stone, exotic hardwoods, and semiprecious stones, which added grandeur to interiors in larger houses and even public buildings. They can look out of place in smaller houses, but many of these finishes are suitable for smaller items of furniture and accessories, and some can also be applied to interior walls and doors.

Textured finishes

These finishes add three-dimensional texture as well as color to interior walls. They can be achieved in a number of ways, either by adding particles such as sand and sawdust to paint, or by applying a textured substance to the walls before painting.

Metallic and pearlescent finishes

The various finishes that come under this heading add a touch of glamor to an interior. Some are achieved in the traditional way by applying thinly beaten metal leaf directly to the wall, while others involve metallic, iridescent, or pearlescent particles suspended in paint or glaze. These effects can be subtle, showing up when the light hits them a certain way.

Stencil brushes

Dragging brush

Stippling brush

Softening brush

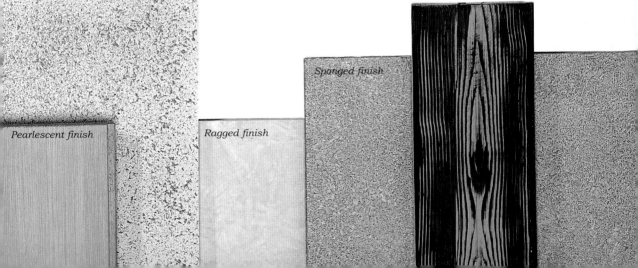

Wood graining

Sponged finish

Pearlescent finish

Ragged finish

When starting a paint effect, make sure that you have mixed up enough colored glaze to complete the job, as it is almost impossible to mix up exactly the same color twice. It is also worth storing a screwtop jar of glaze in case you need to touch up areas of paintwork at a later date.

Graining rocker

Natural sponge

Painting pads

Chamois leather rag

Graining comb

Tools and materials

In order to achieve these paint effects, you will need to invest in specialized tools and materials.

Glazes

These are available in water-based (acrylic) or oil-based formulations and form the basis of broken-color effects. They come in a colorless form that can be tinted with artist's paints, latex paints, or powder pigments or in ready-mixed colors. When painted over a flat base coat they add a transparent veil of color, which can be built up or taken off in layers. Many paint effects depend on manipulating the glaze, and rely on its open time—this refers to the length of time that the glaze can be moved around before it dries. Water-based glazes have a shorter open time than oil-based glazes, but many people find that they are more pleasant to use because they don't have a particularly strong odor.

Base coats

This is the first coat of any paint effect and provides the base onto which the glaze is applied. Vinyl satin or soft-sheen latex (acrylic) is often chosen because its shiny surface covers well and the slippery surface makes the glaze easy to move around. White vinyl satin latex can be tinted with the addition of artist's acrylic paints or colorizers, or you can buy a ready-mixed color of your choice. The base coat is usually a neutral or complementary color to the glaze. It shows through the glaze in places and affects the final look considerably.

Specialized paintbrushes

These are high-quality brushes designed to create particular effects in wet glaze. Because most of them are handmade with natural bristles they are fairly expensive, but are well worth the investment if you are going to get a lot of use out of them. If not, then experiment with different-size standard paintbrushes, trimming the bristles if necessary.

Softening brushes Common softening brushes include badger softening brushes, lily-bristled softening brushes, and decorator's dusting brushes. They are used for eliminating brush-marks from water- and oil-based glazes by gently dusting the bristles over the surface. The most costly is the badger brush, which was traditionally made from badger or, in more recent times, hog hair. If you do not want to purchase a softening brush, it could be replaced by a lily-bristled brush or soft-bristled decorator's dusting brush.

Dragging brushes These brushes have extra-long, straight bristles that are used for dragging through a glaze to produce regular and long brush strokes.

Woodgraining tools These include a rocker, which is a rubber tool that is pulled through a glaze, using a rocking motion to produce a woodgrain effect. Rubber combs, on the other hand, have teeth spaced at different intervals. They are pulled through the glaze to produce grain or moiré patterns.

Lining brushes These brushes are specially designed to paint decorative coach lines on furniture—their long, thin bristles can be heavily loaded with paint to achieve continuous lines.

Stencil brushes These brushes have a blunt, stubby appearance and are used for stippling paint through stencils. They should be used in an upright position.

Stippling brushes These broad brushes contain groups of bristles for creating tiny dots in wet glaze.

Sponges

These are used in broken-color techniques, particularly sponging. Natural sponges give the softest appearance. Synthetic sponges are cheaper, but should only be used if they have had pieces picked out of them to give a more irregular, natural look.

Masking tape

This adhesive crêpe-paper tape is used for masking off any areas you do not wish to be painted. It is available in a flexible form, for curved shapes, and as a "low-tack" tape, which is less likely to damage painted surfaces.

AT-A-GLANCE TOOLS AND MATERIALS

Paint effect	Specialist tools	Specialist materials
Colorwashing	Large brush, softening brush	Glaze, base coat
Dragging	Dragging brush	Glaze, base coat
Stippling	Stippling brush	Glaze, base coat
Ragging	Clean rags, cloth	Glaze, base coat
Rag rolling	Clean rags, cloth	Glaze, base coat
Sponging	Natural sponge	Glaze, base coat
Marbling	Feather, swordliner brush	Glaze, base coat, artist's oil or acrylic colors
Wood graining	Graining comb or rocker	Glaze, base coat
Crackling	Standard brushes	Glaze, base coat, top coat
Combing	Flexible comb	Glaze, base coat
Distressing	Wire wool	Wax, base coat, top coat
Metallic finish	Standard brushes	Metallic paint, powder

Paint effect techniques

Paint effects can completely transform a space, but unfortunately a badly applied technique or an ill considered choice of color can make it ineffective, or can even make the room look worse than it was originally. Take time to familiarize yourself with the tools and materials before embarking on a whole room.

Broken-color finishes

Broken-color finishes all consist of a glaze applied over a base coat. The effect is achieved by disturbing the surface of the glaze with a variety of different tools, allowing the base coat to show through.

Colorwashing

Colorwashing is one of the most popular paint effects today. It is popular for creating a rustic, Mediterranean look, and is brilliant for creating a deliberately distressed look on walls that are less than perfect. Applied carefully, colorwashing can be a very effective finish.

Tools and materials

Paint buckets

Standard latex (acrylic) brush, roller and tray

Large latex (acrylic) brush

Vinyl satin latex (acrylic), matt latex (acrylic), and scumble glaze

Badger softening brush or soft-bristled latex (acrylic) brush

1 Prepare the walls carefully according to the instructions pages 38–42. Apply the base coat vinyl satin latex (acrylic) to the prepared walls, using a standard latex brush, and allow to dry.

Use a standard latex brush to apply the base coat to your walls.

2 Mix the flat latex with the acrylic scumble glaze and a little water until you have a liquid the consistency of thin cream. Take a large brush and apply the glaze using sweeping, random, and crisscrossing strokes, working on a manageable area of about 1 sq yd (1 sq m) at a time.

Hints and tips

If you are attempting to cover a large area, it is easier to work with somebody else, so that one person applies the glaze and the other softens the effect. This will avoid obvious joint marks. In heavy-wear areas, such as kids' rooms and hallways, a couple of coats of flat acrylic varnish applied over the paint effect will give it better durability.

Apply the glaze to the walls using a large brush, and working with random, crisscrossing strokes.

3 Go back over the area of the glaze with the softening or soft-bristled brush, barely touching the surface so that you slightly blur the brush strokes. While working, you should frequently clean the brush on a rag to avoid a build-up of glaze in the bristles as this will result in uneven coverage of the surface.

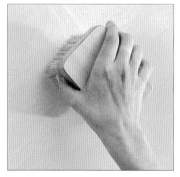

Work over the glaze using a softening brush to blur the brush strokes.

Dragging

This technique is often used to mimic woodgrain or woven fabric, and adds a subtle texture to flat surfaces. An attractive result relies on keeping the brush lines perfectly straight, and looks most effective applied to a limited area, rather than over a complete wall.

Tools and materials

Brush, roller, and roller tray

Paint bucket

Latex (acrylic) and scumble glaze

Dragging brush or long-bristled paintbrush

Rags for wiping brushes

Varnish (optional)

1 Apply the base coat evenly to the wall with your brush or roller, and allow it to dry. Mix up the scumble glaze and paint it onto the wall.

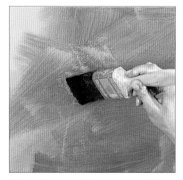

Mix up the scumble glaze and then paint it over the base coat.

2 Take the dragging brush and hold its bristles up against the glaze. Then pull it carefully down through the glaze, keeping it straight until you reach the base-board. After each stroke, wipe the brush clean of glaze to avoid a build-up. Varnish if required.

Next, pull the dragging brush gently down through the glaze.

Stippling

This is a useful, subtle effect that works well on flat surfaces and on moldings, giving an aged appearance. It can also be used for mimicking stone, providing a subtle, mottled effect.

Tools and materials

Paintbrush, roller, and tray

Vinyl satin latex (acrylic)

Acrylic scumble glaze and artist's acrylic colors

Stippling brush or large, flat scrubbing brush

Varnish (optional)

1 Apply the base coat and allow to dry. Paint on the glaze to give even coverage.

Paint the glaze over the base coat and allow it to dry.

2 Use the stippling brush to mark the glaze surface using short, stabbing movements, which will leave a mottled finish free of brush strokes. Allow the surface to dry, and then varnish over the top of the glaze if a tough finish is required.

Mark the glaze by stabbing the surface with the stippling brush.

Textured finishes

These finishes can be subtle by adding fine grains of sand or sawdust to latex (acrylic) base coats, or more dramatic using textured plaster skim colored with pigments and applied with a plasterer's trowel. As textured finishes are hard to remove, first line the walls with lining paper so that they will be easier to strip.

Subtle textured finish

Tools and materials

Vinyl flat latex (acrylic) and sand

Paint buckets

Brushes, rollers, and trays

Tinting pigments

Acrylic scumble glaze

1 Mix vinyl flat latex (acrylic) and sand well in a paint bucket, and apply to the wall. Allow to dry.

Apply the latex (acrylic) and sand mix to the walls with a paintbrush.

2 Mix up a colored acrylic glaze and then brush it at random over the textured surface in order to highlight the lumps and bumps.

Randomly brush the acrylic glaze over the textured surface.

Rough plaster finish

Tools and materials

Paint bucket

Textured paint or other textured finish

Colored latex (acrylic)

Plasterer's trowel

Glaze (optional)

1 In a paint bucket mix the textured finish to a thick, smooth consistency, and apply it to the walls using the smooth edge of a plasterer's trowel. Go back over the surface, adding extra peaks and troughs as required or smooth down any rough areas for the required finish. Allow the surface to dry overnight.

Use a large brush to add additional peaks and troughs if required.

2 Paint the surface with your base coat and allow it to dry. Then drybrush the colored glaze with a large masonry paintbrush over the textured finish, picking out the irregularities in the surface.

Drybrush your colored glaze over the textured wall.

Metallic finishes

Metallic and pearlescent glazes are applied over complementary base coats to produce quite realistic metallic effects. Glitter can also be added to glaze to create a sparkling wallcovering, which is particularly suitable for use in children's rooms.

Using pearlescent finishes

Tools and materials

Complementary base coat

Paintbrush or roller

Pearlescent top coat

Acrylic varnish

1 Apply the base coat using a paintbrush or roller, and allow to dry thoroughly for about an hour before you apply the top coat.

Above: Stenciled leaves scattered across white wood washed floorboards bring nature indoors.

Apply the base coat and allow to dry thoroughly.

2 Apply the top pearlescent coat carefully. Make sure that you work in one direction only, in order to avoid brushmarks.

Use even brush strokes in the same direction to apply the top coat.

3 Allow to dry, then add a couple of coats of flat acrylic varnish.

Apply a couple of coats of acrylic varnish to finish.

Metallic finishes

Tools and materials

Base coat

Paintbrushes

Metallic top coat

1 Begin by applying your choice of base coat using a paintbrush.

Apply a coat of base coat evenly to the whole wall.

2 Once the base coat is dry, apply a top coat of metallic paint, taking care not to leave brush strokes.

Apply the metallic paint, taking care not to leave any brush strokes.

Painting abstract shapes

Effects covering entire rooms are diminishing in popularity and are being replaced with subtler bands of colors or shapes on feature walls, which give the feeling of abstract works of art. The various different shapes can be combined with any of the paint effects outlined above.

Horizontal bands

Horizontal bands around a room will give the illusion of greater width, particularly if painted in pale tones. Dividing up a room horizontally will add interest in a large room. Traditional rooms used to be divided by chair and picture rails, which allowed the use of different bands of color. For a contemporary look, divide the room into bands of varying thickness.

Tools and materials

Level and metal rule

Pencil

Low-tack painter's tape

Latex (acrylic)

Paintbrushes or rollers

1 Measuring up from the baseboard or down from the ceiling will often give you a lopsided line, because floors and ceilings are not always completely level. If you want a true horizontal line, use a level set on a long metal rule to keep the line level. Mark the line around the room lightly in

pencil. Mask off with low-tack painter's tape.

2 Paint or roller the colored bands, pulling off the painter's tape before the paint has dried. Once it is completely dry, apply the painter's tape to the painted section, and repeat.

Vertical lines

Vertical lines around a room help to give the illusion of greater height. They can look overpowering in small spaces, but work well used sparingly on a feature wall. For a contemporary look, vary the widths of the lines and try to use harmonious tones or varying shades of the same base color.

Tools and materials

Chalk line
Low-tack painter's tape
Soft cloth
Latex (acrylic) paints
Paintbrushes or rollers

1 Use a chalk line to mark a straight vertical line quickly. You will need two pairs of hands—one person should hold the line at the top of the wall, the other should hold it tight at the bottom. Then snap the line sharply to leave a pale vertical chalk line on the wall. This can

then be masked off with tape and the chalk line rubbed away with a cloth.

Use a chalk line to leave a vertical chalk mark on the wall.

2 Paint using a paintbrush or roller—remember to remove the painter's tape before the paint has dried. Allow it to dry completely before reversing the process, and applying painter's tape to the finished area to paint the adjacent line.

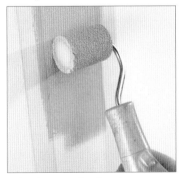

Paint the area that has been surrounded with painter's tape.

Painting circular features

Painted circles are a good way to introduce accent colors and decorative features.

Tools and materials

Hammer
Masonry nails
String
Pencil
Paint and paintbrush
Flexible painter's tape

1 Gently hammer in a large masonry nail at the point where the center of the circle will be. Tie a piece of string to it at one end and knot it around a pencil at the other. Hold the string tight and pull the pencil around to form a circle on the wall. Remove the masonry nail and fill the resulting hole with quick-drying filler.

Pull the string line tight and pull the pencil around to draw a circle.

2 Paint the circle, starting with the outline. You can mask off the line with flexible painter's tape first, if desired. This will give a neater finish.

Now paint the circle, starting with the outline.

Lettering and numbers

Lettering is a popular form of decoration for walls and can look very effective. The effect can be achieved in a number of ways. Lines of poetry or quotes work particularly well in bathrooms—try recipes in kitchens, and numerals in home offices. Experiment with different sizes and typefaces to achieve different styles.

Using plastic lettering

Tools and materials

Level

Pencil

Plastic letters

Latex (acrylic) and small paintbrush

1 Use a level to draw a faint horizontal pencil line in the place where you want the lettering. Large plastic letters are easier to draw around.

Hold your chosen letters to the wall, and draw around each one.

2 Fill in the letters with paint. If needed, make a brush rest using a cane with some packing wrapped in cotton.

Use a small paintbrush to paint the inside of the letters on the wall.

Using a projector

Rent or borrow an overhead projector. Write freehand, or photocopy the writing of your choice onto acetate, then project the writing onto the wall where you want to paint the letters. Draw around the letters with soft pencil, then fill with paint.

Using stencils

Tools and materials

Level

Pencil

Stencil

Painter's tape

Paint and large stencil brush

Varnish (optional)

1 Use lettering stencils to spell out your chosen words along a straight pencil line on

the wall. Apply the paint by dabbing sparingly through the stencils using a large, blunt stencil brush.

Dab the paint through the stencils to color in your chosen words.

2 Remove the stencil carefully by peeling it away, and then varnish over the whole surface.

Once the paint has dried, peel the stencil away from the wall.

Right: If you don't want to use letters, experiment with other shapes, such as this natural vine design.

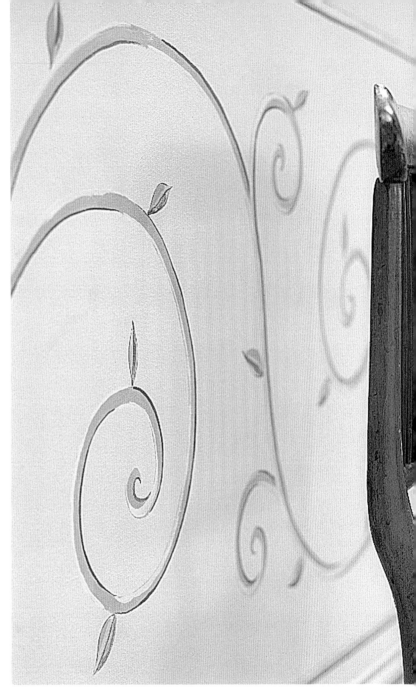

Choosing your
wallpaper

Wallpaper adds softness to a wall and can help reduce echoes and the emptiness of a large room. Papers can be very decorative with a large all-over print, simply striped, or even printed to look like a paint effect such as marbling, so that you get the effect without ever having to dip your brush in a pot.

History of wallpapering

Wallpaper was developed for the middle and upper classes as an inexpensive alternative to wood paneling, tapestry, and cloth hangings, which were favored until the 17th century. But even as a less-expensive alternative, it was still a luxury item printed with hand-applied blocks and intricately carved and color-separated rollers. There are still a few exclusive wallpaper manufacturers who produce luxurious, often hand-colored tableaux panels and papers that are close to the original quality and craftsmanship of the earlier varieties.

Wallpaper grew in popularity in the 19th century when mechanized engraved cylinders could produce continuous rolls of paper. The Arts and Crafts period saw it reach new heights, with the artist William Morris producing many highly colored designs that are still in production today.

Other older styles of paper, such as anaglypta and lincrusta, have also seen something of a revival with people restoring period homes. These papers first became popular in Victorian times and have a stamped pattern that stands out in relief against the background. They were commonly used on ceilings and below chair rails, for example, between the baseboard and waist height. They are sometimes painted today with gloss enamel paints for a high shine, wipeable finish, and sometimes even flat finishes in order to create a chalky appearance.

During the 1950s and 1960s further advances in the production of wallpaper took place. Coatings, such as a fine layer of plastic, saw the introduction of vinyl papers, which were better able to cope with the extremes of temperature and moisture in bathrooms. Metallic-backed papers with silvery backgrounds

Opposite: A simple repeated motif can look elegant and effective as a wallpaper pattern.

Above: Floral patterns work well in a traditional bedroom. If you are using an elaborate pattern, then consider papering just half the wall.

The next step is to look through as many books of papers available as possible. Some sample books have visuals of sets using the various designs, which can be very helpful.

The current trend for paper is to use it as a panel or on one wall, rather than on all four walls. This is mixed with painted surfaces and becomes a highlight or feature of a room, rather than a complete covering.

Lining paper that is left unpainted is another slightly obscure but attractive finish that has been in vogue for a number of years. The paper, which is off-white when applied, ages in sunlight and takes on a yellow, almost parchment-colored hue. Plain brown parcel paper has also been used to great effect as a wall covering, especially in small rooms such as studies or cloakrooms. Good-quality brown paper has a slight stripe in it, and so needs to be hung carefully to be sure that all the lines run in the same direction. The paper itself can be bought in large, commercial quantities.

Jute, silk, and grass have at various times all been applied to paper backings, and these wall coverings are still popular in parts of northern Europe and France.

and iridescent finishes were also produced at this time.

Other wallcovering options include textured woodchip papers, which were popular in the 1950s and 1960s but have been in decline for some time now. They do have some advantages, though, as these thick, textural papers cover over and disguise a multitude of sins, such as cracks and bumps on uneven wall surfaces.

During the 1980s and early 1990s the popularity of wallpaper began to wane, with paint becoming the primary wallcovering, but in the late 1990s a new vogue for papers began to rise once more.

Choosing wallpaper

The wallpaper that you choose will depend on the shape, size, and function of the room being decorated. If the walls are uneven, you may want to choose a thicker paper. In rooms with a lot of pictures, a simple, quiet design will probably be the best choice you can make.

Tools

Pasting table

These light, folding tables are cheap to buy and make wallpapering much easier, as they are just wider than a roll of paper and long enough to spread paste without creasing the paper.

Smoothing brush

This is a wide, slim brush used to smooth paper once it has been hung.

Pasting brush

These large, synthetic-bristled brushes are used to spread paste over paper. It is worth getting one that includes a plastic hook to stop it falling into the paste and making a mess.

Plumb bobs

The simplest form is a weight that hangs from a string, enabling you to mark a perfectly plumb line. It is also possible to buy versions that include a chalk reservoir. This chalks the string, enabling you to snap it against a surface to produce a chalk line.

Seam rollers

These small tools have a revolving roller, which is used to roll over the seams of wallpapers and borders for a flat joint.

Smoothing brush

Electric steamers

These power machines can be bought or rented by the day, and are useful when you are stripping large areas of wallpaper. They are filled with water, which is heated to boiling point. The steam then travels up a rubber or plastic tube to a plate, which is held against the wall, where the steam gets under the paper and loosens the adhesive.

Shears

These scissors have long blades for cutting wallpaper in a straight line. They also have shaped, blunt ends for use when creasing the wallpaper as a guide to cutting.

Adhesives

These include all types of wallpaper paste and come in ready-mixed or powder form. There is also border adhesive, which comes in a tube and is used to stick down paper edges.

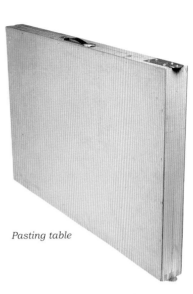

Pasting table

Pasting brush   *Seam roller*

Shears

Types of wallpaper

Before you choose your wallpaper, you must decide what type of paper to use. There is a wide variety of papers available on the market today. They are manufactured in a number of ways and produce different effects on your wall. It is important to bear in mind the decorative style that you are trying to achieve when choosing your paper—for example, a heavy, embossed paper will look fine in a period setting, but may be at odds with a minimal, contemporary design.

Standard wallpaper

Standard printed rolls of wallpaper are $20^3/_4$in (52cm) wide. They come in an enormous variety of colors and designs, usually with a flat finish.

Hand blocked/ printed wallpaper

This has standard dimensions, but the designs have been printed by hand, making it much more expensive than standard varieties.

Vinyl wallpaper

Designs consist of a paper backing with a printed vinyl top coat. These papers are easy to hang and strip, and are also very durable and resistant to being scuffed. They can look shiny.

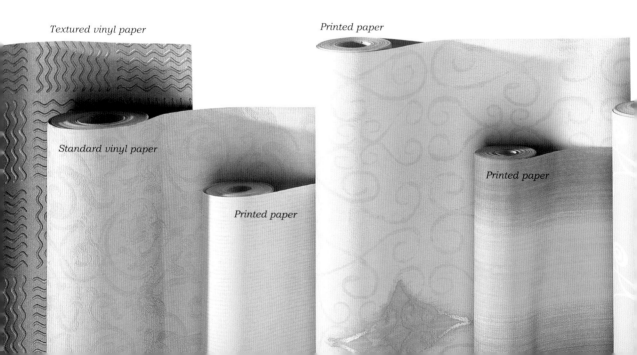

Textured vinyl paper

Standard vinyl paper

Printed paper

Printed paper

Printed paper

Textured/emboss-ed papers

These papers are ideal for using on walls that are slightly uneven, as their raised surface pattern disguises minor imperfections. They are hung in the same way as standard wallpapers, but often require longer soaking, so always follow the manufacturer's instructions.

Anaglypta and lincrusta

Anaglypta is an embossed paper, which was first used by the Victorians and is made from a combination of cotton and paper pulp. This is passed through patterned rollers when wet, which press out the design onto the paper. It is particularly popular for heavy-wear areas such as hallways, as it is resilient to knocks and bumps. It comes uncolored, so you can paint it to match your color scheme—it can also be used as a base for creating a number of broken-color effects. Lincrusta is also an embossed wallcovering, but is made from a linoleum mixture and is super-durable.

Woodchip wallpaper

This is a favorite in the refurbishment trade, as the small chips of wood can hide a multitude of sins, giving walls an oatmeal-like texture. Take great care when removing woodchip wallpaper, as it may well be holding the plaster behind it together, and by removing it you run the risk of exposing a wall that may need professional replastering.

Blown vinyl wallpaper

This is a vinyl paper with a raised pattern created by a special printing process—on being heated, the printed area expands, giving a three-dimensional effect. Designs used to be old-fashioned, but newer ranges include mosaic tiles, and natural fibers.

Standard vinyl paper

Anaglypta

Printed paper

Standard vinyl paper

Printed paper

Wallpapering techniques

Many people are wary of using wallpaper because there is a persistent belief (mainly among those who have never tried) that it is incredibly difficult to put up. In fact, hanging wallpaper is not only quite straightforward if approached in a methodical manner, but also immensely satisfying and fun to do.

Starting points

Traditional advice recommends starting the run of wallpaper by centering it at a focal point such as a fireplace. This makes sense if you are using a paper with an obvious pattern, because it will make the design look balanced. However, if it is your first attempt at wallpapering, there is no harm in starting with the longest wall, which does not have any obstacles. This will give you the confidence to handle other obstacles as you work your way clockwise around the room.

Preparation

Strip the walls of any existing paper and patch up any cracks or holes in the plaster (see pages 38–42). Before painting or wallpapering the walls, size them with diluted wallpaper paste, which gives them good slip and allows the paper to be moved about. Then line the walls with lining paper. This is available in different weights—the heaviest gives the best coverage and the smoothest surface to work on. If you are painting the walls, hang the lining paper vertically, fill and sand any small gaps between the joints first, and follow the instructions for normal wallpapering (see pages 68–9).

Cross-lining walls with lining paper

If you are wallpapering you should cross-line the walls—this means hanging the paper horizontally. The reason for doing this is to avoid the joints of the lining paper and wallpaper lining up. If you don't feel confident about cross-lining, hang the lining paper vertically, but take care when positioning the wallpaper on top of it, making sure that the joints don't line up.

Tools and materials

Tape measure
Level
Soft pencil
Shears
Wallpaper paste
Old paintbrush
Lining paper
Paste brush
Smoothing brush
Putty knife
Utility knife

1 Measure the width of the lining paper and, using a tape measure, mark this measurement at intervals, starting at the top of the wall. Use a level to draw horizontal lines across the room with a soft pencil. Measure the length of each wall and work out the number of lengths of lining paper that you need to cut (allow several inches or centimetres excess at each end).

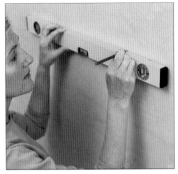

Draw a horizontal line around the room, using a level and pencil.

2 Measure and cut the lengths of lining paper. Paste the first length, taking care to cover the edges. Once pasted, fold the paper into an accordion shape (paste against paste) and allow to soak for the recommended time. Paste the second length while the first is soaking.

Fold the paper into an accordion shape, ready to hang on the wall.

3 Start hanging the accordion pleat of lining paper in the top right-hand corner of the room, smoothing it into the corner with a smoothing brush. Then gradually smooth the paper across the wall, unfolding the lining paper as necessary. When you reach the other end of the room, trim the paper to fit.

Hang the accordion pleat of lining paper, smoothing it across the wall.

4 Hang the second length of paper, butting it up to the first piece. Continue around the room, smoothing it into place and working in the same way as for the first length. Paper one wall at a time. When you reach the baseboard, use a putty knife to push the paper into the angle between the baseboard and the wall. Hold the paper firmly in place, and trim using a sharp utility knife. Ensure the edge is hidden behind the baseboard.

Buying wallpaper

When buying wallpaper, take along a note of the dimensions of your room and the height of the ceilings—the store should be able to advise you of the number of rolls to buy. Always buy a couple more than you will need, because these can be stored in case you need to make any repairs. Check that all the rolls of wallpaper are from the same batch or print run—this should be marked clearly as a batch number on the side of the packaging. If you run out of paper and need to buy more, make sure that you get the same batch, because colors on different batches always vary slightly because of the printing process.

Butt the top edge of the second piece up to the bottom edge of the first.

Hanging wallpaper

Tools and materials

Tape measure

Level

Wallpaper

Shears or utility knife

Pasting table and brush

Wallpaper paste

Plumb bob

Metal straightedge

Smoothing brush

1 Measure the drop from the ceiling to the baseboard and add about an inch (a few centimeters) top and bottom. If the paper is patterned, remember the repeat. Cut the first few lengths and lay them on the pasting table. Paste out from the center, with the edge overlapping the table slightly so you don't get paste on the table.

Apply paste from the center outwards towards the edges.

2 Making sure the first drop is hung straight is vital and, as most walls are not completely square, you will need a plumb bob. At a point in the room that is close to the darkest corner, measure just under a width of the wallpaper away from the corner. Hold the string at the top of the wall, let the plumb fall to the baseboard, and wait until it has stopped moving. Mark with a pencil at intervals along the string. Join up the line with a metal straightedge.

Use a plumb bob to ensure that you hang your paper perfectly straight.

3 Starting at the top, smooth the paper onto the wall, allowing an overlap of about an inch (a couple of centimetres). Use the smoothing brush to smooth the paper from the center outwards, squeezing out any air bubbles. The paper should be worked well into the corner, overlapping the adjacent wall by about $^1/_2$ in (1cm).

Use a smoothing brush to squeeze out any air bubbles.

4 Use the rounded tip of the shears to crease the paper at the point where it meets the ceiling. Slowly pull the wallpaper away from the wall at the top, and use the shears to trim away the excess. Then carefully smooth the paper back down the wall, using the smoothing brush. Repeat the process at the point where the wall meets the baseboard.

Make a crease in the paper where the wall meets the baseboard.

5 Hang the second drop of paper by carefully aligning it with the edge of the first drop and sliding it up against it to achieve a butt joint (the two edges should meet without any trace of a gap at all). If you are using a patterned wallpaper, then you will need to slide the paper along the wall until the two halves of the pattern meet up at the correct position.

6 Trim the top and bottom of the paper as shown in step 4. Repeat around the whole room. Make sure that the last drop of paper overlaps the corner by approximately $\frac{1}{2}$ in (1cm) and is pushed well into the corner using the smoothing brush. Finally, finish off by wiping away any wallpaper paste that may have been left on the ceiling or cove and baseboard using a clean, damp sponge.

Papering around corners

Once you have mastered a straight run of wallpapering, turning corners shouldn't be a problem. The key is to allow $\frac{1}{2}$–1in (1–2cm) overlap.

Inside corners

Tools and materials

As for Hanging wallpaper (see opposite)

1 When you have hung the last drop of paper before reaching the corner, stop and measure the width of the next drop. Do not assume that the wall is completely true—measure the gap at the top, bottom, and middle, and add about an inch (about 2cm) to the largest measurement.

Measure the width of the drop you need to reach the corner.

2 Lay the paper on the floor or pasting table and, using a straightedge, mark the paper and cut with shears. Make sure that the cut edge is the one nearest the corner that will be covered. Paste and allow to soak. Reserve the scrap if it is a decent size.

3 Hang the paper as above, pushing it well into the corner with the smoothing brush. If it creases where it turns the corner, make a few snips along the edge with shears, and smooth into place.

If the paper creases at the corner, snip into the edge with shears.

4 If the cut lengths before the corner left you with a decent-size scrap, use this piece to continue—if not, begin with a fresh length. Measure the width of the scrap and hang a plumb bob at this distance from the corner on the new wall. Paste, soak then hang over the overlap, level with the corner, with the cut side nearest the corner. Continue the process.

Hang the next piece so that the cut side is nearest the corner.

Outside corners

Outside corners are usually in rooms with fireplaces. If you start papering in the middle of a chimney breast, cut the paper before the corner so it is wide enough to wrap around the corner with an inch (a couple of centimetres) spare as an overlap. If you are approaching a corner from an alcove, use the following steps.

Tools and materials

As for Hanging wallpaper
(see page 68)

1 Measure the depth of the chimney breast at three points, then cut a length of paper that width plus 1in (2.5cm), which will be wrapped around the corner. Paste, soak, then hang as described above, using the brush to smooth the cut edge gently around the outside corner.

Use the smoothing brush to smooth the paper round the corner.

2 Measure the scrap and plumb a line as described above on the new wall. Paste, soak, then smooth in place, covering the overlap. Trim on the top and bottom.

Put the scrap in place on the new wall, covering the overlap.

Papering around obstacles

The same principles apply to papering around most obstacles. The key is to crease the paper carefully around the object.

Papering around a fireplace

Tools and materials

As for Hanging wallpaper
(see page 68)

1 Smooth the paper down towards the top of the fireplace stopping 1ft (30cm) above it. Smooth it into the corner where the edge of the fireplace meets the wall.

Use the smoothing brush to smooth the paper into the corner.

2 Use a sharp utility knife or pair of shears to make a horizontal slit along the center of the mantel shelf from the point where the fireplace meets the wall.

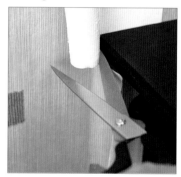

Use shears to cut a series of slits in the wallpaper.

3 Smooth the paper above the shelf, and trim. Use your fingertips to press the paper around any moldings below the mantel, and trim with a utility knife.

Smooth the paper, trimming around any moldings on the fireplace.

Papering around a recessed window

Tools and materials

As for Hanging wallpaper
(see page 68)

1 Make sure that the final drop is wide enough to cover the depth of the recess. Smooth the paper over the window, then cut horizontal slits across the top and bottom of the window to the corners of the recess. Fold the flap over into the recess. Trim, but don't smooth.

2 Cut a small length of paper 1in (2.5cm) deeper and wider than the area left at the top of the recess, and smooth it under the long drop. Cut a small triangle off the corner of the paper to fold it neatly over the edge of the recess. Smooth the long drop over it.

Alternative method

There is an alternative method for papering around wall switches and receptacles. Turn off the power at the fuse box and unscrew the front of the switch box just enough to push the excess paper underneath.

Papering around a door (or window without a recess)

1 Cut a length of wallpaper to hang over the door, and apply paste to it, avoiding the area that will be cut away. Hang it loosely over the door and cut away the area over the door, leaving 2in (5cm) overlap. Use the smoothing brush to push the paper into the recess between the door frame and the wall. Make a small diagonal slit in the wallpaper to the corner of the door frame.

2 Use the smoothing brush to smooth the paper around the frame, and trim using a knife.

Papering around wall switches and receptacles

Tools and materials

As for Hanging wallpaper
(see page 68)

1 Hang the paper loosely over the switch, and use the brush to locate the switch position through the paper. Use a utility knife to cut two diagonal slits from corner to corner of the switch.

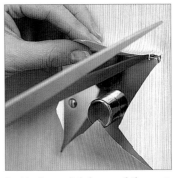

Locate the switch box, and then cut diagonal slits in the paper.

2 Fold back the paper triangles and smooth the paper around the switch box with the brush. Use a utility knife to trim the triangles as close to the switch as possible.

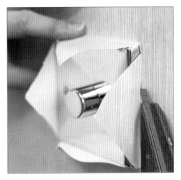

Fold the triangles back, and then trim them as neatly as possible.

Choosing your tiles

Tiles have long been a standard wall covering for bathrooms and cloakrooms, as well as kitchen surfaces. The advantage of these glazed or vitreous ceramic squares is that they are waterproof, durable, easy to wipe clean and dry, and come in a huge range of colors.

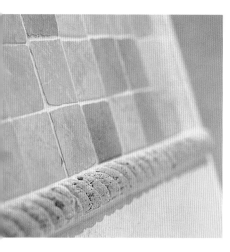

History of tiling

Although these days tiles are machine-made in many materials, originally they would have all been ceramic, handcrafted from local clay, and baked in a fire or, later, a kiln. Ceramic tiles are made in virtually every country in the world, and the ceramic tradition dates back thousands of years. Among the most widely found base for tiles is terra-cotta, a low-fired red clay. In its basic form this tile can be simply glazed or waxed to cover the porous surface, but in more sophisticated realms it can be highly decorated with painted designs in many colors. The Greeks and Romans both used this type of decorated tile in the interiors of their homes, and examples of fine mosaic patterns, made from hundreds of tiny colored tiles, can be seen in ancient sites throughout the world.

Other tiles were made with an earthenware base. During the 16th century this type was favored by the craftsmen in the

Above: Edging tiles with diagonal grooves give a rope-like effect and add a textured dimension.

Right: Small mosaic tiles are very popular in bathrooms today. Mix and match colors to create a pattern.

Opposite page: These matte tiles are made in very subtle, neutral coloring, which provides a sense of calm.

town of Delft, in southern Holland, where the tiles were glazed with a white background and decorated with patterns in various depths of blue. For over 400 years this blue-and-white configuration has been popular, and tiles are still made to this scheme.

Choosing your style

There is a wide variety of tiles to choose from, and you should select yours to suit the size of the room you are decorating, as well as to complement your scheme.

In a large bathroom walls of tiny mosaic tiles may look bitty and lost, and conversely, in a small room large ceramic panels may make the room feel smaller. Therefore, you should ensure that you choose the right size of tile to be in proportion to the setting. In most bathrooms it is usual to panel the area above the bathtub and sink with tiles in order to protect the immediate surrounding wall from water splashes and dampness. The walls, and even the ceiling and floor, of a shower stall may also be covered in tiles for the very same reason.

Tiles can be chosen to be plain and innocuous so that they are simply a background or you can select them to enhance and endorse a particular design. For example, in a Moorish bathroom tiles will be a feature – they are not only popular in the indigenous decoration of the country and are therefore appropriate when recreating such a style, but they are also colorful, incorporating dramatic, geometric patterns for added effect.

Small mosaic tiles can be used to form patterns or create pictures. Some of the popular patterns made using these small tiles include the ombre or shadow effect, which is a gradation of a single color that starts with dark toned tiles near the floor and gradually fades to the palest shade near the ceiling. If you are using blues you can create an underwater effect so that, when lying in the bathtub, it is as if you are at the bottom of a lagoon looking up to the sky above.

Larger, traditional tiles (4 x 4in/10 x 10cm) can be laid in regular lines parallel to the surface or floor, or set on their points to form a diamond pattern. You may also mix two or three shades of the same color, or contrasting shades such as black and white or blue and orange, to form a checkerboard effect.

Left: Here is an example of a strong, colorful Moorish bathroom tile design. Why not try incorporating such tiles in your own bathroom scheme and make a feature of them?

shade, different pattern or even paint or paper.

Most ceramic tiles are machine-made so that they are exactly the same size, thickness and color, which makes them easy to lay and provides a uniform finish. But, for more rustic or bohemian settings, there are also hand-made tiles and those that are manufactured so that they appear handmade. The surface of these tiles is uneven, slightly undulating and the colors vary a little too.

Matte finished tiles are ex-tremely popular today. These tiles date back to Victorian times when they were manufactured as encaustic tiles. They were especially favored by architects such as Pugin, who used them in grand civil buildings such as the Palace of Westminster, in London, England.

The pattern on these original, and now reproduction, Victorian tiles is made by inlaying contrast-ing colors of clay into the surface of the tile. This is then fired and the colors are fused and set. Some of the matte finish tiles have a sandstone appearance,

Another way of dividing up a large expanse of tiles is to create a frieze or border. This can be done by introducing a narrow band of smaller tiles such as mosaics, a contrasting line of narrow, linear tiles or a slightly raised feature tile that will form a divide between the upper and lower levels on the wall. The lower level may be in one color or size of tile while above there may be a deeper

Profiler

Tile-cutting tool

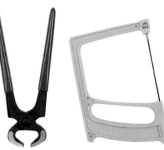

Tile nippers   *Tile saw*

and can be used in conjunction with other natural tiling material such as stone, slate and even cement in more contemporary style settings.

Tools and equipment
Tile-cutting tools

A variety of methods can be used for cutting tiles. The cheapest and simplest is a handheld tool that scores through the glaze of the tile, which will then snap along the line when pressure is applied. A sturdy version of the same tool incorporates a measuring gauge for accurate cutting and has a lever-operated snapping tool, which grips the tile. For thicker tiles, including quarry tiles, it is worth buying or renting an electric tile cutter, which incorporates a water reservoir, making cutting easier. Tile nippers and tile saws can be used for cutting irregular shapes

from tiles, but both methods require practice.

Tile spacers

These small plastic crosses act as spacers, making sure that each tile is an equal distance from the next. Different sizes are made to suit wall and floor tiles. They are pressed into the tile adhesive, making sure that they are below the surface of the tile so that when grout is applied, they are hidden.

Grout and adhesive

Adhesive is spread directly onto the wall surface with a notched spreader, which is often supplied with the adhesive. Tiles are pressed into the adhesive, which is allowed to dry before grout is applied. Grout is applied over the tiles with a smooth-edge tool that forces it into the spaces between the tiles. It is important to choose the correct adhesive and grout for

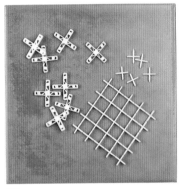

Tile spacers

the situation. Areas that will get very wet, like shower stalls, should be tiled using waterproof adhesive and grout, which will prevent water seeping through the grout lines into the wall. Areas like kitchen backsplashes, which will occasionally be splashed with water, do not require a waterproof grout and adhesive. Grout is available in a variety of colors, and you can also buy touch-up pens to refresh worn or dirty-looking grout.

Types
of tiles

Tiling is the most popular choice for protecting the walls in kitchens, bathrooms, and other areas where water is in use. When tiles are properly applied to a wall they provide a water-resistant barrier, which is easy to clean and maintain. Tiles of different sizes, made from many different materials, are now widely available. Tiling a small, regular-shape area is a fairly easy task, although you should be aware before starting that you will need to leave sufficient drying time between tiling and grouting.

Handmade tiles

These ceramic tiles are made by hand, from slabs of clay, which gives them their characteristic individual appearance. Slight differences in thickness and size will be noticeable, and, as they are glazed and fired in small batches, colors will vary from batch to batch. This variation is part of the appeal for many people. They are more expensive than mass-produced equivalents because they are labor-intensive.

Machine-made ceramic tiles

These tiles are made in large batches, often using liquid clay poured into a mold to be sure of the right consistency. Many have a printed surface decoration, which mimics expensive materials such as marble and stone.

They come in a large variety of different shapes and sizes, from conventional squares to large, rectangular slabs. Some manufactured tiles have a raised surface decoration, which is

Mesh-backed mosaics

Paper-backed mosaics

Machine-made ceramic tiles

applied before firing. Some have an undulating surface and uneven edges to mimic hand-made tiles.

Mosaic tiles

Mosaic tiles or tesserae come in a wide variety of materials, including glass, ceramic, and stone. The most expensive tesserae are made from a thin layer of gold leaf sandwiched between two pieces of glass. Most often associated with swimming pools, their versatility has made them increasingly popular in private homes over the last few years. Although mosaics appear in ultra-contemporary interiors, they have been used since Roman times in elaborate floor designs. Tesserae are smaller than conventional tiles and are often supplied on a paper or woven-fiber backing sheet. Mosaic tiles can also be purchased in loose form.

New materials

Designers are constantly exploring new materials, which can be made into tiles. Metal tiles or tiles with a metallic glaze have become a popular choice to complement stainless-steel and industrial-style kitchens. Resin tiles are available in a wide range of colors and have an opaque quality that suits contemporary interiors. Glass artists have developed a range of tiles, which fuse clear glass with other decorative materials. Printing techniques can also be used to apply a photographic image to your tiles.

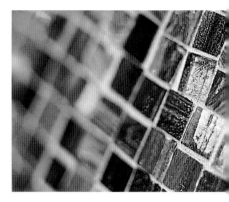

Above: Modern mosaic tiles come in a very wide range of colors and effects. They are made from glass and stone as well as the more common ceramics.

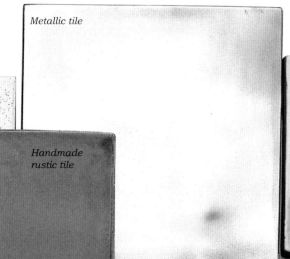

Metallic tile

Handmade rustic tiles

Machine-made rustic-style tile

Handmade rustic tile

Tiling techniques

To achieve a perfect tiled surface, plan your tiling scheme carefully to avoid awkward cuts and joints in obvious places. Make sure that you have ordered sufficient tiles for the job—always order around 10 percent extra to allow for any breakages. It is also a good idea to keep some spare tiles, for future repairs.

Cutting tiles

To cut tiles into regular shapes, score and cut with a tile cutter. To cut away irregular shapes, follow the instructions below.

Tools and materials

Tile cutter

Tile nippers

1 Score the glaze with a series of crosshatched lines.

Score the glaze with the scorer part of the tile-cutting tool.

2 Use tile nippers in order to "bite" away the pieces of unwanted tile. Carefully position the nippers before cutting.

Use tile nippers to break away the unwanted pieces of the tile.

Tiling a standard wall

Tools and materials

Level

Furring strip (optional)

Nails

Hammer

Notched trowel or spreader

Tiles and spacers

Adhesive

Grout

Flexible spreader

Cloth

Tiling difficult areas

If you are tiling difficult-to-reach areas such as the wall above a bathtub, sink, or kitchen worktop, it is important to check the level with a level before you begin tiling. Also, make sure that you take time to plan the spacing before you begin, so that you can avoid awkward tile cuts.

1 If you are tiling onto a blank wall, you should first establish a level by nailing a furring strip onto the wall, which will provide your starting point.

Nail a wooden strip to a wall in a straight line for a starting point.

2 Use a notched trowel or spreader to apply an even layer of tile adhesive to the wall. Work on an area of 1 yd sq (1 m sq) at a time —any larger, and the adhesive will dry before you can apply the tiles.

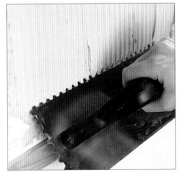

Use a notched trowel to apply adhesive to the wall.

3 Apply the first row of tiles so that they butt up against the strip. Then remove one prong from each spacer to form a T shape and push the spacer into position. If you need to use any half tiles or cut tiles, make sure that you position these in the darkest corner of the room, where they are least likely to be seen. Before positioning the second row of tiles, push whole spacers in place to make sure that they are evenly spaced. Allow the adhesive to dry thoroughly overnight before you begin to grout.

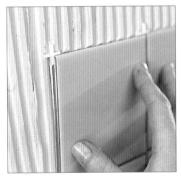

Cut spacers into a T shape and position them between each tile.

4 Use a flexible spreader to apply the grout, pushing it down well into the gaps between the tiles. Remove any excess with a damp cloth and allow the tiles to dry. Polish the tiles to remove any remaining film.

Use a flexible spreader to apply grout between the tiles.

Tiling a kitchen worktop

If you are tiling an awkward-shape object, such as a kitchen worktop, make sure that the top is completely level by using a level before you begin. If the surface is not perfectly flat, you may have to fit a piece of plywood to the top before you can begin tiling.

Tools and materials

Glue solution
Paintbrush
Tiles
Notched trowel or spreader
Adhesive
Spacers
Grout
Tile cutter
Cloth

Left: Blue is a popular color for a bathroom and these variegated tiles give a shimmering effect.

1 To be sure of the best finish, it is worth laying the tiles out dry before applying any adhesive. By doing this you can plan the design and work out the ideal places to use cut tiles. It is best to begin with full tiles along the front edge of the work surface, so that any cuts can be planned to appear along the back junction with the wall. Likewise, if the work surface includes a corner, it is best to start with a full tile in the corner, and build up the rest of the design from this point.

2 To make the tiling easier, apply a coat of glue solution (1 part white glue to 5 parts water) to the plywood surface. This helps to seal the board, making it easier to spread adhesive. Allow the glue to dry before proceeding to tile.

3 Use a notched trowel or spreader, ideally a large one, to spread adhesive across the plywood surface. Do not spread more than about 1 yd sq (1 m sq) at a time. Use the notches to maintain a consistent depth of adhesive, which helps to ensure a consistent tile level.

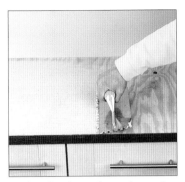

Apply adhesive to the surface using a notched spreader.

correctly, and use spacers to keep all gaps consistent. Spacers will also be required, albeit temporarily, along the junction between the edge tiles and the wooden edge strip, to ensure the lines of tiles are kept consistent.

5 Once the adhesive has dried completely, grout the tiled surface with an epoxy grout. This type of grout is more durable than standard grout, and more hygienic for surfaces upon which food will almost certainly be prepared. It is best to concentrate on small areas at a time, since epoxy grout can be difficult to work with, and also tends to dry extremely fast. Make sure that you force the grout firmly into every joint, removing any excess as quickly as possible with a damp sponge before it has had a chance to dry.

4 Apply the tiles, pressing them down into the adhesive with a slight twisting motion. Since the tiles are applied to a horizontal surface there is no risk of them slipping down, but it still pays to be vigilant. If rows of tiles are allowed to go out of square, this will affect the finish and lead to some unsightly tile cutting. So take time to position the tiles

Use spacers to ensure that the gap between tiles is even.

Spread the grout, taking care to force it into the joints.

6 Wait until the grout has completely dried out, then give the tiled surface a final wipe before polishing with a cotton cloth. This will help to remove any remaining grout residue, and will leave a clean and bright-finished surface.

Hints and tips

Preparation is essential when tiling. Before they can be tiled, walls must first be prepared so that they are in a sound condition to receive the adhesive. Before applying the adhesive, therefore, remove wallpaper and fill any holes (see pages 38–42).

Keeping the area and your tools clean is also essential. Have a bucket of warm water and a sponge to hand at all times when you are tiling. Keeping your hands and tools as clean as possible will also help make the job easier as you can work with precision.

Cutting tiles is probably the most difficult part of the job when tiling. If you have a lot of tiles to cut, it is worth renting an electric tile cutter with a diamond cutting wheel from your local tool rental store. Electric tile cutters work with water for lubrication, and make cutting tiles quick and easy.

Choosing your
flooring

Flooring comes in a wide range of finishes, from natural wood and stone to the woven fibers of coconut husks and jute stems that form coir and sisal. These surfaces can be plain or decorative, rough or smooth—whichever you choose, make sure that it has the durability required for your room.

History of flooring

The earliest homes had beaten mud floors covered with hunks of grass or rushes, but as time went by flagstones were hewn and laid, and mats woven of rush became more commonplace. Clay tiles were used in Egypt and the Romans developed concrete for their decorative mosaic tile floors.

Wood has also been popular for centuries, from simple, wooden plank arrangements to the more ornate herringbone, parquet, and even inlaid floors dating back to the Tudor and Stuart periods. In the early 18th century woven carpets were popular in grand homes. Less expensive painted canvas floorcloths were also popular in America and Britain at this time.

Animal skins and hides have also been used as floor coverings through the ages and, like a woolen mat or rug, can be used to bring warmth and softness to an area of hard stone or tile covering.

Although pile carpets were developed in India before the 12th century, most floor coverings in the West were flat-woven until the 19th century.

In the 1840s a revolution started that brought the luxury of carpets and rugs to a far wider audience, when a steam engine was used to power a loom. By the 1950s the high-speed tufting machine was developed and the rug and carpet industry took on the mass market. With the ability to manufacture carpet by the mile new, cheaper, synthetic fibers were also introduced. These fibers, such as nylon and acrylic, brought the prices down even further.

Choosing your style

When choosing flooring, make sure that you incorporate the floor coverings into the overall

Above: Limestone floors look stylish and are also easy to look after.

Opposite: Neutral colored natural fiber floor coverings can tie in with any color scheme.

Above: The grain patterns in timber floorboards can be very decorative.

Opposite: The expanse of these large white tiles has been broken up by using small black tiles.

Choosing the right floor for each room

Different areas of the home will require different types of flooring to suit the demands of the room. For example, kitchen and bathroom floors have to be easy to wipe clean and capable of putting up with water splashes and drips. In a bedroom the floor covering should be warm and comfortable under bare feet. Hallways may be carpeted, but if you want to protect the main track or pathway acrpss the room, you could lay a runner or rug over the wall to wall floor covering.

decorative scheme. As a general rule, it is best to have a mix of pattern and plain in a room—for example, plain walls look good with a patterned floor, as does a plain floor with patterned walls. Avoid using pattern on all surfaces because it can be overwhelming. It may also be appropriate to consider the style and period of your home, and the furniture that is to be used in the room where the floor covering is to be laid.

Natural floor coverings have become increasingly fashionable and include wood, cork, coir, various stones, and terra-cotta and brick tiles. Wood generally has a warm color, is pleasant to walk on, and when polished reflects light back into the room. When installed in large rooms or areas it softens sounds, and is less likely to cause echoing than harder surfaces such as stone. As a rule, wood improves with age as the color mellows and becomes richer. Dents and marks only add

to its character, and some contemporary floor suppliers distress their new wood floors to give them a worn and vintage appearance. Wood is also a good canvas—it can be stripped, sanded, and stained. Paint borders around the edge, or choose an all-over pattern.

Another natural floor covering is natural matting, which is made from coir, sisal, and jute. Some mats have patterns woven or printed onto the edges, creating a traditional effect, and colored bindings of leather or woven wool can be used to link in to the color theme of the whole room.

Marble, granite, limestone, and slate have natural decoration in the veins and striations of their formation. Stone floors tend to be expensive, but withstand hard treatment and are easy to clean. To soften hardness and reduce echoing, use kelims and mats to break up large areas.

The rich, red color of brick and terra-cotta tiles adds warmth to any room. Brick comes in a variety of shades, from yellow through to browns and red, and these shades can be used to create patterns—or single-colored bricks can be laid to form a herringbone design. These surfaces are ideal for halls, kitchens, cloakrooms, and conservatories.

Types of flooring

When deciding on the flooring for each room of your home, it is important to consider the amount of wear and tear each area will receive, and choose a floor type accordingly. Flooring falls into several categories, ranging from soft flooring, which includes carpets and rugs, to hard flooring, which includes wood, stone, and tile, at the other extreme. Semi-hard flooring is the intermediate category, which includes materials such as vinyl, linoleum, and rubber.

Soft flooring
Carpet
Carpet is one of the most comfortable and luxurious floor coverings. The best-quality carpets have a high wool content—wool fiber repels dirt naturally, is soft underfoot, and has a long life span. Synthetic fibers take color well, and can be treated to make them resistant to stains. They are often combined with wool to produce durable carpets for areas of heavy wear. Common types of carpet pile are twist and velvet—twist pile is denser and more suitable for heavy-wear areas, while velvet pile is longer and softer, making it the ideal choice for bedrooms.

Coir, sisal and jute
Natural floor coverings have become increasingly popular in recent years. Natural matting made from coir, sisal, and jute can be laid like a carpet or used in bound squares or runners for halls, stairways, or as a central panel over a wood or stone floor.

Wood veneer tongue and groove flooring

Marble floor tile

Terra-cotta quarry tile

Slate floor tile

Ceramic floor tile

Most natural-fiber floor coverings have a vinyl rubber backing and require specialized fitting. Some combine the toughness of natural fibers with the softness of wool carpeting on a jute backing. There are also unusual woven-paper floor coverings available, which are tough and durable due to the tightness of the weave. These come from renewable sources so are environmentally sound, but, because the material is dried, it is not advisable to use natural fibers directly in front of a fireplace where sparks may tumble out and burn it, or by a sink where water will splash and cause damage.

Hard flooring
Wood

There are various types of wood used for floors. The more expensive are the hardwoods such as oak, ash, walnut, iroko, elm, and maple. The cheaper softwoods such as pine are often stained or decorated because they lack the rich color of hardwoods. Left in its natural state, wood flooring can be laid in herringbone patterns, in parquet-style designs or as planks in a staggered configuration so that a pattern is formed by the wood.

Wood is a "living" material and so should be properly treated and dried before being laid. Central

Alternative flooring

New technology is bringing exciting advances in floor coverings. Cork floor tiles that combine natural material with photographic images of subjects such as pebbles, grass, and leaves are available. Vinyl floor tiles that mimic materials such as mosaic, exotic woods, and metal give the appearance of the materials they imitate without the hardness underfoot. Floor coverings that utilize the large amount of waste plastic we produce are also being pioneered.

Natural sisal
(front example has colored weft)

Wool twist carpet

Ribbed wool carpets with a sisal weft

Mosaic-style vinyl

Self-adhesive vinyl tile

heating can cause the boards to dry out and shrink whereas a spillage of water, such as a regular leak from a pipe, will make the boards swell. New wood floors should be left for at least 48 hours to acclimatize to a room's environment before being laid.

As an everyday surface, wood is comparatively easy to clean—you can simply brush it or wipe over the top with a damp cloth or mop. Depending on the finish of the wood it may need to be wax polished every month or so or, if it is varnished, stripped and recoated about every ten years, depending on its location and the wear that it takes.

A cheap alternative to wood is laminate flooring. The laminating process involves taking a photographic image of woodgrain, printing it onto paper that is then sandwiched between chipboard and a plastic-coated surface to make a realistic-looking plank of flooring.

Stone

One of the advantages of stone is that it is virtually indestructible, making it an ideal choice for the kitchen. On the negative side, it is unforgiving to items accidentally dropped onto it. Also, stone can feel cold underfoot, although this can be easily remedied with radiant heating systems, which make it pleasant to walk on with bare feet. Because of the cost of stone, it is advisable to have it laid by a professional.

Tiles

Tiles come in a huge variety of designs, many of which mimic stone and marble. Glazed ceramic floor tiles can be fitted by the competent DIY enthusiast and are less costly than other hard floor coverings. The tiles should be made specifically for floor use, as tiles destined for wall or work surfaces (see pages 76–7) will not be as thick or heavy and will, in time, crack and break if used underfoot. The shiny surface of ceramic tiles makes them very easy to clean but they are prone to breaking and chipping if a heavy object is dropped on them or if they are laid on anything other than a perfectly flat surface.

Industrial-style floors

Industrial-style floor coverings have also crossed over into the home and include hard materials such as concrete, stone, metal and rubber. Concrete can be colored and polished to a high sheen, when it will take on a highly decorative appearance and can therefore work well in homes.

Metal treadplate tiles have become increasingly popular in kitchens—they complement stainless steel accessories and add to the professional appearance of a kitchen. Rubber flooring, which has long been associated with schools and hospitals, is now valued in the home for its warmth underfoot and non-slip qualities, making it an ideal choice for the bathroom.

Semi-hard floorings
Manufactured floor coverings

These include linoleum, rubber and vinyl tiles. They can be laid in many patterns, the most common being the black and white checkerboard design. Linoleum, vinyl and cushioned vinyl floor coverings also come by the roll and can be cut and fitted like a carpet. Most are hardwearing and low on maintenance but the surface may be harmed by a sharp or hot object. Linoleum was developed in the late 19th century but went out of fashion until recently—it is now definitely back in vogue. This type of flooring is regarded as being utilitarian so is most appropriate for bathrooms, kitchens and hallways.

Cork

Cork, which is also returning to popularity, is usually treated with

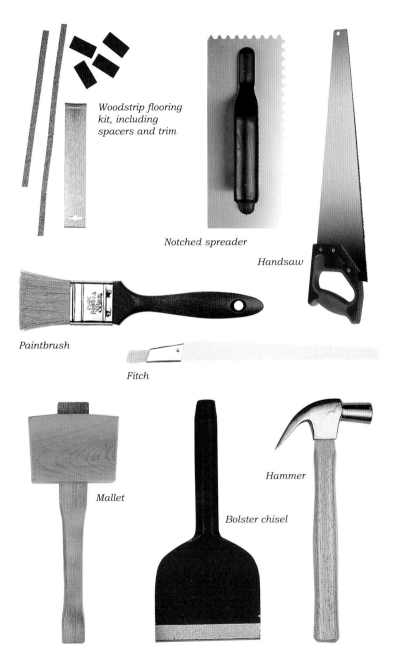

Woodstrip flooring kit, including spacers and trim

Notched spreader

Handsaw

Paintbrush

Fitch

Mallet

Hammer

Bolster chisel

a rubber backing and a surface sealant (especially if in tile form) to prevent it from becoming damaged by water or moisture.

Cork comes from the outer bark of the cork oak tree, which regrows, so is a renewable resource. It is also a soft surface to walk on and it has good insulating properties.

Essential tools

When fitting carpet, in addition to a utility knife for cutting the carpet, you will require a knee kicker to stretch the carpet as well as a bolster chisel and mallet to anchor it over tackless strips.

Installation kits for tongue-and-groove wood and laminate flooring include plastic spacers, cork expansion strips and a metal edging device used with a hammer to fit the plank nearest the wall. You also need a handsaw to cut the final planks to the correct size.

Use a large notched spreader to apply the correct depth of adhesive when laying a tiled floor. For thicker tiles it is worth hiring a tile cutter or angle grinder.

Paint, stain or varnish can be applied with brushes or small rollers. For a clear finish, such as a varnish, it is worth investing in a good quality woodcare brush. Use a smaller brush if you are painting a detailed pattern.

Flooring techniques

Before installing a new floor or refurbishing an old one, you must first consider the length of time that the room will be out of use, as this may affect the technique that you choose to use. You also need to remove all furniture and fixtures, before beginning to install anything. It is also a good idea to draw a floor plan on a piece of graph paper to enable you to work out the quantities needed with accuracy.

Electric sanders

Make sure you rent sanders from a reputable company who will explain the safety drill and controls before you start. Most rental stores rent floor sanders and edging sanders as a package you pay for by the day or the weekend—you will pay extra for the sanding disks and belts. It is essential to wear ear plugs, dust mask, and goggles while operating the machines. Tape a plastic drop cloth over the door to the room in which you are working, to prevent sawdust spreading to other rooms.

Wooden floorboards

Wooden flooring is a practical choice for every room. Most older houses have floorboards through-out, which, if you are lucky, will be in good enough condition to restore. There are a number of different ways in which you can finish floorboards that have a build-up of years of old finishes. Sanding them back to bare wood is quite a labor-intensive job, but it gives you the choice of applying a natural finish or tinting with a translucent varnish in a variety of shades. If you do not want the disruption of sanding the floor, there are specialized floor paints available in a wide range of colors, which can be painted directly onto unstripped floorboards. This is a quick method, but it is an opaque finish, so will not show the grain. On the plus side, it gives you the chance to apply a decorative pattern or motif to the floor.

Preparation and repair of floorboards

Tools and materials

Hammer

Blunt chisel and pliers

Nail set

Spiral nails

1 If the room is carpeted, roll up the carpet and remove. Jute-backed carpet will have been tacked in place with carpet tacks or tackless strips—work your way around the edges of the room with a hammer, blunt chisel, and pair of pliers, pulling up the tackless strips or tacks that held the carpet in place.

2 Use the hammer and nail set to drive down any nails that are sticking above the surface (this is very important if you are going to be using an electric sander, as rogue nails can tear the sanding belt and damage the machine).

Push down any nails that are sticking above the surface.

3 Check for loose floorboards, and secure them to the joists with spiral nails.

Applying a painted finish over old floorboards

Tools and materials

Floor cleaner

Sanding block and coarse-grit abrasive paper

Flexible wood filler and knife

Painter's tape

Paintbrush, or roller and extension pole, and paint

1 Vacuum to remove dust, then clean the floor thoroughly with a commercial floor cleaner that will remove traces of old wax or polish. Allow to dry. Use a sanding block and coarse-grit abrasive paper to remove any stubborn marks and areas of raised grain that might show through the paint. Use flexible wood filler to fill in any gouges or holes that will spoil the finish.

2 Mask off the baseboards with painter's tape and prepare to apply the paint, starting from the corner of the room farthest away from the door. You can use a large paintbrush or, if you prefer, a roller attached to an extension pole. Work quickly in the direction of the grain. Allow the paint to dry, and repaint if necessary.

Use a roller to paint the floorboards in the direction of the woodgrain.

Stripping and finishing floorboards

Large electric sanders can look somewhat daunting, but they do make stripping floorboards a much less arduous task. Most homeowners would prefer to rent one (see box, opposite page).

Tools and materials

Electric floor sander

Abrasive paper—from coarse-grit through to fine

Steel wool, cloth, and mineral spirits

Floor finish

Paintbrush

1 Fit the floor sander with coarse-grit abrasive paper. Position it in the corner of the room so that you will be able to work your way across the room in diagonal strips. Holding the machine by the handle, tilt it back so that the sanding belt is off the floor. Turn the machine on and lower the machine so that the sanding belt makes contact with the floor. Begin pushing the machine forward immediately, because if you leave it stationary in one place, it will sand a deep gouge in the floorboards. When you reach the end of the room, tilt the machine

Use the sander in a diagonal direction across the floor.

back and reposition it to sand the next strip. Work your way diagonally across the room. Change to medium-grit abrasive paper and work back at right angles.

2 Use the edging sander around the edges of the room, working your way through the grades of abrasive paper. Finish any tricky inside corners by hand with steel wool and a little mineral spirits, or with the pointed end of a shaped electric sander. Complete this task before finishing off with the drum (step 3) so that you will avoid walking across the finished boards unnecessarily.

Work around the edges of the room using the edging sander.

3 Finish off with fine-grit abrasive paper attached to the drum sander, and work your way back and forth along the floorboards in the direction of the grain for a really smooth finish. Allow the

dust to settle, vacuum thoroughly, then wipe away any residue of sawdust with a cloth dampened with mineral spirits.

Finish the sanding by fitting the drum with fine-grade abrasive paper and working with the grain.

4 Seal with the finish of your choice. There are a large number of different varieties of floor finish available—the most durable types are oil-based with a gloss finish; acrylic-based finishes dry more quickly, making it easier to complete the job in a single weekend. Some finishes are completely clear while others are tinted, stained, or dyed, which will subtly change the final color of the floorboards. Apply the floor finish with a large, good-quality paintbrush, working from the corner of the room toward the door. Leave the finish to dry completely, and then reapply floor finish if necessary.

Apply your chosen floor finish with a good quality paintbrush.

Tongue-and-groove wood and laminate flooring

Tongue-and-groove flooring is available in many different varieties. The most expensive is solid wood, which is both attractive and durable, and can be sanded and refinished if necessary. Most manufacturers recommend tongue-and-groove flooring for every room except the bathroom, where water could cause warping. Wood veneer varieties are mid-priced and have a surface of real wood on a composite base. Laminated designs vary enormously in price —the really good-quality ones are virtually indistinguishable from real wood, and they are also almost indestructible.

When laying laminate floors, some systems require the tongue-

and-groove joints to be glued and left overnight to dry. The newest varieties on the market simply click together and can be walked on immediately.

Tools and materials

Laminated strips and padding
Handsaw or jigsaw
Plastic spacers and tool
Hammer
Metal S-shape tool
Quarter-round molding
Miter saw
Brad nails

1 Unpack the flooring and leave it in the room for 24 hours—this allows it to acclimatize to the temperature. If possible the baseboards should be removed so the expansion strip can be fitted underneath. If it is not possible to remove the baseboards, use a

quarter-round molding to hide the expansion strip. Lay the padding —this usually consists of a poly-thene vapor retarder followed by a cushioning foam layer.

2 Cut the first board using a sharp handsaw or jigsaw, follow-ing the instructions on the pack-et. Place the cut end in the corner of the room, with the same end against the wall. Apply the recom-mended wood glue sparingly into the groove of the floorboards.

3 Continue adding planks of flooring, following the pattern set out in the instructions. Use plas-tic spacers around the outside edge of the floor between the boards and the wall. This will become an expansion gap. Use the plastic tool provided to join the planks by tapping gently with a hammer.

Laying laminate flooring

Do not attempt to lay one of the more expensive tongue-and-groove floors yourself, as you may actually invalidate the manufacturers' guarantee if you make a mistake. The cheaper, laminated varieties are relatively easy to lay yourself with a bit of planning (see steps, left).

4 When you get to the end of a row of planks, hook the metal S-shape tool over the edge of the last plank, and gently ham-mer against the other end of the tool to fix the plank in place.

Use the S-shaped tool to fix the last piece of floor into place.

5 Repeat the whole process for the next row of planks and continue until the floor has been laid, using

Lay down the foam padding before you start.

Join the planks together by tapping on the plastic tool with a hammer.

the same method. Then remove the plastic spacers and push the cork expansion strips between the last plank and the wall.

Lay down the cork expansion strips, pushing them between the last plank and the wall.

6 Replace the baseboard, or add quarter-round molding against the baseboard, using brad nails, to cover the expansion gap. Cut the molding with a miter saw to fit inside and outside corners.

Fit quarter-round molding between the flooring edge and baseboards.

Concrete floors

Concrete is gaining popularity as a flooring material, particularly in areas with an industrial feel, such as catering-style kitchens. On the down side, it is fairly cold underfoot and unforgiving to items dropped on it. It can also stain easily if not sealed properly.

Concrete can look very attractive when polished to a sheen, providing it is in good condition. Using a self-leveling floor compound will sort out any uneven areas. For larger areas, it is advisable to call in the professionals, who will lay the floor and polish it. They can also supply more exotic concrete-based finishes such as terrazzo, which is a concrete-and-marble-chip composition, polished to a high shine. Plain concrete floors provide a good base for a painted design. Some floor paints are specially formulated for painting onto concrete, although the colors tend to have an industrial feel.

Using a self-leveling floor compound

This simple product is great for use on existing concrete floors that have seen better days. Mix the compound according to the

Left: Tongue-and-groove flooring creates a clean and contemporary look in any room.

manufacturer's instructions, then pour over the floor, leaving it to find its own level. Various decorative effects, such as flagstones, can be achieved by using a stick to make regular patterns in the compound as it starts to set.

Tools and materials

Bonding agent and brush

Self-leveling floor compound

Mixing bucket or trough

Stirring stick or drill attachment

Plasterer's float

Stick for flagstone effect (optional)

Paint, brush, or roller/tray (optional)

1 Clean the floor, brushing away any loose or flaking areas of concrete. Paint bonding agent (a solution of white glue and water) over the floor.

Mix up a solution of white glue and water, and paint it over the floor.

Preparing concrete floors for a tiled finish

For a good quality tiled floor you must first have a level surface. The best way to make sure of a completely level, flat floor is to apply a self-leveling compound over your existing concrete floor. See this page for instructions on using it. Seal the completed level surface with a solution of bonding agent to prevent the tile adhesive from drying out too quickly.

2 Mix up the floor compound then carefully pour it over the floor, working from the far corner toward the door. Use a float to smooth the compound into every corner, then allow it to settle.

Smooth the self-leveling compound using a float.

Finding the center point of a room

Draw two intersecting diagonal lines from each corner of the room. The point at which they meet is the center point. An alternative method is to use a steel rule—find the center of the room by marking a line vertically and horizontally. The point where the lines meet is the center of the floor.

3 To create a flagstone effect on your floor (optional), use a stick to mark out the lines between 'stones' in the compound.

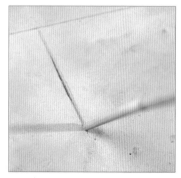

Mark the flagstone "lines" with a stick to create a flagstone effect.

4 Alternatively, if you want to paint the floor, wait until the compound has dried out thoroughly, then seal the surface with dilute white glue or a multi-purpose

primer, and allow to dry. Paint using special floor paint for concrete floors, applying it with a broad brush or roller. Start in the far corner of the room, and paint out from there.

Use special concrete floor paint and apply with a roller or brush.

Tiled flooring

Before tiling a floor, you will need to be sure that the tiles have a completely flat, sound surface to adhere to. How you prepare the floor will depend on the finish that is currently in place.

Preparing floorboards for a tiled finish

Wooden floorboards expand and contract in different temperatures and flex underfoot, which means that before laying ceramic, stone, or quarry tiles on this type of floor you will need to lay a more rigid surface of plywood sheets over the floorboards.

Tools and materials

Graph paper and pencil
Plywood sheets
Jigsaw
Cordless drill/driver
Screws, hammer, and nails

1 Sketch the dimensions of your floor on graph paper to work out the quantity of plywood you will need. It comes in standard 4 x 8ft (1.5 x 2.5m) sheets, although many lumber merchants will cut it to your specifications. Lay the sheets out over the floorboards, trimming with a jigsaw where necessary.

2 Start in the corner of the room, then screw in place every 6in (15cm) until the whole floor is covered. Seal with a solution of bonding agent before tiling.

Screw in the floorboards at 6in (15cm) intervals with a screwdriver.

Before you begin laying floor tiles, ensure that your floor is perfectly flat.

Laying ceramic tiles

These are thin, glazed tiles that often mimic more expensive slate, stone, or quarry tiles. Being thin, they are easier for the home handyperson to cut and lay than thicker tiles.

Tools and materials

Tiles

Wood strips and metal rule

Adhesive and notched trowel

Plastic spacers

Level

Tile cutter

Grout

Cloth or sponge

1 Start by establishing the center point of your room (see box on opposite page), then lay out a practice run of tiles, allowing $^1/_8$in (3mm) for grout lines. This allows

Work out where the tiles will fall around the room.

you to establish the size of the edge tiles.

2 Nail two straight wood strips to the floor at the point where the last row of whole tiles ends. Check the angle between the two strips is exactly 90 degrees so the run is completely straight.

Nail wood strips in place where the last row of tiles will end.

3 Working in manageable areas of approximately 1 yd sq (1 m sq),

Spread the tile adhesive out over the surface of the floor.

spread the tile adhesive evenly over the floor, using the notched spreader to achieve a good and even coverage.

4 Place the first tile at the point where the two strips meet, pressing it firmly into the adhesive. Use plastic spacers between tiles to be sure of even spacing, and then continue to lay all the whole tiles using the same method. Check for level with a level.

Put the first tile in place where the two strips meet, and push down.

5 Work out the sizes of the tiles to be cut by placing them over the last whole tile, butting another tile up to the skirting board and using it as a cutting guide. Allow an extra $1/8$ in (3mm) space for the grouting. Cut the tiles by gripping them in the tile cutter and using the cutting blade to score the glaze.

Score the glaze of the tile with the cutting blade.

6 Snap the tile cleanly in two by placing it in the relevant part of the tool.

Cut the tiles by snapping them cleanly in the mouth of the tool.

7 If the gap where the cut tiles are to go is small, carefully butter the tiles with adhesive before fixing them in place. Leave the tiles to dry overnight. Do not walk on the tiles during this time or you may dislodge them.

Butter the cut tiles with adhesive before laying if the space is small.

8 Next apply the grout over the surface of the tiles using the smooth edge of the notched trowel to achieve an even, level coating of grout.

Apply the grout over the surface of the tiles using a notched trowel.

9 When the grout has hardened clean off any residue from the grout with a clean cloth. Allow the tiles to dry and then give them a good polish.

Clean off any ground residue using a cloth and then polish.

Cutting round obstacles

Cutting tiles into regular shapes is fairly straightforward—once the glaze has been scored they will break cleanly along the line. Cutting tiles into irregular shapes is much more difficult, and most methods are fairly labor intensive. It pays to plan your tiling carefully to avoid having to make awkward cuts. Straight lines can be cut with an electric tile cutter, which works using a blade lubricated with water. These can be bought or hired from a tool rental outlet. Irregular shapes, such as curves around pipes, can be cut with a tile saw. Alternatively, you can score the tile with a tile cutting wheel then use tile nippers to gradually chip away the unwanted part of the tile.

Using a profiler

This clever tool uses a series of plastic rods to transfer the shape of the obstacle onto the tile to ensure accurate cutting.

1 Line the profiler up with the tile to be cut, then push the profiler against the obstacle. This will cause the rods to form a template of the obstacle on the tile. Use a pencil to draw carefully around the template.

Use a profiler to measure the space around awkward obstacles.

2 Grip the tile carefully in a vice (padded with an old cloth), then use a tile saw to cut away the waste part of the tile carefully.

Laying slate and stone tiles

Slate and stone slabs are hard, natural materials, which make excellent heavy-duty floor coverings. Although they are laid using virtually the same technique as ceramic floor tiles they need to be bedded into a thick, cement based adhesive. The irregular thickness of the slabs and their cost makes laying these materials a tricky job, which is best left to experts. If you do choose to lay them yourself seek specialist advice from your supplier. Work slowly on a small area, checking the level of each slab carefully as you work. Slabs will vary in thickness, which means you will have to vary the thickness of the cement bed. Stone and slate also require the use of specialized cutting tools, such as angle grinders, which shear through the extra tough slabs. They may require sealing once laid, to avoid surface staining.

Laying mosaic flooring

Before laying a mosaic tiled floor the surface should be prepared in the same way as for a standard tiled floor (see pages 95–6). Mosaic tiles come in a variety of different materials, including ceramic, glass, and stone. The individual tiles are called tesserae and are sold loose or stuck to a paper or mesh backing. For a large floor area it is best to use the tesserae with a backing. Many come in blends of toning colors mixed randomly on a sheet.

If you wish to lay the tiles in a pattern plan the design carefully first on a piece of graph paper. There are two methods of laying tesserae: the direct method where the tiles are laid directly in place in the adhesive and the indirect method, where tiles are stuck back-to-front on gummed brown paper and then pressed in place in the adhesive.

For an expanse of tiles with a simple pattern, use sheets of single-colored tiles on a backing material and carefully pick off some of the tiles and replace them with other colors to build up a pattern.

Laying sheet mosaic with a pattern

Tools and materials

Steel rule

Floor tile adhesive

Notched spatula

Mosaic tiles

Newspaper and painter's tape

Scissors or utility knife

Tile nippers

Sponge and abrasive pad

Floor grout and spreader

Soft cloths

1 When using the direct method, plan your mosaic design before you start to lay the tiles.

Plan your design while the tesserae are attached to the backing paper.

2 Prepare your floor as described above. Find the center point (see page 96) and, working from there outwards, spread the floor tile adhesive to cover about 1 sq yd (1 sq m) at a time. Use the notched side of the spatula so the tiles will stick easily. Lay the sheets of mosaic tiles, one at a time. Make sure that they are pushed well into the adhesive.

Lay the sheets of tiles one at a time and push firmly into the adhesive.

3 Work your way to the outer edges of the floor, using the same method until you are left with any areas that will need to be covered with cut sheets. Mask off the baseboards with newspaper and painter's tape, then work your way around the edges of the floor, applying the adhesive as described above. Cut any sheets that require trimming with a sharp pair of scissors or a utility knife and lay the sheets as described above.

4 Any tiles that require cutting should be stuck last of all. Use a pair of tile nippers, and cut the tiles to size. If you work with the direction of the grooves (if using glass tesserae), you should find that the tiles snap cleanly. Shaping tiles to form irregular shapes with the nippers will take a bit more practice. Use them to

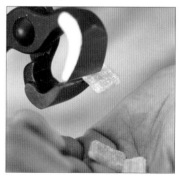

Any individual tiles that need cutting should be cut with tile nippers.

nibble away at the tiles a bit at a time. Allow the adhesive to dry overnight before continuing.

5 Soak the backing paper using warm water on a sponge; allow to soak. Gently peel off the backing paper. Remove any stubborn areas of paper with an abrasive pad.

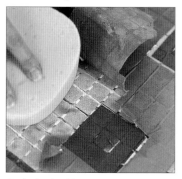

Soak the backing paper with a sponge, let it soak in well and then peel it away.

6 Mix up the floor grout following the manufacturer's instructions, and apply it to the tiles with a grout spreader, making sure that you work the grout well in between the tessarae. Allow the grout to dry for about twenty minutes. Wipe off the excess grout with a soft cloth before it is completely dry. Once the grout has dried completely, you can use a clean cloth to polish the tesserae to a final shine.

Spread the floor grout over the tesserae with a grout spreader.

Vinyl floor coverings

Vinyl is an ideal floor covering for kitchens and bathrooms because it is resilient and easy to clean, and it now comes in a multitude of different designs. Vinyl flooring is available in sheet or tile form. The sheet vinyl comes in a standard thickness or it can be cushioned with the addition of a foam padding sandwiched between vinyl. This makes a very comfortable floor surface on which to walk or stand while you are working in the kitchen.

Make sure that the floor is properly prepared (see page 90) before laying the vinyl as described below. The vinyl should be left loosely rolled in the room for 48 hours before laying, because this will increase its suppleness and ensure that it lies flat.

Laying sheet vinyl

Tools and materials

Measuring tape, paper, and pen

Vinyl flooring

Sharp utility knife

Vinyl flooring adhesive and spreader, or heavy-duty double-sided flooring tape

Scissors

Profiler (if there are obstacles in the room)

Metal straightedge

1 Measure the room and draw a rough plan on a piece of paper so you can plan any joins. Cut the vinyl roughly to size, allowing about 1ft (30cm) all round, and lay in position. Cut away squares at each corner and make a series of release cuts, which will allow you to push the vinyl right into the baseboard. Trim away the excess with a sharp utility knife.

Trim away the excess vinyl at each corner.

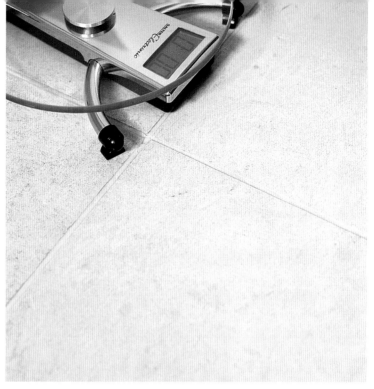

2 To fit the vinyl against an uneven wall, use a scrap of wood, and rest the pencil against it while you slide it along the length of the wall. Your pencil line will follow the contour of the wall—use this pencil line as a guide, and trim the vinyl with a sharp utility knife or scissors so that it fits neatly against the wall.

Stone tiles are particularly suitable for use in kitchens.

Use a wood scrap and pencil to mark against an uneven wall.

3 When you come across obstacles such as doorways make release cuts in the vinyl on each side of the frame, or for more complicated shapes use a profiler, which is pushed into the molding and then used as a template for cutting. For simple, larger items like bathroom fixtures, you can simply make a series of release cuts around the object, then trim the vinyl so that it makes a close fit for the item.

When you reach an obstacle, make cuts in the vinyl, then trim to fit.

4 To make perfect joints in two lengths of vinyl, overlap them, making sure that if the vinyl is patterned there is a match between them. Use a utility knife and metal straightedge to cut through both thicknesses of vinyl.

Cut through the overlapped pieces of vinyl with a sharp utility knife.

5 Pull back the edges of the strips and stick down with double-sided flooring tape. Alternatively, you could use vinyl adhesive spread and apply it with a notched spreader.

Laying vinyl, rubber, or cork floor tiles

Vinyl and cork floor tiles are laid using exactly the same method as has just been described. Some have a self-adhesive backing covered with paper, which is simply peeled off when you are ready to stick it down. Other tiles will have to be stuck in place with the manufacturer's recommended adhesive or double-sided flooring tape. Always make sure that you have a clean, level surface to work on, although soft floor tiles are more forgiving of slight irregularities in the surface than hard tiles are.

Tools and materials

Steel measuring rule and pencil

Vinyl tiles

Adhesive and spreader (optional)

Scissors or sharp utility knife

Paper (if there are obstacles)

1 Find the mid-point of the room (see box, page 96). Lay out the tiles in a "dry run," working from the center point outwards. If you find that you are left with small fiddly cut tiles around the edges, adjust the start line, moving it further away from the wall. Half tiles laid against opposite walls will look better than a tiny strip against one wall.

Use a steel tape measure to work out the center point of the room.

2 If you are using adhesive work on 1yd sq (1m sq) of floor at a time, allowing you time to position the tiles perfectly. If you are

Lay the first tile carefully along your center line.

using self-adhesive tiles, simply peel away the backing and position along the center line, making sure that each tile butts up closely to the next. Press down firmly with your hands to make sure that all areas of the tile have stuck to the floor surface below. Continue until all whole tiles have been laid.

3 You can achieve an accurate cut by positioning a whole tile on top of the last tile, and then adding another whole tile butting up to the baseboard. This will leave part of the tile below exposed. Draw along this line, and cut with scissors or a sharp utility knife for a perfect fit. If fitting a tile around an outside corner, simply move the tile into position over the last whole tile on the other side of the corner, and repeat the process.

Use a tile butted up to the base-board as a guide when cutting tiles.

4 When cutting a tile to fit round a large obstacle like a sink or toilet suite, cut a sheet of paper to the size of a tile and make a series of parallel cuts to the depth of the obstacle. Push the paper up against the obstacle, and fold back the cut strips at the points where the obstacle touches the floor. Use this as a paper pattern for cutting the tile. To get round smaller obstacles such as pipes, use a tape measure to accurately gauge the position, then use a coin of a similar diameter to cut a perfect circle. Cut a slit from the edge of the tile to the circle and slot it into position.

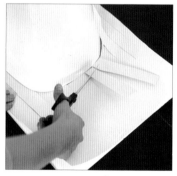

Make a paper template to measure the size of a large obstacle.

Carpet

There is a huge variety of carpet designs available, but they will all be either jute- or foam-backed. Of the two, jute-backed carpet is generally better-quality and more expensive. It requires a padding that adds a cushioning layer, making it more comfortable to walk on. Using padding is important for a variety of reasons—it prevents dirt and dust working its way up from beneath the floor, it stops wear patterns developing along joints in the floorboards and adds a layer of soundproofing.

Foam-backed carpet is made with foam rubber backing, which acts like an in-built padding. Before laying a foam-backed carpet it is a good idea to cover the floor with a paper or fiber sheet—this will stop the foam-rubber backing sticking to the floor, and make it easier to remove when you change the flooring.

Fitting carpet and underlay

Tools and materials

Carpet
Padding
Pliers
Tackless strips
Hammer
Nails
Utility knife
Staple gun
Bolster and mallet
Knee kicker
Scissors
Hacksaw
Threshold strip
Screws and screwdriver
Straightedge

1 Give the room a thorough sweep and vacuum, then remove any old carpet tacks with pliers. If tackless strips were originally used and these are still in good condition, they can be reused. You should not reuse padding, as it will begin to show the previous areas of wear through the new carpet. Nail tackless strips to the floor about $1/4$ in (0.5cm) from the baseboard all the way around the room.

Nail tackless strips securely in place around the room,

2 Roll out the strips of padding and cut them with a sharp utility knife so that they butt up to the tackless strips. Join the individual widths of padding with a staple gun to stop them sliding around.

Use a staple gun to hold the padding in place.

3 Unroll the carpet and lay it loosely in place. Fix the machine-finished edge against one wall by pressing it into the teeth of the tackless strips. Smooth the carpet across to the opposite wall, then use the knee kicker to nudge it onto the tackless strips, but do not secure firmly until the carpet is evenly stretched along the wall.

Using the knee kicker, nudge the carpet onto the tackless strips.

4 Next, cut triangular release notches into each corner and continue around the room, stretching the carpet into the corners, until you are completely happy that it is evenly tensioned throughout. Use the bolster and mallet to push the carpet firmly into the angle between the floor and baseboard, taking care not to hurt your fingers when doing this. Trim with a sharp utility knife if necessary.

Use a bolster and mallet to hammer the carpet securely into place.

5 To finish off the doorways, use a threshold strip suitable for the flooring that you are attaching to (for example, a strip made for carpet to hard flooring). Cut it to fit the doorway using a hacksaw, and screw in position on the floor. Cut the carpet to fit around the door frame then, using a straight-edge, make a single cut across the doorway and tuck the carpet edge neatly under the threshold strip.

Using your bolster chisel, tuck the carpet under the threshold strip.

Loose-laying carpet on a straight stair run

Wall-to-wall carpeting of stairs is a job best left to the professionals, as it could be extremely dangerous if it is not completed properly, but if you have a straight run of stairs you could loose-lay a strip of carpet with finished edges, and hold it in place with decorative stair rods.

Laying carpet

There is quite a knack to fitting a properly stretched carpet, but you can do it yourself if you have a small, regular-shape room that does not require any carpet jointing. You will need to rent a knee kicker, which is a professional tool for stretching carpets.

Adjusting doors

When you have added extra layers to your flooring, you may find that doors no longer fit easily over the surface. If this is the case, you will need to have the doors removed from their hinges and a few fractions of an inch or milli-meters shaved off the base, otherwise the doors will stick and the constant dragging of the door over the carpet sur-face will cause marks and eventually wear it out.

Tools and materials

Fabric measure or string

Carpet

Padding

Sharp utility knife

Carpet tacks

Hammer

Drill

Screwdriver

Screws

Stair rod clips

Stair rods in your chosen finish

1 Use a fabric tape measure or a piece of string to measure the length of carpet required, allowing around 1ft (30cm) excess for turning under at the bottom.

A piece of string can be used to measure the length required.

2 Cut pieces of padding slightly narrower than your carpet, and nail to the stair tread using car-pet tacks.

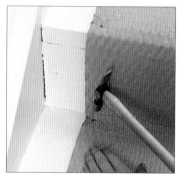

Use carpet tacks to attach your padding in place.

3 Start the carpet by nailing it to the back of the second tread—it is normal for the landing carpet to cover the first riser. Smooth it over the nosing, and anchor in place by pushing the rod into the

clips. Continue down the stairs, turn excess under at the bottom, and nail in place. To spread the wear, you can adjust the carpet by moving it up or down a tread.

Nail the first section of carpet to the second tread.

4 Use a drill and screwdriver to attach the stair rod clips just outside the width of the carpet.

Secure the carpet by screwing a stair rod over the top into the clips.

Right: Wall to wall carpeting is best left to a professional.

Windows and
dressings

Windows are said to be the eyes of a room—they allow you to see out, and let light in. Traditionally, windows were small because glass was expensive and could only be made in small panes. Now, panes have become larger, enabling whole walls to be replaced by a sheet of tempered glass.

Above: Modern window dressing designs are often quite simple. Here, shades have been matched up with plain, no-sew curtains that run on a chrome rod.

Assessing your windows

Before embarking on window dressing assess the style, shape, and number of windows in the room. Think about how much sunlight your room receives. If it only has one or two small windows, your priority should be for a window dressing that does not restrict or hinder the small flow of natural light available. If you have many tall windows and the room is orientated so that it receives plenty of daylight, then you can afford to go for more complex dressings and valances that will, to some extent, inhibit the flow of light.

Window shapes and styles

The windows themselves may be of an interesting shape or style that makes them a feature of the room in their own right. To make the most of such a window, the dressings should be minimal. Use simple curtains, shades or drapes to accentuate the shape. Modern double-hung and casement windows without muntins, or vinyl frames are rarely worth making a feature of, so their edges can be camouflaged by fabric.

Interesting windows and window features include French doors that open out onto a balcony or into a garden. These should be carefully dressed so as not to hinder access. Period double-hung windows with six, eight, or twelve panes of glass date from as far back as the 18th century, and even single-paned lower sashes, which came into popularity in the mid-19th century, are worthy of curtains that highlight their graceful appearance.

If you have unusual-shape windows, such as round, oval, or arched, you may prefer not to dress them with drapes at all. Alternatively, you can simply use an arrangement of flowers, a piece of sculpture, or a decorative object placed on the sill to fill the window space, so that it is like a painting within a frame.

Bay windows are also features that are often found in a living room or bedrooms. This style of window is generally made up of three or more individual frames set in a bow that curves outwards in a graceful semi-circular shape. This can be a difficult structure to dress well. One solution is to place a shaped rod along the upper edge of the window with a running valance placed to hang three large curtains or a pair of curtains for each window. An alternative is separate shades or shutters for each window.

Sloping attic windows or skylights pose a dressing problem but curtains can be held back against the sloping ceiling or wall with fine rods or corbels that are fixed to the wall. In the case of a large attic window, a shade can be fitted to the top of the actual frame and fixed to a pair of clip retainers at the bottom. Or, a solid panel can be made to fit inside the frame with fasteners that clip from the frame over the panel.

There are other types of windows where the practical aspect of hanging a window dressing is worth thinking about. For example, the best window dressing for a site above a kitchen

or bathroom sink may be recessed or on the window itself. In this case, a shade may be better than a pair of well-pleated curtains that will hang out over the edge of the window sill and be in danger of getting splashed or stained by sink activity. Or you may want to

Above: The slats on Venetian shades can be opened and closed, depending on whether you want to allow light in or block it out. Here, the light streams in through the slats and is reflected off the contemporary glass blocks.

Above: Roman shades create an accordion effect when folded away.

Opposite: A decorative voile can soften the angular lines of a Venetian shade.

consider a simple cellulose glass covering to avoid any kind of dressing.

Window dressings

When planning your window dressings, you should also consider the style of the whole room and the rest of the decoration. Ornate and fussy curtains will look at odds in a room where everything else is plain or minimal, and plain white or cream drapes may make the windows look bare and underdressed in a room where there is plenty of color and pattern. Try to achieve a balance between the strength of color, pattern, texture, and weight of fabric throughout the room.

The view is another consideration. If your view is less than desirable, you will want window dressings that obscure or camouflage the view without cutting back too much of the natural flow of light.

You may find it useful to build up layers of window dressings. To obscure the view and to provide privacy, a plain roller shade or a sheer curtain is ideal. These will produce a light covering that does not hinder the daylight completely. Then, for decoration and a link with the main colors and styles of the room, you may add a more formal set of outer curtains.

Shades and voiles

Standard roller shades fit into the recess of the window and, when extended, cover the whole window. There are a number of more ornate shade designs. Deep, horizontally pleated Roman shades are made with cords and rods attached on the reverse of the fabric, so that when the cords are pulled the shades fold back neatly into accordion-like pleats. The fussier, ruched festoon is also known as an Austrian shade. Venetian and vertical-louvered shades are also popular and can be used not only to screen windows but also as retractable room dividers. There are many materials to choose from when ordering Venetian shades, including wood, metallic finishes, and vivid plain colors.

Although voiles are most commonly white or off-white it can also be interesting to have colored or ombre-effect sheers. Many contemporary window dressings feature voiles and shades that have cut decoration. This allows a glimpse of outside and means that interesting shadows and patterns are formed as the light passes through.

With simple shades it is possible to give the window frame a little more dressing by adding a soft cascade or swag of fabric draped around a pole or simply pinned with small tacks to the upper edges of the window frame. In France, Belgium, and other parts of Europe half curtains are a popular way of restricting the view but still allowing light to shine through the upper levels of the window.

Shutters

Shutters are popular in America, Australia, and southern Europe. In warmer climes, it is most common to have external shutters—these are used to reduce the access of sun and heat into the house and are also a security measure.

Above: Holdbacks work well with fabrics that hang nicely when scooped over and around them, like this sheer fabric does.

Internal shutters tend to be finer. In the classic style they are generally paneled and fold back into recesses on either side of the window. Louvered shutters are also popular. These can be made to fit almost any window and divided into sections so that you can open them from side to side and up and down.

Curtains

By far the most common window dressing is the traditional curtain. No-sew curtains are currently fashionable because they are so easy to hang and change—they are simply secured in place by clipping to curtain hooks or eyelets. Ready-made curtains come in standard sizes and widths, which fit the majority of commercially produced window frames.

Linings Lining curtains contribute to a more professional finish and give extra weight and density, which makes them hang well. There are several different types of lining—among them is the standard white or off-white cotton, which is perfect for putting with lightweight cotton. Insulation linings are thicker, and suitable for medium to heavier curtains. Blackout curtains are useful for children's bedrooms and those who need total darkness to sleep.

There are also those who prefer colored linings rather than the traditional white or cream. A colored lining can be arranged so that it curls around over the inner side of the curtain.

Headings The traditional gathered heading produces neat narrow pleats and is best where a valance is going to be used so that the top of the curtain can be concealed.

Pleated headings come in a variety of styles—from pencil pleats, which are evenly spaced, to triple pleats in groups of three.

Simple, contemporary headings include the turnover top, where an extra 4in (10cm) is stitched down to form a deep envelope or tube but leaving the ends open.

Tie-tops are also popular. Pairs of equal length ties are stitched to the top edge of the curtain and then tied to the pole.

Tab headings are now popular in ready-made curtains, but are simple to make yourself. This type of heading can only be used with a straightforward rod or pole support. To calculate the number of tabs you need, you should allow for one every 4in (10cm) along the finished width of the curtain. You will also need to place one at the beginning and end of the material.

Valances, tiebacks, and other dressings To complete a formal or traditional window dressing it is customary to add valances and cornices. These can also help to reduce the height of a tall window as well as give a more decorative appearance to the curtains.

Valances can be made in the same material as the main curtain, in a contrasting fabric, or in a matching plain shade selected from the pattern or color of the curtain. Valances are usually rigid —they can be mounted on a thin wooden board or made with a self-adhesive backing or stiffener. They are applied to the window with a box or bracket method that lifts the valance free of the bunched fabric of the curtain when drawn back. The edges can be left plain or decorated with fringing or braid, or cut to form scalloped or crenelated edges. Soft valances are generally padded to give them body and to help them stand proud of the curtains.

Cornices are another option but work better with shades and small curtains. They are fixed valances that follow the frame of the window. They sometimes extend down to the sill and can add something extra to a window where only a shade is practical. Cornices are made on a backing of light board or a self-adhesive plastic coated sheet that can be stuck directly onto the fabric.

Another type of window dressing involves arranging the pleats of the curtains themselves—this can be done with tie-backs and holdbacks. Tie-backs are used to scoop the edges of the curtain back and create a curvy frame around the window. The top edges of the curtain remain drawn together or slightly parted.

Tie-backs are usually crescent moon-shapes and can be made of the same material as the curtain or in a plain color picked from the pattern. The fabric is stiffened with an adhesive crinoline or lining, and a loop is sewn at either end. These loops, usually small metal circles, are then slipped over a hook secured to the wall behind the far edge of the curtain. Other types of tie-backs

Attaching lining and hanging curtains

Once you have selected your lining, you can attach it fastened or loose. Fastened lining is sewn inside the curtain and held in place by being stitched into the hems at the top, bottom, and sides of the curtain. A loose lining is separately hemmed all the way round then just the top edge is joined to the curtain so that the lining hangs loose inside the curtain, rather than being part of it.

When calculating the length of the rod or pole to be attached above the window, allow space at both ends for the curtain to be pulled back beyond the edge of the window. Heavy fabrics or curtains that are lined and interlined will need more space, as they are bulkier when pulled back.

This highly decorative carved wood valance works well in a period setting.

include twisted silk cord and tassels, plaited rope or cord, and needlepoint tapestry.

Holdbacks create the same effect as a tie-back but are rigid brass or wooden arms fixed to the wall. A holdback can be a simple wooden knob or more decorative. The curtain is scooped up and placed behind the holdback.

Window dressing techniques

Before you think about how to decorate your windows, repair any damage, particularly if you have original period windows, which you will need to maintain in order to prolong their life. Make sure that you choose a dressing that fits in with the rest of your room and meets your needs for privacy.

Stripping and finishing windows

Windows need to be carefully maintained to keep them looking good. It is traditional to paint window frames and surrounds in the same paint color. White or off-white colors are most popular and give rooms a clean simple look. You could choose a more dramatic look and follow the example of earlier periods when woodwork was often painted a darker color than the walls. If you are going to put all the time and effort into fully stripping your windows, you may decide you like the look of the bare wood and go for a clear protective finish.

Wooden windows

Wooden windows are traditionally found in older and wood-frame houses. The most common types of wooden window are double-hung windows, which operate on a corded pulley system contained within the frame, and casement windows, which are hinged. Double-hung windows need to have their cords replaced periodically to keep them running smoothly—this is a job best completed by a specialized carpenter. All types of wooden window are at risk of rotting if they are not properly maintained.

Metal-framed windows

These types of windows are most commonly found in houses built from the 1920s through to the 1950s. Metal frames are susceptible to rust, which will attack areas of exposed metal if the painted surface is damaged.

Before repainting metal windows, any patches of rust should be removed with a rust inhibitor/remover. A chemical stripper in gel or paste form is the best way of removing a build-up of paint. Do not attempt to use a heat gun on a metal window frame, because the metal will conduct the heat from the gun and shatter the glass. It is important to use a metal primer that will ward off rust under the paintwork.

Vinyl windows

These windows are most commonly found in new homes or when double-glazed units are installed in older houses. They are made from tough vinyl, usually in white or wood effect and need very little maintenance. However, they can ruin the look of period houses, so think about this before installing them.

Vinyl can also discolor with time and begin to look shabby, but specialized paint is available for this. Vinyl windows can be prone to mildew, so make sure you clean the frames regularly with mild detergent.

Stripping with chemical stripper

If you plan to leave your windows with a translucent finish, it is best to strip them using a method that will not harm the surface of the wood, so use a chemical stripper in a gel or a paste form. Bear in mind that this method is labor-intensive and may require several applications before you finish off with steel wool and fine-grit abrasive paper.

Tools and materials

Heavy-duty rubber gloves
Putty knife
Chemical stripper
Shaped paint scraper
Fine steel wool

1 Wearing rubber gloves, use a putty knife to apply a thick layer of the stripper onto the window frame. Leave it in place for the manufacturer's recommended time.

Using a putty knife, apply a generous coat of chemical stripper.

2 Carefully remove a small area of stripper with the paint scraper to check if the paint has been removed as well. Re-apply paint stripper to the window frame if necessary. Finally, remove any stubborn areas of paint with fine steel wool dipped in liquid stripper, or with a metal cabinet scraper.

Remove the stripper from the surface using a shaped paint scraper.

Stripping with a heat gun

Heat guns are another effective way of stripping wooden window frames. However, care must be taken not to singe the wood by directing the flame at one area for too long. When working on the glazing beads it is essential to use a special metal attachment, which deflects heat away from the glass as the glass could break otherwise.

Tools and materials

Glass shield
Heat gun
Shaped paint scraper
Fine-grit flexible abrasive paper
Cloth and mineral spirits

1 Fit the glass shield to the heat gun and hold it up to the window

Measuring for Roman shades

Roman shades are attached to a wooden strip, which is then attached to the top of the window frame. Measure the drop from the top of the wood to the sill, and the width of the window frame. To estimate the amount of fabric needed to make a Roman shade, allow 3in (7.5cm) for the dowel or strip casing, and the dowels should be evenly spaced at approximately 8in (20cm) down the shade, leaving 4in (10cm) for the last dowel and bottom edge. Also add 2½in (6cm) for the heading and hem.

frame at a 45-degree angle so that paint does not drip back into the heat gun.

Hold the gun at a 45-degree angle to stop the paint dripping back on it.

2 When the paintwork starts to blister and bubble, remove with the paint scraper, or integral scraper on the gun. Continue until all the paint is removed. Any remaining slivers can be removed with a sharp cabinet scraper. Pull the scraper down across the grain holding it at a 30–45-degree angle. Sand with fine-grit abrasive paper, then wipe with a cloth dipped in mineral spirits.

Remove the stripper from the surface using a shaped molding scraper.

Stripping with an electric sander

Sanding is a good option if you want to "key" a painted surface for a new coat of paint. There is a wide range of electric sanders on the market. Some have shaped attachments to fit different molding profiles. Sanding back to bare wood with an electric sander will remove most of the surface patina of the wood. Hand

sanding is a gentler method, although not recommended if you have a heavy paint build up.

Tools and materials

Electric multisander with shaped attachments

Abrasive paper in assorted grits from coarse to extra fine

1 Sand any flat surfaces with the main sander attachment, starting with the coarsest abrasive paper to remove a build up of paint. Work your way through the grades, finishing with extra fine.

2 Attach the sander attachment to suit your window's moldings and work your way through the grits of abrasive paper.

Attach the sander attachment and then sand the moldings.

Painting windows

If you are painting windows choose a fine day so that you can leave them open while they dry. Begin with the parts that will meet the frame so they dry first. Accidental drips of paint that end up on the glass can be removed when dry with a utility knife blade. Use a good quality paintbrush with bristles that come to a point to get into tricky corners.

Tools and materials

Window guard or low-tack painter's tape

Small paintbrush

Gloss enamel or satinwood paint

1 Mask the windows with low-tack tape allowing a fraction of an inch (a couple of millimetres) of glass to remain visible. You should paint over this area of glass to help form an airtight seal between the glass and the frame. Pull the tape away before the paint dries completely or you will pull off the paint.

Tape around the window edge before painting the frame.

2 Alternatively, you could use a plastic window guard that you simply hold up against the frame while you paint it.

Hold a window guard up against the frame and then paint the frame.

Decorative techniques for windows

The most common ways of dressing windows are with curtains or shades. In order to buy them to fit correctly you will have to take accurate measurements of your windows. It is also important to choose the correct fastenings and fixtures for your type and shape of window.

Measuring for and fitting shades

Some windows are recessed. This recess is often called the reveal, which means that they are set back into the wall and have a sill or ledge. With this type of window

it is usual to fit a shade within the reveal, which makes accurate measuring crucial. Other window frames are fitted level with the wall, meaning that shades are fastened onto the frame or on the surrounding wall. In this case measuring is not as crucial. Shades often contain fastening brackets that give the option of top fastening, side fastening, or face fastening. Shades over 3ft (1m) often have a central support bracket as well as end brackets. Top fastening means drilling into the reveal above the window, side fastening means drilling into the side of the reveal, and face fastening is fastening directly to the frame or wall. Ready-made shades include roller shades, metal and wooden Venetian shades, Roman shades, and roll-up shades. Roller shades can be cut to size but most other shades cannot. If your window is not a standard size you can order a shade for a perfect fit.

Tools and materials

Tape measure

Roller shade and brackets

Pencil

Screws

Drill with masonry bit

Wall plugs

Level

1 Measure the window within the reveal and note down the dimensions. Buy a shade to fit or cut one to size. Hold the brackets in place and mark screw positions with a pencil, making sure the marks are level. Fit a suitable sized masonry bit into the drill and drill holes. Then fit the wall plugs into the holes and screw the brackets in place.

Screw the brackets into the surface of the frame using a masonry drill bit.

2 Finally, slot the shade into position and, if it is outside the reveal, check that it is level with a level.

Slot the blind into position within the brackets.

Measuring for and hanging curtains

There are curtains available to suit most interior styles, from elaborate swags and tails to simple tab-topped panels. Voile or muslin curtains let light through while maintaining privacy, and curtains in heavier materials, such as velvets and damasks, block out light and act as efficient draft excluders. More expensive curtains tend to be lined, which improves the way they hang. The most sumptuous curtains are interlined, meaning that they have a thick, fleece-like material sandwiched in between the lining and the fabric to give extra fullness. The area above the window can be difficult to drill, so it is a good idea to fit a wooden furring strip to which any window treatment can be attached.

Curtains can be various lengths from just above the sill, just below the sill, or floor length. It is a good idea to buy or make curtains slightly too long to allow for any shrinkage during washing. When measuring a window for curtains begin the measurement at the curtain pole or rod, from which they will hang.

Curtain poles

Curtain poles are available in wood or metal, and in a multitude of finishes. They are often used in conjunction with curtain rings, which fit onto the pole. The hooks on the curtain heading are then suspended from a small metal loop at the bottom of the ring.

Curtain poles are held on brackets, which are attached to the wall or a wooden strip about 6in (15cm) above the window. Special poles with flexible or angled sections are available to fit angular bay windows. Generally curtains on poles are simply drawn by hand, although some more expensive tracks are corded—opened and closed with a cord system.

Fitting a curtain pole with concealed fastenings

Tools and materials

Tape measure

Level

Curtain pole

Fastening plates and brackets

Masonry bit and drill

Screwdriver

Curtain rings

1 Use a tape measure and level to mark the positions of the brackets in pencil. The brackets should be at equal distances from the corners of the window. Poles over $6^1/_2$ ft (2m) long should also have a central support bracket to prevent bowing under the weight of the curtains. Use a masonry bit to drill the holes, then join with suitable wall plugs. Screw fastening plates firmly in position.

Use a screwdriver to fasten the plates securely in place.

2 Slot the wooden bracket over the fastening plate then tighten the screw, which anchors it firmly in place.

Attach the wooden bracket in place over the fastening plate.

3 Attach the pole in position with the curtain rings in place. Remember to leave a ring on the bracket side of the pole to hold the curtains in position. Tighten the small screw on the underside of the bracket, which holds the pole in position.

Secure the bracket and curtain pole with a screw.

Traverse rods

Traverse rods are an alternative to poles and are available in plastic or heavy-duty metal. They have hooks, which are looped through the curtain heading tape and slide along the tracks. Corded versions, which work on a pulley system, are also available. Most versions simply slot onto brackets.

Tools and materials

Tape measure

Level

Drill

Wall bracket

Screwdriver

Hacksaw

Traverse rod

Curtain hooks

1 Use a tape measure, level and pencil to mark the position of the brackets at equal intervals. Drill, plug, and screw into place.

Screw the wall brackets to the wall at equal intervals.

2 If necessary, use a hacksaw to cut the traverse rod to length, then fix the end stop in place by tightening the small screw.

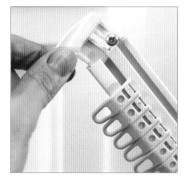

After cutting the traverse rod to length, fasten the end stop in place.

3 Finally, slot the traverse rod into place on the brackets.

4 To hang the curtains, simply hook the metal or plastic curtain hook over the sliding runners.

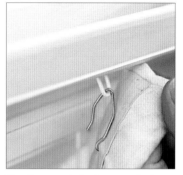

Slot the curtain hooks onto the integral sliding runners.

Fitting tension wire

This is a recent invention, which will give your lighter weight curtains a more contemporary look. Steel wire is stretched on a tension system between walls, or between brackets. The curtains are held on small rings with pincer-style clips, which grip the fabric and slide along the wire.

Tools and materials

Tension wire
Wire cutters
Hex key
Drill
Screwdriver
Wall brackets and cover pieces
Curtain rings and pincer clips

1 Cut the tension wire to length with a pair of wire cutters and use the hex key provided to fix the end piece in place at each end.

Once you have cut the tension wire to length, fasten the end pieces.

2 Drill, plug, and screw the two wall brackets in place on opposite walls.

Use a screwdriver to fasten the wall brackets in place on opposite walls.

3 Screw the cover piece in place over the wall bracket. Feed the

curtain rings onto the wire, and then fix the other end to the opposite wall. (If you are using tab-top curtains, thread them onto the wire first.) Pull the wire tight.

Fasten the torpedo cover pieces over the top of the wall brackets.

4 Use the pincer clips attached to the rings to secure your curtain panel in place, clipping them onto it at equal spacings along the top of the panel.

Attach the curtains to the rings using the pincer clips.

Above: A metal pole and matching rings clipped to the curtain can give a stylish look to your room.

Alternative window treatments

Curtains and shades are not the only methods that you can use to screen or dress your windows— the only limit is your imagination. New, exciting materials to treat glass are available, allowing you to create your own etched or stained-glass effects. If you prefer something more substantial, shutters are a good solution and give your windows a bit of additional security.

Shutters

Although most traditional shutters are made from wood, modern ones can be made from a variety of materials including acrylic sheet, MDF, and metal for a look that is suitable for any room in the house.

Tools and materials

Tape measure
Shutters
Screwdriver
Hinges
Awl
Level

1 Measure your window carefully and order the correct size shutters—the supplier will advise on the best way of fastening them to your window. Screw hinges in equidistant positions from the top and the bottom of the shutters.

Fasten hinges halfway between the top and bottom of the shutter.

2 Use an awl to make pilot holes and then screw the hinges in place at the top and bottom of the window.

Screw the hinges to the side of the window.

3 Fit furring strips to the sides of the windows if required. Check with a level to ensure that they are straight.

Creating a frosted window panel

Frosted windows can give bathrooms a more contemporary look than old-fashioned textured glass. Cellulose frosting spray gives a temporary finish that will stand up to cleaning but can be removed with a sharp blade if you feel like a change.

Temporary frosted finish

Tools and materials

Glass cleaner

Cloth

Cellulose frosting spray

Clean the window thoroughly with glass cleaner to remove grease and grime. Spray the frosting evenly all over the window. Use two thin coats rather than one heavy coat to avoid runs.

Spray frosting spray onto the window, aiming for even coverage.

Semipermanent frosted finish

Tools and materials

Glazier's frost film

Straightedge

Sharp utility knife

Cloth

Squeegee

1 Cut the frost film to size with a straightedge and utility knife. Wet the window with a damp cloth.

2 Peel off a corner of the backing film and position the film in one corner of the window. Gently peel away the rest of the backing.

3 Use a good quality squeegee to smooth the film gently in place—the water will act as a lubricant. Force all bubbles away to the sides of the film.

Use a squeegee to remove all the air bubbles from beneath the film.

Shutters are not only an attractive window dressing, they can also increase security.

Fires and fireplaces

Fireplaces were once the sole source of heat in a room. Now they are mainly decorative, as central or radiant heating systems provide warmth. There are ornate period fireplaces, classic molded surrounds, and modern versions using gas flames and ceramic shapes to create the effect of a real fire without the work and bother.

Types of fireplaces

Although there have been many innovations in the world of heating, with hot air and convector heating and the revival of radiant heating, there is something special about the glow of an open fire that still holds universal appeal. The flicker and appearance of the flame may still look to us as it did to prehistoric man, but there have been many developments in how the fire is fueled and laid. Coal and wood are traditional fuels, while in most cities gas and electricity now supply the power. The modern fake fire is often chosen over the traditional variety because it provides all the color, glow, flicker, and warmth without the soot, ashes, and effort of having to light the fire and refuel it.

Early log fires consisted of chunks of wood laid on earth, but sometimes the wood was raised up from the floor by fire irons or fire dogs. This allowed the air to

circulate through the wood. Later, fire dogs were replaced with a basket, then a grate. The latter comes with a façade that forms a panel inside the surround. Fire baskets are now placed on a non-combustible base made of marble, stone, or granite.

Structure of a fireplace

Fireplaces usually come in two main sections: the surround and the jambs. The surround is made from stone, such as limestone or marble, or wood such as pine. The jambs are the two upright sides of the fireplace, which often have foot blocks at the base. The jambs line up on either side of the opening to support the shelf, which runs across the top.

The details found on large fireplaces include a mantel, a fire front, and the grate (the cast-iron part), which holds the coal or wood. The hearth is the area set into the floorboards and is often

Above: This elaborate carved fireplace is a focal point of this dining room.

Opposite: The jamb (the upright part of a fireplace) can be engraved to match other architectural features in the room, such as a chair rail or cove.

Safety tips

For safety, always have a secure firescreen or guard in front of a fire when children are in the room or if a real fire is to be left unattended, as hot coal or logs may tumble out onto the floor in front of the fireplace. You may consider installing a fire alarm to give you warning should a fire start. Carbon-monoxide alarms are also available, and can be a useful check on air level. You should also ensure that there is good ventilation around your fireplace. An air brick in the wall of the room will ensure a through flow of fresh air.

made of stone or marble, or tiled, which protects the floor from falling coals. In bedrooms you usually find smaller fireplaces, cast in one piece out of molten iron and called registers.

In recent years the fireplace has been reinvented, so you will find that a basic hole-in-the-wall look is becoming popular.

Fireplace style

Fireplaces vary widely in style, from rough-hewn oak or wooden beams with a brick or stone interior in a rural home or farm-house, to ornately carved marble in a period house. Surrounds can be simple, with little detailing, or highly ornate, with swags,

cameos, mythical scenes, recesses, foliage, and urns carved into the jambs and shelf. The most important thing when buying a fireplace is to choose a style, size, and shape that sits comfortably within the room it is to be positioned in. If the room is small, choose a neat, simple design that will be a focal point but not overwhelm the space. If the room is large, with period features, try to match the decoration of the fire surround to the other features, and choose a material that is also in keeping.

The classic style of fireplace, with jambs, columns, and pilasters, is still popular and found in many homes today. Salvaged originals command high prices, and even modern reproductions are far from cheap. Marble fire surrounds are among the most expensive, but a cheaper pine or more inexpensive carved wood surround can be painted to look like marble. Pine can also be stained and waxed in order to give it the appearance of a richer wood, such as mahogany.

Some modern fires use geometric ceramic shapes, called geologs, that sit in a stainless-steel or black geometric grate. Gas flames flicker around the geologs, which come in matte black, orange, blue, green, and yellow. Alternatively,

you can choose to have flames coming from a hearth of pebbles.

Restoring or replacing your old fireplace

Putting a new fireplace into your home has its own set of complications, while reviving one that has been boxed or painted over by a previous owner provides a different agenda. If an old fireplace has been boxed, you may be lucky and find that it is in good condition and needs nothing more than a thorough clean. However, if it has been painted over, then it will require some work to restore it.

First of all, you need to establish what sort of material the fireplace is made from. In an area

Above: When choosing a fireplace, be sure that it will suit the décor of the rest of your room. This impressive example would look good in a large, period-style room, but might look out of place in a small, minimalist setting.

Opposite page: An open fire makes a dramatic feature in a contemporary, hole-in-the-wall fireplace.

Above: In the summer months, you can create a display in your fireplace, such as these logs.

near the wall on the base of the footblock, take a sharp knife and scratch away the upper layers until you come to the original surface. Once you have established what it is made from, you should be able to find a proprietary paint stripper or peeler that will remove the paint (see pages 130–1 for further details on how to do this).

Modern gas fires can run off main-supply or bottled gas, and will have automatic lighting and a flame-failure device as well as an oxygen depletion sensor.

Looking after your fire

With real coal and log fires the chimneys should be regularly swept by a professional who works to an authorized code of practice—otherwise soot will build up and may lead to a chimney fire. Smoky fires can be caused by the material you burn, such as damp logs, or perhaps through poor ventilation. Another reason can be the incorrect ratio of distances between the hearth, the chimney opening, and the chimney top. This latter problem can only be remedied by a craftsperson who may raise the hearth, add extra height to the chimney, or put a baffle or shield on the front of the hearth.

Dressing your fireplace

There are a number of dressings and accessories associated with the fireplace, including the fender, a metal frame that prevents coals that spill out of the fire from falling on the carpet. In the 19th century the small border fender grew into a surround with leather padded ends that doubled as a stool.

Fire dogs may no longer be required for their original purpose of supporting burning logs off the earth floor, but they can be a decorative feature and may now be used to prop up a fire poker, tongs, and shovel.

Even when the fireplace is not being used, you can employ the mantelpiece or shelf as a focal point and decorate it accordingly. In the summer months the black

hole can be camouflaged with a screen, decorative tray, or panel. Alternatively, you can place a wicker basket of logs in front, or position an arrangement of branches or wild grasses in the empty grate. You could also make a decorative feature of the space by placing church candles or a display of fossils and pebbles in it, or by storing books or magazines in an unused grate.

Above: Marble is a particularly attractive material to use for fireplaces.

Fireplace techniques

Restoring an existing fireplace, or installing a new one will require the services of a craftsperson, if you want it to function as a fire. However, there is nothing to prevent you from preparing a reclaimed fireplace ready for installation. Make sure that the grate you have chosen will fit your chimney breast. If there is no breast, then you could always construct a simple surround, which will be used for show purposes only.

Safety tips

Make sure that you wear tough household gloves when applying paint stripper, and take care not to splash any on your skin.

If you are painting a working fireplace, do not paint the parts that will come into direct contact with the fire. You must also be sure that you choose paint that has been specially formulated for heat resistance for the surround.

Restoring fireplaces

Fireplaces that have been repeatedly painted lose sharpness of detail. If you have a chimney breast missing a fireplace, it can be cheaper to buy an unrestored one from an architectural salvage company, than to install a reproduction. In either case, it is worth spending the time and effort to strip the surround and restore it in a sympathetic manner.

Before starting the restoration, identify the material of the fire surround. The most common materials are wood, cast iron, marble, stone, and brick, while in houses built in the 1920s and 1930s stepped tiled designs often held electric fires. Each material needs to be treated differently during restoration. Wood surrounds can be stripped using chemical paint stripper in a gel or paste form—stripping with a heat gun is less advisable because of the danger of scorching. Cast iron can be stripped using a heat gun, but take care as the surface is prone to scratching—the best option is to use a paste stripper.

Marble, stone, and brick are porous materials and prone to staining, so check the recommendations of any chemical stripper before you use it.

Wooden fire surrounds

Tools and materials

Chemical paint stripper in gel or paste form

Heavy-duty rubber gloves

Paint scraper

Fine steel wool

Neutral wax polish and soft cloth

1 Apply the paint stripper according to the manufacturer's instructions—use a paint scraper to push the stripper into any crevices and moldings. Leave for the manufacturer's recommended time, when the paint will blister.

Use a paint scraper to push the stripper into the crevices.

Above: A cast iron fireplace restored to its former beauty is magnificent.

2 Remove the paint from the wood carefully with the paint scraper, and reapply stripper if necessary. Remove any stubborn traces of paint using fine steel wool that has been dipped in liquid stripper. Neutralize the wooden surface by wiping it over with a rag that has been well moistened with mineral spirits.

Use the paint scraper to take off the stripper and paint layers.

3 If you want to achieve a more natural finish for your wooden fireplace, continue working on it by sanding the surface lightly with fine-grit abrasive paper, and then simply applying a neutral wax polish with fine steel wool. Allow this wax polish to dry thoroughly before polishing it with a soft cloth.

Apply a neutral wax polish and, once this is dry, polish with a cloth.

4 If you prefer a painted to a wooden finish, apply a quick-drying primer/base coat and gently sand with silicon carbide paper. Finish with a satin paint of your choice. Apply two coats, and sand with silicon carbide paper between coats.

Cast iron registers and grates

Tools and materials

Liquid or gel chemical stripper

Old paintbrush

Heavy-duty rubber gloves

Paint scraper

Fine steel wool

Stiff wire brush

Rust-inhibiting solution

Grate polish

Soft cloths

1 Apply the paint stripper thickly, following manufacturer's instructions, using an old paintbrush to work it well into any crevices.

Apply the paste stripper to your fire-place using an old paintbrush.

2 Wait for the recommended time to elapse. When the paint begins to blister and bubble, remove the stripper and old paint carefully with a paint scraper, taking care not to gouge or scratch the surface.

Use a paint scraper to take off the layers of stripper and paint.

3 Re-apply the stripper to the cast iron where necessary. If any stubborn paint residue remains, remove it by working carefully with fine steel wool dipped in stripper.

If there are some stubborn areas, use steel wool and liquid stripper.

4 Before re-finishing the fireplace you should remove any rust. First brush away any flaky rust and corrosion from the surface with a stiff wire brush.

Remove any rust and corrosion with a wire brush.

5 Paint on a rust-inhibiting solution—choose one that also inhibits new rust forming. Leave for the recommended time, then clean with fine steel wool.

Use the old paintbrush to apply a rust-inhibiting primer.

6 To retain a cast iron finish on your grate, apply black grate polish to the cast iron using a shoe brush or cloth. Leave the polish to dry thoroughly, prefer-ably overnight.

Apply black grate polish with a soft cloth.

7 When the polish is completely dry, use a clean soft cloth to buff to a graphite sheen.

When the polish is dry, polish to a graphite sheen with a soft cloth.

Changing fireplaces

If you wish to use a fireplace that has been boarded up or is not active, it is important to get professional advice. Have the flue checked for obstacles and ensure the fireproof lining is intact. A chimney that has been unused for several years will almost certainly need to be swept. A simple test to see if a chimney is drawing properly (removing smoke) is to hold a lit spill in the opening—the flame should be noticeably drawn upwards. If the flame splutters or dies, it clearly indicates a lack of oxygen, often caused by blockages further up the chimney.

Once your chimney and flue are in working order you can then consider the type of fireplace you wish to install. A gas fire is a popular choice for many people. Many cities also have a smoke ban, meaning the only coal that can be burnt on an open fire is an expensive smokeless variety. However, real fires are appealing if you live in an area without a smoke ban as nothing can beat the evocative smell and sound.

Period fireplaces are not to everyone's taste—heavily tiled, dark marble, and overornate fireplaces can dominate a room and make it difficult to create a contemporary look. However, many people consider removing a period fireplace as sacrilege, and before taking this drastic step you should consider carefully how it could affect the value of your home. Period features are a highly sought after selling point and, although it may not appeal to you, your period fireplace could be highly appreciated by the next owners. If you find a fireplace too overpowering to live with, consider less drastic ways of disguising it.

Painting over a tiled fireplace

Nineteenth and early 20th century fireplaces often have tiled slips set into a cast-iron insert. If the colors

Painted finish

For a painted finish on a cast-iron grate, first apply a rust-inhibiting base coat/ primer, which is formulated for ferrous metals, and allow to dry. Apply two coats of your chosen paint color.

of these tiles are not to your taste, they can be painted over in a more neutral shade. 1920s- and 1930s- style fireplaces, which are often tiled in murky colors, can be painted in the same way to make them less obtrusive.

Tools and materials

Tile cleaner/detergent and cloth

Tile primer

Specialized tile paint or gloss enamel/satinwood paint

Two small foam rollers and trays

Low-tack painter's tape

Silicon carbide abrasive paper

1 Clean the tiles thoroughly to remove any traces of dirt or grease. Mask off the tiles that are to be painted.

2 Apply the tile primer sparingly to avoid drips, using a foam roller. Allow to dry. If the pattern or color has not been covered, apply a second coat.

3 Sand lightly with silicon carbide paper. Apply the top coat using a foam roller and allow to dry. Sand again lightly with silicon carbide paper before applying a second coat.

Making a simple MDF surround

This plain surround will not dominate a room but provides a focal point to display a few carefully chosen items. It can be used to dress up a bare chimney breast where there is no working fireplace, or be made to fit over an existing fireplace that you do not like. This type of surround is purely decorative and should not be used in conjunction with a working fire.

Tools and materials

Paper and pencil

One sheet of ¾in (18mm) MDF

Several lengths of square-dressed lumber

Electric jigsaw

Electric screwdriver with countersink bit

Screws with countersink heads

Mirror plates

Wall plugs

Masonry drill bit

Wood filler

Paint of your choice

Straightedge

1 Sketch out a plan for your fireplace, taking into account any existing fireplace you wish to cover. The dimensions will vary according to the width of your chimney breast. If there is no existing fireplace the new version should sit comfortably in the available space, allowing about 1ft (30cm) of space each side. Draw out the components of the new fireplace on the sheet of MDF. You will need a front piece, two side pieces, three inside pieces and a top piece cut from the $^3/_4$ in (18mm) MDF. Use a straightedge clamped to the MDF to make accurate cuts—alternatively ask your local lumber merchant to cut the pieces for you.

2 Apply wood glue and clamp the timber frames to the outside and inside of the front piece of the fireplace.

Glue the frames to the fireplace and fasten in place with a clamp.

3 Make pilot holes and use a countersink bit. Screw the outside and inside panels in place in the same way.

Screw the panels in place using a screwdriver.

4 Fill all the screwholes with wood filler, allow to dry then sand until smooth.

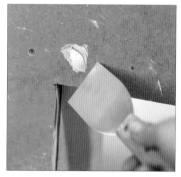

Fill all the screw holes that you have made with wood filler.

5 Prime and then paint in a color of your choice, using a paintbrush or roller. Leave it until it is completely dry. Sit the new fireplace on the hearth that has been cut from a piece of thick MDF, then attach to the wall using mirror plates screwed to the inside of the fireplace. Once the fireplace is securely fastened in place on the wall, touch up any areas of paint as needed.

Above: You can paint your fireplace, or retain the original stone finish.

Prime and paint the fireplace in a color of your choice.

Fitting a salvaged fireplace

When shopping for a salvaged fireplace, take the dimensions of the existing hole with you. Choose a style appropriate to the age of house if you want it to look original—and consider the hearth material. If you want the fireplace to be a working one, consult a builder or gas installer before purchasing it. Make sure that a salvaged fireplace is complete—it can be tricky finding items such as grates to fit if they are missing when you buy it. If you are choosing a wooden surround your salvage merchant should be able to recommend a cast-iron insert.

Tools and materials

Brick chisel

Mallet

Mortar

Electric drill with masonry bit

Suitable wall plugs and screws

Screwdriver/electric drill bit

One-coat plaster

Plasterer's trowel

Stiff brush

Level

Abrasive paper

Latex (acrylic) paint and paintbrush

1 Remove the existing hearth. If it is concrete, chip it out with a brick chisel but, if tiled, use a blunt chisel to lever them up. Mix a dryish mortar and apply to the hearth, using a piece of wood notched to the thickness of the new hearth as a depth gauge.

2 Lay the new hearth material in place and tamp down firmly with a rubber mallet, using a level for accuracy. Allow the mortar to harden. Mark the position of the new fireplace in the center of the chimney breast. Note the height of the fastening plates and use a brick chisel to remove some plaster from around the fastening. Make a hole with a masonry bit, fit a wall plug and screw in place.

3 Use a plasterer's trowel to apply a one-coat plaster mix over the fastening. Allow it to harden a little, then level off with a dampened trowel. Sand and then paint.

Architectural
features

Many architectural features started life as purely practical fixtures—a crown molding around a window helped to hold it in place and reduce drafts, and picture rails were used to hang pictures.

Fitting stair carpets

When it comes to decorating a staircase, safety must be foremost in your mind. Whichever floor covering you choose, it should be well installed so that there is no overhang or surplus on the nose or edge of the step. This is the surface that is most prone to wear, as it receives most of the weight and frequent rubbing from shoe soles. If it has not been installed properly, it may also cause someone to slip.

Opposite: Staircases need not just be a practical feature—be bold and make a feature of them.

Decorative moldings

Moldings have always played a fundamental role in the quality period house. They were usually applied to conceal the joint between the wall and ceiling, and they added relief and embellishment to plain areas.

There are various types of molding, which are generally applied in three main areas. First is the cove, which is positioned over the joint between the walls and ceiling. Second is the baseboard, which runs between the wall and floor. Third is the crown molding, between the door surround and the wall.

As well as their practical purpose, moldings were also used to add to the grandeur and status of a room. This can be clearly seen in the panel work and ceilings in grand period homes and important civic buildings.

Baseboards

Although decorative molding is rarely found in modern homes, baseboards and shoe moldings have survived the test of time because they are practical. They provide a neat joint between wall and floor, and also protect plaster and paintwork from knocks from feet and furniture. They can also be used to hide wiring or a safety deposit box.

Restoring or adding moldings

To restore existing ornate plasterwork, it is best to employ a craftsperson. For smaller cracks and repairs, you may be able to do it yourself with a thick mix of filler. If your moldings suffer from years of overpainting, take the time to strip them back.

If you have a room without any such architectural features, then you can add simple detailing with cove. This is essentially a straightforward plaster curve that arcs between the wall and ceiling—simple and cheap versions of these are easily glued in place and then painted over. Ceiling roses and cove at the upper levels

Ancient influences

It is said that the level of the chair and picture rails, as well as the cove and baseboard, echoes the various levels and elements of a classic Greek or Roman column. This reference to classic style shows how many of the traditional elements of interior design are based on ancient logic, form, and scale.

of a room are not subjected to close scrutiny, so cheap, imitation products can work well. Wooden quarter-round molding can also be used to create paneling on doors and walls.

Chair and picture rails

In some classic or period style homes you will find that walls are divided and decorated with chair and picture rails. Originating in the 18th and 19th centuries, these rails had a practical purpose too. The chair rail, which is roughly at hip height, protected the fragile wall finish of the time (which was made from horse hair, lath, and plaster) from being damaged by

people or furniture banging or bumping against it.

These days chair rails are often employed for cosmetic or decorative purposes, to divide up a large wall or to create a two-tone or bi-colored scheme for a hall or stair-case. You can also create interest by using textured wallpaper above and below the rail. A chair rail can easily be applied to a wall using both glue and screws.

The picture rail was also a functional feature in such homes, providing a hanging point for pic-tures. Today, pictures are hung from deep brass clamps that clip over the thickness of the rail, which is now often metal. Modern picture rails tend to stand out from the wall rather than being an integral part of it.

Staircases

In many period houses the main staircase was often a show piece with decorative carved wood or iron balusters (the vertical sup-ports for the handrail).

In modern homes, the staircase is not just a means of getting from one level to another, it is a way of making the most of available light. Light from a skylight above can

Right: Splitting color above and below a rail will help you to break up a large expanse of wall.

filter down through many levels if the staircase is of an open construction. As such, high tension steel wire, like yacht rigging, and reinforced glass paneling is popular for the sides of staircases.

Restoration and decoration

If you are restoring or repairing an existing staircase you may need to replace some of the balusters or change them completely. Wood is the most common and cheapest material used for these supports and it can be fashioned either into simple, four-sided pillars or more ornately carved and turned balusters. When it comes to decorating, the wood can be left plain, painted, or stained.

Iron is also a common feature of period houses—staircases used to be edged with ornate balusters. Iron balusters can be found through salvage specializers or new ones can be made by a blacksmith. The last baluster on a flight of stairs is usually finished with a thicker post, which is often decorated with a knob or carving.

Architectural features techniques

Many people are put off by the prospect of adding architectural features to a room because they think that this may entail major structural work. In fact, the opposite is true—it is relatively easy to install moldings and wall paneling. Make sure that you choose a feature that is in keeping with your style of house.

Matching moldings

If you have an older house you may need to replace damaged or missing sections of molding. Plaster modeling factories and outlets stock a wide range of ornate moldings that may match your original. Otherwise a new piece of molding can be made to match. Check your local telephone directory for a plaster modeler.

Opposite: Elegant cove such as this can add the finishing touch to your living room.

Fitting decorative moldings

Most decorative moldings are installed using the same methods. In period houses these moldings were simply nailed into wooden plugs, which were fastened into the masonry. Recent advances in adhesives mean that nails can be replaced with adhesive applied with a caulk gun. Alternatively, you can countersink screws into the moldings and fill with wood filler. The most important device to master is using the miter block, which allows you to cut perfect inside and outside corners.

Installing a chair rail

Tools and materials

Tape measure

Miter box

Hand or back saw

Caulk adhesive

Brad nails and hammer

Drill with countersink wood and masonry bits

Screws with countersunk heads

Wall plugs

Chalk snap line

Pencil

Wooden moldings

Pliers

Filler

1 Use a tape measure to measure the length required, and cut using the miter box to achieve an inside or outside corner.

Use a miter box and saw to cut the corners.

2 Use a level and tape measure to mark a straight line to indicate the bottom of the molding. If this is a chair rail like that shown here, it should be positioned a third of the way up the wall from the floor. Tap small brad nails along the length of the line.

Tap a line of brad nails along the line marking the bottom of the molding.

3 Apply the adhesive with a caulk gun along the entire length of the wooden molding.

Use a caulk gun to apply adhesive to the molding.

4 Press the wooden molding firmly into position against the wall. The brad nails will support it and hold it firmly in place while it dries. Do not try to work any further on the molding until it has completely dried.

5 When the molding is dry, remove the brad nail from below the molding carefully, using either a pair of pliers or the end of a claw hammer.

Use pliers to remove the brad nails when the adhesive is dry.

6 Fill the holes that are left behind with a quick-drying, ready-mixed filler.

Installing baseboards

Tools and materials

Tape measure

Miter box

Hand or back saw

Drill with countersink wood and masonry bits

Nails and screws

Wall plugs

1 Measure and cut the boards as above. Predrill holes near the ends and near the center of the boards.

Drill holes near the ends and center of the baseboards.

2 Use a nail to mark the corresponding position for the holes on the wall.

With a nail, mark the corresponding position on the wall.

3 Drill holes with a masonry bit and tap a plastic wall plug in place. Glue as shown above but use screws to ensure a firm fixing. Fill and sand screw holes before painting or staining with a color of your choice.

Tap a wall plug into place before fastening the baseboard in position.

Wall paneling

Wall paneling is a common period feature in older houses. It reached the height of popularity in the late 18th century when the main reception rooms of a house were often paneled up to chair height. By the mid-19th century paneling had become rarer and was made of softwood, which was then painted to mimic more expensive hardwoods.

Installing tongue-and-groove paneling

This common wall paneling is made up of thin planks of wood, which slot together with the tongue of one plank fitting into the groove of the next. It is an excellent way of covering up a less than perfect wall surface and is commonly used to modernize kitchens and bathrooms as it can be treated with a water-repellent varnish. It can be painted to suit any color scheme or given a clear finish, which allows the grain to show through. There are various types of tongue-and-groove paneling—some incorporate a rounded bead between each plank. Most types of tongue and groove can be fitted vertically or horizontally, and it can be used on ceilings as well as walls.

It pays to buy quality tongue-and-groove paneling as the cheaper, thinner varieties tend to warp and bow. It can be attached using a variety of methods, including secret nailing into the tongue of the boards. Some varieties have special clips, which are metal fasteners that hold each board in place. For quick results you can also use panel adhesive to stick the boards directly onto the wall. Vertical tongue-and-groove paneling is usually finished off with a baseboard at the bottom and a rounded or quarter-round molding on top.

Tools and materials

Level

Furring strips

Jigsaw

Tongue-and-groove paneling

Wood screws

Wall plugs

Nail set

Long brad nails or panel adhesive

Tack hammer

Neutral-color wood filler

Quarter-round molding

1 Decide on the height of your tongue and groove—it is available pre-cut to chair-rail height—and cut it to size if necessary. Use a level to mark two lines on the wall, one toward the top and the other toward the bottom of where the paneling will sit. Cut the furring strips to size, then drill, plug, and screw them in place.

Screw the furring strips, checking that they are straight with a level.

2 If your room has outside corners, use one as your starting point so that any cut boards will be hidden in the corner of the room. Start with the groove of the board lined up with the outside corner. Use the tack hammer to knock the brad nails in place, and a nail set to make sure that the heads of the brad nails are knocked below the surface of the wood. Fill with a neutral-color wood filler.

Use a nail set to knock the head of the nail below the surface.

3 Continue along the wall, and when you reach the corner, cut the tongue off the final board to be sure of a good fit. To turn the corner, butt the groove of the next board against the previous board and nail in place.

4 To turn an outside corner, cut the tongue of the first board and butt it up to the groove of the previous board to form a neat corner. Cover the corner of the paneling with a piece of right-angled molding.

Use right-angle molding to cover outside corners.

5 When the paneling has been completely fastened in place, cap it with lengths of quarter-round molding. Then miter the capping at the corners and hold it in place using a panel adhesive or brad nails.

To finish the paneling, apply lengths of molding to the top.

Plaster moldings

The term plaster moldings encompasses all the many different types of decorative architectural details used in the home that are made from plaster and plaster composites, including cove, cornice, ceiling roses, corbels, pediments, and niches.

These moldings are commonly found in period houses. If you have damaged moldings it is possible to have them copied by specialized companies that will make a mold from a cast of the existing molding and reproduce it. This can be a costly process, but there is a wide range of standard mass-produced reproductions available.

Putting up plaster cove

Putting up plaster cove will help to soften the gap between wall and ceiling. There are lightweight varieties available made from a number of different materials. It is advisable to choose the most authentic-looking design for the style of your house—an ornate, period-style cove will look out of place in a contemporary interior. If you do not feel confident about mitering corners, some manufacturers make inside and outside corner pieces, which fit snugly over the gap.

Tools and materials

Paint scraper
Straightedge
Level
Adhesive
Plaster cove
Putty knife
Small nails or brad nails
Decorator's caulk
Caulk gun

1 Remove any loose or flaking areas of plaster or paint and use a straightedge and level to mark the position of the cove on the wall and ceiling to provide you with guidelines.

2 Mix up the adhesive following manufacturer's instructions and carefully butter it onto the back of the cove, using a putty knife.

3 Press the cove firmly into position on the wall and gently tap small nails or brad nails above and below it, to support it while the adhesive dries.

4 Remove the nails and fill the resulting holes. Use excess adhesive or flexible decorator's caulk applied with a caulk gun to fill any gaps between the cove and the wall/ceiling.

Fitting a decorative ceiling rose

Ceiling roses were traditionally positioned above the light fittings in period houses. When installing or replacing a ceiling rose, it is important to identify the position of the joists in the ceiling so that you can make a firm fastening. You can do this by lifting up the floorboards in the room above, or by using an awl to pierce the ceiling until you find a joist. There are also various different electronic gadgets available that locate the presence of metal in walls or ceilings, which may help you to locate the joists.

A ceiling rose will look best in the center of the room. Make sure that if there is a working light fixture where you want to install the ceiling rose that you turn off the mains electricity supply and disconnect the fixture before you start drilling in the area.

Tools and materials

Ceiling rose

Pencil

Drill with countersunk drill bits

Specialized plastic cove adhesive

Screws with countersunk heads

Screwdriver

All-purpose white filler

1 Carefully hold the ceiling rose in position and draw around it using a soft pencil. The rose can be heavy so you may need two people for this job—one to hold it and one to draw.

Hold the rose in place on the ceiling and draw around the shape.

2 Drill holes to accommodate the wiring for the light fixture (if required) and also make a hole on one of the flat areas on each side of the rose.

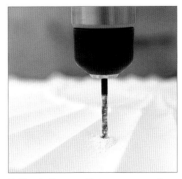

Drill a hole on a flat area on each side of the ceiling rose.

3 Mix the adhesive following the manufacturer's instructions and spread it carefully on the back of the rose. Then press the rose firmly into position on the ceiling.

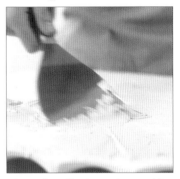

Mix up the adhesive and spread it on the back of the rose.

4 Use two long countersunk screws to support the rose. Screw them directly into the joist. Fill over the screw head with white filler.

Use countersunk screws to fasten the rose securely in place.

Living rooms

Planning your living room

A living room is a relaxing space where family and friends meet, but it is also a public room where the interior decoration should make a statement. As such, planning is essential—for example, furniture should be arranged in sociable groups, yet without obstacles blocking any pathways.

Planning your space

Unless you are fortunate enough to have a den or private space where you can closet yourself away, the main focus for daytime relaxation in the home tends to be the living room. But the living room is a hybrid space, often a public venue where, at certain times, guests and friends are entertained. It is also a family room where group, as well as individual, rest, and leisure time is spent.

Because the living room is a shared space, it is usually the focus of communal family gatherings and a place where a number of activities take place at the same time. Children may play games or watch TV while adults read or listen to music.

As well as being adaptable for day-to-day family life, the living room should also be able to cope with the changes that are brought about between being a night and daytime venue, as well as a summer and winter location.

During the day the room should be a bright and enjoyable place to be, lit by natural light. In the evening, with curtains or shades drawn, the emphasis is on a more cosy and secure environment. During this time, different levels of lighting that are focused on the

various recreational tasks and activities that take place in the room are important.

In the summer, the room should be appealing because it is cool and fresh, and in the winter, a comforting place into which you can retreat, leaving the cold and dark outside.

For all these reasons the planning and furnishing of the space needs to be thought out carefully, so that the room can cope with the requirements and levels of wear and tear.

Above: This traditional room has chairs and sofas arranged near a natural light source.

Opposite: It important that the main pathway through the living space is free of clutter and obstacles, so that a person entering can reach their destination easily.

Above: You can make the most of period features in your living room, such as this elaborate fireplace, and draw attention to them by arranging the seats nearby.

Opposite: A raised area in a bay window creates a private sitting place with a 180-degree view.

History of the living room

In centuries gone by, the furniture in the living room was arranged around the walls. This, the main entertaining room, was a formal place for people to gather and talk, so the center of the room was left empty to enable people to walk around or stand still and converse.

In the 18th and 19th centuries, the living room became a drawing room or salon in the homes of the wealthy and the middle classes. This room was used only for special entertaining or for adult family gatherings. The drawing room or, more properly, withdrawing room, was the place that the ladies withdrew to as the men smoked cigars and drank port after a meal. In more humble homes this room was known as the parlor, but nevertheless it still had the formal, rather straight-laced approach to relaxation time.

In grand houses the drawing room was often on the first floor and in some modern homes this layout has been adopted in order to make the most of a view or to raise the room above street level and car noise.

Instead of the nursery, play room, morning room, study, and parlor being separate spaces and in different parts of the house, some or all of these functions are now housed in the living room. A lot more is expected of the contemporary space and, in turn, the general decorative style has become more simple and streamlined. Beneath the layout, however, storage and planning have become more complex.

An effective layout

Current interior-design thinking advocates making rooms within rooms, and this can work well in a large living area. Furniture and rugs can be used to delineate different areas—for example, if there is a fireplace, that will probably be the focal point of the room around which people gather. The fireplace area can be defined by a large rug on which a U or semi-circle arrangement of sofas or armchairs are placed around a central coffee table. The U shape may have to be broken to allow access, but its outline marks the sociable area, where people will sit.

Arranging seats

Make an effort to avoid long or continuous lines of seats—this is visually uninviting, but also makes it difficult for a group to communicate. Arrange chairs and sofas so that they form a unit enabling people to talk to those opposite them, or at an angle to them. Also, avoid placing small tables between every chair, or setting a chair in a space on its own, because this creates a barrier between those sitting in the main seats and a feeling of isolation for those on their own. The backs of the chairs and sofas form a visual barrier, making suggested walls that enclose the space in front.

Elsewhere in the room, perhaps by a window or French doors, there could be a chaise or recliner that is specifically placed on its own, denoting another "room" reserved for private reading or contemplation. In a different area

Creating play areas

It is useful for children to have their own play space. In an ideal allocation of rooms, the play area should be separate from the bedroom so that it is not associated with play or entertainment at all.

If children can have their own play area, this will give them freedom to make noise and play without restrictions. It will also leave the main living area for mostly adult use.

However, you can create a play area within a living room by using a screen or mobile divider to partition off an appropriate space.

there could be a TV and bean bags, or a small, two-seat sofa for children to sit on and watch TV or play with games.

By dividing the room into sections you can accommodate various requirements. The only problem that will occur is in volume control when all three divisions of the room need to be used at the same time—this is when headphones can be useful.

Another configuration that works well is the extendable seating unit—this can be L-shape, with a short side in front of the window (so as not to block out too much light), or near a wall with the long back of the seats placed across the open room. The open end of the sofa, without an arm, makes it accessible and open to those arriving in the room. This configuration does not create such an enclosed space as the U shape, but the long back of the sofa or the backs of a similar arrangement of chairs still provides a delineation between one part of the room and another. The corner of the L also creates a small, more intimate space where people can sit side by side to talk.

Another option is the parallel-line configuration. This lines up a matching pair of sofas or a sofa and two armchairs on either side of a fireplace or central room feature, providing two equal-size and equal-space seating areas that connect face to face.

Heavier pieces of furniture, such as sofas and armchairs, can be supplemented by lighter, easier to maneuver chairs that can be kept against a wall or in an arrangement by a table or light, and brought into the main space when guests arrive. In a small apartment or living area, these chairs could be foldaway. Chairs without arms will look less bulky.

If your setting is contemporary or you want a feature chair, then opt for a work of a classic, modern designer—such as Arne

Jacobsen's series 7 chair or Tom Dixon's S chair.

Adjustable and adaptable furniture is important in a living room. There may be times when you need to clear the center of the room for a drinks party or social function. Some chairs and smaller sofas can be moved more easily if put on casters or wheels, which enable them to be pushed without much effort. The wheels or casters may need to be placed in cups—solid-plastic dishes that go under the wheels—to protect a deep-pile carpet or valuable rug.

Positioning tables

Smaller pieces of furniture, such as tables, should serve as useful accessories, rather than cluttering the limited space or becoming obstacles to easy movement.

The positioning of side tables is particularly important. To encourage and promote relaxation, a table should be within easy reach of the person in an armchair or on a sofa. For example, a good reading light should be to hand on a table in order to avoid eyestrain. There should also be space where a drink can be

Above: The sofas in this room are arranged in an inviting manner so that people can talk to each other easily while relaxing in a comfortable seat.

Opposite: This U-shape configuration of built-in seating maximizes a small space and forms an intimate salon away from the main living room.

Glass-topped coffee tables are extremely popular because the material is attractive to look at, and can make a pleasant feature in a room. However, it may be dangerous, so make sure that you buy a table that incorporates laminated or tempered glass, which are both tough and resilient and can withstand most knocks and bumps.

Another style of table that is useful in a living room is a console table, which has a narrow format. Traditional styles are supported by brackets fastened to the wall, while modern console tables are usually freestanding.

Subconsciously, many people prefer to sit with their backs to a wall and to have a clear view of anyone entering the room, but in a circular or group arrangement of chairs and sofas, this is not usually practical. To create a barrier between the back of a sofa and an open space behind, a console table can be placed so that it butts up to the back of the seat. This creates a screen or small wall-like feature, which makes the sitter feel less vulnerable and the room less open. The console table is also an area where small displays of photographs or treasures can be displayed, but the number of artefacts should be limited so as to

Above: This period-style room has a large ottoman for books and a small console table against one wall for holding ornaments.

Opposite: In a split-level space like this, it is important to have schemes that work together because you can see both areas at the same time. Here, the spot-decorated cushions act as a link between the upper and lower levels.

placed or where a book, newspaper, pen, or pencil can be laid. To meet these requirements you may need a series of small tables, which are more formally known as occasional tables, or you could use a nest of tables—tables of graduated sizes that fit on top of each other. When selecting or buying this type of table, be sure it is at the right height for the chair. In a family room, the tables should also be robust, with good, solid legs to make them resilient to the occasional knock or bump.

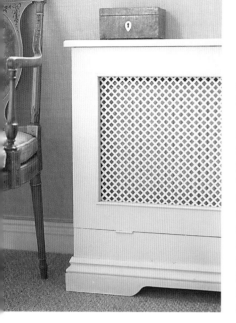

avoid it becoming cluttered and a hazard for people walking past.

It is worth thinking carefully about where you place your tables, and how many of them you use. If you have a long wall with a doorway in the center, or a fireplace with space on both sides, then you can position a table on either side of the feature and use it to support a pair of table lamps or a pair of artefacts, such as marble columns or large glass vases. The pleasing nature of matching items appeals to our sense of symmetry and proportion, which alludes to Classical style.

Traffic paths

One of the most important factors in arranging a busy area such as a living room is to work out the traffic paths. People will need access from one side of the room to another as well as to bookcases, TV, and other elements within the space. Your priority should be to avoid arranging the main seating area so that it has

Above: A radiator cover can be used as a display surface instead of a side table.

Right: This coffee table is positioned within easy reach of the daybed, so that the person seated there can reach it without getting up.

Opposite: The layout is arranged so that there is room to move between the tables and chairs.

a path of through traffic, entering and exiting, as this will be disruptive for those sitting there, and awkward for those who are passing through.

Try to map out the areas where a clear pathway is necessary, and arrange the placement of the furniture to accommodate this. If the room is small, then there may be only one main thoroughfare, but in a large room there may be several routes. The journey around a room should be simple and easy

to execute, not an assault course of low stools, haphazardly arranged side and coffee tables, and baskets of newspapers, magazines, or logs for the fire. Try to place small objects adjacent to the large one they are meant to be used with. For example, slot a foot stool under a seat or coffee table so that it is out of the way when it is not in use. A log basket should be set right beside the fireplace. Baskets of magazines and newspapers should be regularly edited

so that only a few relevant issues are kept.

Focal points

In a living room a focal point, such as a fire or a particular painting, can be attractive as well as reassuring. There should be at least one object that draws the eye and on which the mind can focus. This helps in the calming procedure and the process of unwinding, as well as providing a center of attraction for the space.

Above: The fireplace is the focal point in this room, and the side table and pictures have been arranged symmetrically on both sides to bring the eye back to the center point.

Opposite: This small, modern niche fireplace breaks up an expanse of wall and, although there is no traditional fire surround, a single painting hung above the fire alludes to a more conventional setting.

If the fireplace is the focal point of the room, the area around it should be well planned. The space directly in front of the fire may be a hearth or stone block that protects the floor from sparks. On each side you could build seats, under which you could have cupboards. These seats would allow the sitter to use the wall as a back support, and should have a padded cushion on the base to make it comfortable. Scatter cushions, or a covered pad suspended from hooks or a pole attached to the wall, would also

work well. In a contemporary setting this could be a low, wide wooden shelf that doubles as an occasional sitting area as well as a place for display.

In a traditional style of sitting or living room, there are often deep recesses on both sides of the chimney breast. These areas are commonly filled with bookcases or cupboards at the lower levels and with shelves above. In a classic setting, the top shelf may be finished off with a decorative feature such as a pediment or broken pediment. This is a triangular or pyramid-shaped feature originally used to crown the top point or level of an important Grecian or Roman building. The arrangement of shelves can vary in width to accommodate differing heights of books and artefacts, but the shelves should be equally spaced on both sides of the chimney breast so that they form a continuous line. Having them staggered or at irregular distances will upset the harmony and balance of the room's layout.

If the fireplace is opposite a window, an appropriately framed mirror can be a useful feature to reflect and increase the effect of the daylight. The space opposite a fireplace could alternatively be used to display a painting or print. As this wall space is usually quite substantial in size, the picture could be large. Although

elsewhere in the room groups of pictures may be arranged to create a feature, the area above the fireplace is generally reserved for one single, impressive image.

When framing an overmantel mirror or picture, take a reference for the frame from the fire surround itself. If the surround is simple with geometric or linear detail, then the frame of the picture should complement that. On the other hand, if the fire surround is ornate (such as one carved with swags and cherubs), then the picture frame you choose can also afford to be a lot more decorative.

If your living room doesn't have a fireplace, there are other ways to create a focal point. First, the arrangement of furniture will draw the eye to a certain point in the room. For example, if most of

Incorporating sounds and scents

Scents and sounds can be used, like color, to create the perfect atmosphere. Scents are very personal—some people love a room richly scented with perfumed room candles and the oriental aromas of sandalwood and musk, while others prefer the fresh smells of pine, lemon, lime, and orange peel.

Sounds can be therapeutic and relaxing, too. The tinkle of a water feature outside a window, or the gentle movement of wind in the trees serves as a reminder of nature and open spaces. A favorite piece of music played at a gentle volume may be all that is required after a busy day.

At-a-glance color guide

Traditional colors that suit sitting rooms are red, against which gilt-framed pictures and mirrors work well, blue, which is attractive with silver accessories, and bottle green, which is often associated with old-style private clubs and gentlemen's studies.

Mid-shades, such as yellow and magnolia, are classic and help to bring a subtle form of light and color to a room, while still providing a presence in the background.

Contemporary sitting rooms often have minimalist white or off-white walls.

Right: This contemporary radiator has a sculptural quality and sits low on the floor, and does not interrupt or impinge on the wall space.

Opposite: This vibrant color scheme works well because of the natural light that pours in through the wall of sliding glass panels.

the chairs and sofas are arranged around a coffee table, then that will become a focus. A piece of sculpture or art that is well-framed and highlighted by a picture or task light will also draw the eye.

A room that has no focus will feel unsettling and vacant, but if you want to opt for a minimalist style of decoration then use color to create interest. In a room that is all white or decorated in neutral colors, a bowl of bright red flowers on a table, or a group of vivid blue cushions on the end of a sofa will catch the attention of the person entering the room.

It is best to keep the focal point at standing eye level. If you use a mat or rug, too much attention will be drawn to the floor. Conversely, a wild-colored central lightshade will cause people to look upwards, rather than at your intended feature.

Communal living areas

The living area of a home may also be linked to another room. It is increasingly common in contemporary homes for an open-plan living area to incorporate the dining and/or kitchen space too. The barriers and walls that once divided these different rooms are being knocked down to provide large, through spaces. These large, all-in-one living areas need to be linked by decoration because it looks odd if the kitchen

Above: This central, contemporary fireplace brings the focal point of the room away from the walls and into the center. It is a useful way to divide up a large room and create a cosier sitting area in a corner, rather than in the middle of the space.

is a cool, minimal contemporary scheme, while the sitting area is decked out in full-blown 19th-century drapes and rich colors. The key is to find a base color that works in all areas, and then to use accessories to vary the tempo and mood in each space.

The simplest way is to choose a neutral base scheme, for example, a beige or pale gray for floors and walls, throughout, with white woodwork and detailing.

Using color

To create a truly relaxing environment, you need to think about color. Depending on the size of the room, your character, and your likes and dislikes, you may find that rich, warm colors help to create a calm atmosphere. Deep reds or dark blues can be enveloping and give a sense of security, but conversely these colors may also make some people feel boxed in and uneasy, especially in a small space. Those who prefer lighter colors may find a mousy mid-brown or a muted shade of green much more comforting and relaxing.

You may, however, choose to paint your living room white. There are actually many shades of white available today that have a hint of another tone—for example, stone-white, which is slightly muted with gray, and sand white, which has a soft brown tinge.

Stenciled fall leaves floorboards

Use this simple idea to create the illusion of colorful fall leaves that have been blown in by the wind. You will need to start off with new or unfinished floorboards that can be washed white. Then simply gather fallen leaves and flatten them for a few days inside a heavy book before using them as templates.

Positioning the leaves

1 Space the flattened leaves out, and place a sheet of glass over the top of them.

Tracing the leaves

2 Place the cellulose acetate sheet over the leaves, and then use a china marker pencil to draw carefully around the outline of each one.

3 When the stencil cutter has heated up, use it to trace along the pencil lines. Then carefully remove and discard the scrap pieces of cellulose acetate.

Smoothing the floor surface

4 Fill any holes or dents in the floorboards with wood filler, and sand until smooth.

Materials

Pressed leaves of various shapes and sizes
Sheet of glass
Cellulose acetate sheet
Wood filler
Wood wash in white, terra-cotta, amber, and driftwood gray—buy ready-made or use diluted latex (acrylic) paint
Spray adhesive
Satin floor varnish

Tools

China marker pencil
Stencil cutter
Putty knife
Fine-grit abrasive paper with sanding block or electric sander
Large brush
Stencil brushes
Fine paintbrush

Space out your chosen leaves in a row so that you can place a piece of glass over them.

Place a piece of cellulose acetate over the top and draw around the leaves with a china marker pencil.

Applying the wood wash

5 Apply white wood wash in the direction of the wood-grain over the floorboards.

Fixing the stencil to the floor

6 Use spray adhesive to stick the stencils to the floor.

Coloring the leaves

7 Dab the colored wood washes with a dry stencil brush and apply the wash to the leaves, working away from the edges of the stencils.

8 Use pale gray wood wash to paint shadows on each leaf. Allow to dry, then varnish with satin floor varnish.

Once you have filled any holes or dents with wood filler, sand the surface until smooth.

Using a large brush, apply white wood wash over the whole surface of the floor.

For a realistic effect, add shadows on the leaves, making sure that they fall in one direction.

Creating your
own wall art

Materials

1 x1½in (2.5 x 4cm) wood
Scrap masonite
Brad nails
Fine-gauge artist's canvas
Gesso primer
Selection of latex or artist's
acrylic colors
Low-tack tape
Texturizing medium
Coarse sand
Gilt transfer leaf

Tools

Miter saw
Jigsaw
Hammer
Scissors
Staple gun
Spray gun and water
Paintbrushes
Palette knife

Finding the perfect piece of artwork to complement your interior can be difficult, so why not create your own? You don't have to be a talented artist, just choose colors that inspire you and work well together. You can buy ready-made canvases, but it is much more economical to stretch your own canvas before you begin to decorate it. And don't be afraid to experiment with color and texture. You can create impact by hanging several similar-size canvases side by size, or create one giant canvas that will give dramatic impact to your room.

Establishing frame dimensions

1 Decide on the dimensions of your frame and cut the wood to length with a miter saw to ensure close-fitting miter joints.

Making the frame

2 Cut the masonite into triangular pieces using a jigsaw. Then butt the corners of the frame together and place the pieces of triangular masonite over the top

Use a miter saw to cut the four pieces of wood, making sure that the joints are tight.

Position the triangular pieces of masonite over the wooden joints, and use brad nails to secure.

of the joints. Use brad nails in order to secure the masonite in position.

Stapling the canvas

3 Cut a piece of canvas that is large enough to fit over the whole frame, then secure the canvas on the reverse of the frame using a staple gun. You should work systematically around the frame, pulling the canvas tight to be sure that it is evenly stretched over the frame. You should also make sure that the corners of the canvas are neatly folded under.

Preparing the canvas

4 Spray the canvas with a fine mist of water to make the cotton fibers shrink slightly. This will improve the overall tension of the canvas. Once dry, prime it with two coats of gesso primer, and allow this to dry for approximately one hour.

5 Paint the entire canvas, including the edges, with a base coat, which will be the dominant color. Allow to dry.

Applying color

6 To add a block or stripe of texture, mask off an area with low-tack tape. Then mix your second chosen paint color with the texturizing medium and apply this to the canvas with a flat palette knife. Before the medium has set, pull away the tape so that you avoid pulling away dried paint.

Staple the canvas into place on the back of the frame using a staple gun.

Paint the whole surface of the canvas with gesso primer, and allow it to dry.

Choose your dominant paint color and cover the whole area of the canvas with it.

Adding texture

7 When the second color is dry, mask off different areas of the canvas. Choose another paint color and mix coarse sand into it. Apply this to the masked off areas and allow to touch dry. Again, be sure to remove the masking tape before the medium has dried so that the paint is not peeled off with it.

8 Finally, add the finishing touches to your wall panel by giving it some gilt highlights. To do this, carefully press squares of gilt transfer leaf onto areas of paint while the paint is still sticky. Smooth the squares of gilt leaf down with your fingers, and then peel off the backing paper to reveal the gilt.

Mix your second color with texturizing medium, and apply it using a flat palette knife.

Mask various areas of the canvas and apply paint mixed with coarse sand into them.

Use gilt transfer leaf as a highlight over the design, and then peel off the backing paper.

Alternative

A single, large-scale painting can look just as effective as a group of smaller paintings. Creating a canvas of simple stripes in colors that complement your interior is an ideal way of using up leftover household paint.

A quick alternative to stretching your own canvas is to use a piece of lightweight MDF instead, which can be attached to the wall using screw eyes or mirror plates.

Lightly sand then seal the MDF with a base coat of multi-purpose primer or a slightly diluted coat of standard latex (acrylic) before you begin. Choose the color that you wish to dominate the painting, and apply it with a brush or small roller to the MDF surface and allow it to dry. Decide where you would like to position your stripes, then draw them in lightly with a soft pencil and a set square. Mark out the stripes using low-tack painter's tape, then apply the different colors. Finally, pull off the masking tape before the paint dries completely.

Decorative screen with colored panels

This practical screen has many uses in the living room. It is both light and easy to move, and the semitranslucent panels make it suitable for positioning in front of a window if you require extra privacy during the day but do not want to lose any light. It is also excellent as a room divider, so can be used to screen off a dining or home office area. We have constructed the screen using simple butt joints, and used a natural beech woodstain to color the frame, though you may prefer to paint or stain it in a darker shade. Feel free to experiment ...

Planning the screen

1 Start by drawing a plan of your screen. To work out the spacing of the horizontal wood strips, multiply the thickness of the wood by six. Take the resulting number away from the height of the vertical uprights. Now divide this number by five to find out the inside height of each square. (If you are using the suggested wood, this measurement should be

Materials

12 pieces 6ft (1.8m) long of dressed 2 x 2in (5 x 5cm) softwood
Wood glue
Wood screws
Wood filler
Square beading to form the rabbets
Brad nails
Mineral spirits
Beech varnish
8 sheets of polypropylene in various colors
9 flush hinges

Tools

Paper and pencil
Handsaw or electric jigsaw
Set/combination square
C-clamp
Drill
Screwdriver
Palette knife
Tack hammer
Medium- and fine-grit abrasive paper with sanding block
Cloth
Paintbrush
Sharp utility knife
Staple gun

Work out the length of each strip and then, using a handsaw, cut the strips to size.

With a pencil, mark the positions of the horizontal strips on the vertical pieces.

Know your materials

Polypropylene is a type of plastic sheet, thin enough to cut with scissors or a utility knife, but stiff enough for use in this screen project. It comes in a variety of translucent and opaque colors and textures. Because light filters through polypropylene, it is also suitable for making modern lamp-shades, window hangings, and mobiles. It is readily available from all good art-materials suppliers.

1ft/30cm). Use a sharp handsaw or electric jigsaw to prepare the 16 wood strips, which should also be 1ft (30cm) long, and cut these out in the same way.

2 Mark the final positions of the horizontal strips on the vertical pieces of wood, using a set square (see picture bottom right, page 171).

Fastening the joints

3 Clamp the joints together using a C-clamp, then drill a pilot hole in the center of each joint using a small wood bit. Make sure you use a countersink bit so that the screw head sits beneath the surface of the wood. This is important because you don't want

the screw heads to be visible on the finished screen. Spread a thin layer of wood glue over the joint, then make sure the screw is firmly in place. Continue this process at each joint until all the panels are complete.

4 Fill the countersunk screw holes with a neutral-color filler. Allow the filler to dry (following the manufacturer's instructions), then sand the surface smooth.

Attaching the rabbet strips

5 Cut the rabbet strips to the required lengths. (You will need eight pieces per screen square.) Use a tack hammer and

Use a C-clamp on the joints, and then drill a pilot hole for a screw to hold them together.

Fill the countersunk screw holes with a neutral-color filler and leave it to dry.

Cut the rabbet strips to the correct lengths and then hammer them into place.

brad nails to fasten the strips in place, slightly inset around each square in order to form a rabbet on the front of each panel. (Blunt each brad nail by tapping the point with the hammer, which will help to prevent splits in the wood.) The second set of rabbets will be made later to hold the polypropylene in place.

Varnishing the screen

6 Sand the whole surface of the panel frames thoroughly using medium- then fine-grit abrasive paper wrapped around a sanding block. Once you have finished, remove any remaining sawdust with a cloth that has been dampened in mineral spirits. Next, apply beech varnish to the panel frames using a 1in (2.5cm)

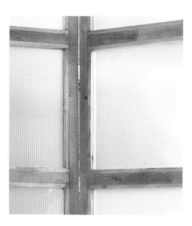

paintbrush. Allow the varnish to dry, then lightly sand over the areas. Apply a second coat of the varnish in the same way.

Stapling the sheets

7 Carefully cut the sheets of polypropylene so that they will

sit neatly over each square, using a sharp utility knife. Then attach the sheets in place against the rabbet using a staple gun. For a tidy finish you should now fit the second set of rabbets in place on the back of the screen, using the pin hammer as before.

Assembling the panels

8 Attach the screen panels together to create the large screen. This should be done using three flush hinges screwed at equidistant points along the length of each panel. Hold the hinges in place, and mark the positions of the screw holes. Drill the holes and screw the hinges firmly in place so as to complete your screen.

Sand the panel frames, apply two coats of beech varnish, and allow to dry.

Cut the polypropylene sheets to size and then staple them to the rabbet strips.

Use three flush hinges on each panel, and screw them into place to complete the screen.

Alternative

Decorative screens can make ideal display panels for photographs—you can make a simple display screen using MDF.

Get your lumber supplier to cut one 4 x 8ft (1.2 x 2.4m) sheet of ½in (12mm) MDF into three equal pieces along its length. Mark out five photo openings and the feet of each panel, using a pencil and set square. Drill a pilot hole in the inside corner of each square, then use a jigsaw with a sharp blade to cut out the openings and around the feet. Sand lightly, then apply several coats of black eggshell paint with a small paintbrush or mini gloss roller and allow to dry. Get a glazier to cut sheets of clear acrylic sheet or safety glass just under 1in (about 2cm) larger than each opening. Enlarge the photographs so they are the same size as the glass or acrylic sheet. Cut stiff cardboard to fit the back of each, and use metal mirror corner plates to fix the glass, photograph, and cardboard on the back of the screen.

Furnishings and
textiles

Furnishings and textiles are like the makeup, shoes, and belt that go with a dress—they are the finishing touches that create individual style and appearance. Furniture should be selected for comfort, quality, and shape, while textiles can introduce fashionable or seasonal colors and patterns.

Choosing your furniture

The type of furniture you choose for your living area should be conducive to relaxation. When trying to imagine a place for unwinding, the first thing that comes to mind is a huge, squashy, enveloping sofa, but this type of seat can be uncomfortable and detrimental to relaxation.

Finding the right sofa

You should take your time and try out plenty of sofas before buying one. You may want to rush out and buy the inviting-looking, squashy sofa mentioned before, but there is often no proper lumbar support on this type of seating, unless of course you lie flat on it and arrange cushions to provide specific underpinning to the right areas of your body. If the seat is too deep, then you will perch on the edge, sit back, and tuck your legs underneath you to provide an anchoring point, or

dangle your legs, unsupported, in the air. If two people sit beside each other on an overlarge sofa, they tend to sag toward each other or end up slumped up against an arm at one end, which means that their spines will be curved and unsupported.

A smaller, two-seat sofa with a seat that is just deep enough to accommodate you comfortably in the sitting position is a better choice. It may not look as inviting as an oversized three-seater, but it can be more comfortable, and ultimately more relaxing, too.

Armchairs and footstools

Similar criteria also apply to a single armchair. Big, deep, cosy chairs may look the best, but in

Above: A sofa with high arms is easier to get in and out of. Cushions on sofas can be used not only to provide color, but also support.

Opposite: Choose a sofa carefully— too big and it will overpower the room, but too small and it will look lost or insignificant in a large space. The most important thing, however, is to choose one that has proper lumbar support for the spine.

Above: Fun fabrics, such as this dalmatian print, are ideal for accessories if used in moderation.

Right: A simple bucket chair can offer good support and has a raised shape.

fact a neat, upholstered and well-proportioned chair will be better for you in the long term, as it gives you good support.

The ideal relaxing sitting position should allow the feet to rest lightly on the floor, with an angle of slightly more than 90 degrees between the hips and the lumbar region of the spine. The back of the chair should support the whole length of the spine as well as the base of the head. If the seat is too low, you will feel the need to cross your legs, which is bad for blood circulation.

Upholstered furniture with arms not only makes you feel more enclosed and secure in the seat, but also helps you get in and out of a chair. For older people, a chair with a high frame and raised arms that meet the elbow will make getting in and out of the chair easier.

"Putting your feet up" has long been an expression used in conjunction with having a rest, and there is a lot of truth in it. For those who spend a lot of time standing at work or around the house, or people with leg problems such as varicose veins, putting their feet up while sitting is beneficial. An ottoman or foot-stool at the same height as the edge of the seat of the chair is ideal, as your legs will be straight out in front of you. If you have a circulatory problem in your legs, it can be beneficial to raise the height of your extended legs above your hip level for some time to help blood flow. There are a number of chairs designed with retractable footrests, which slot neatly into the base of the chair when not in use, but are easily raised by means of a lever at the side of the chair when wanted.

Electrical considerations

Television and video equipment are almost always located in living rooms today. The positioning of such equipment is very important, not only for aesthetic reasons, but also for your health. First, try to avoid glare on the screen, which can cause eyestrain and headaches. Also, reduce the effect of the radiation given off by the screen by sitting well back from it. Radiation diminishes by the square of the distance and a mini-mum of 6ft (180cm) is suggested. The level of light when watching TV should also be regulated. The intensity of light in the room should be similar to that emitted from the screen. It can be quite

detrimental to your vision to watch TV in a dark room (see Lighting your living room, pages 187–8).

Another electrical consideration is the management of wiring and cables in living rooms. There will be cord for table lamps and lamp-stands, for TV, hifi, and other electrical items, which all require access to a socket and a clear route to their base. Never over-load a socket, especially with adapters—by all means use one single adapter to extend the use of a single socket to two plugs, but don't put one adapter into anoth-er, because you may not only overload the circuit and cause the power to trip the fuse, but you may also, inadvertently, cause an electrical short circuit, which could start a fire.

If running electrical wiring, such as a cord for a side light, under a rug or carpet, make sure the cable is properly insulated, and that it does not run under a wheel, caster, or any other sharp or heavy object that may cut or damage the wiring or its casing.

Textiles

Textiles and textures play a vital part in encouraging relaxation. However, the practical element of wear and tear must also be kept in mind.

Above: This simple, turned hold-back allows a light voile curtain to be drawn back from the edges of the window and arranged in a soft drape.

Upholstery

Soft and sensual fabrics such as silk, velvet, and wool can be comforting, especially in the fall and winter, when it is icy and dark outside. However, these fab-rics are very delicate, and so are best used for incidentals and accessories, where they will not become worn.

An increasingly popular materi-al for upholstery, and even floors and wall panels in living areas, is leather, which can be used to cover traditional, as well as more contemporary, furniture. This

Above: Raw silk cushions have an interesting slub texture and sheen.

Right: By mixing shapes, you can bring a change of emphasis to a minimal look.

Opposite page: The bold shapes and colors on the furniture and accessories act together as an effective contrast to the basic minimal look of this room.

material is great for upholstery, as it is soft but durable.

If you choose to upholster your furniture in pale shades, be sure that the fabric has a stain-retardant or repellent finish. Light colors can form a good, neutral background to a room, but will easily become stained and marked. These protective finishes create an invisible coating on the fabric, preventing spills from soaking into the weave or texture of the fabric, and making it easy to wipe them clean.

Another option is to have loose or removable covers. These are fitted to the shape of the chair or sofa, but can be removed by unzipping or untying. Depending on the fabric, loose covers can be washed in a machine or dry-cleaned. The main thing to be wary of is to check that they are prewashed or shrink-tested—there is nothing worse than trying to refit a loose cover after it has been washed and discovering that it has shrunk! Dry-cleaning is usually the safest option. Manufacturers make many textiles suitable for upholstery in heavier weights, such as wool weaves, jacquard, and damask self-patterned designs, as well as textured cotton or canvas. When looking in a fabrics store or department, ask to be directed to the fabrics that are specifically designated for this type of use.

Floor coverings

These days living room floors are most often carpeted or covered in a hard surface such as wood. A luxurious wool or wool-mix pile carpet is still among the most popular of finishes, but is best used in a room that is not subjected to heavy use, as the pile will eventually wear. Heavy traffic areas or main walkways can be

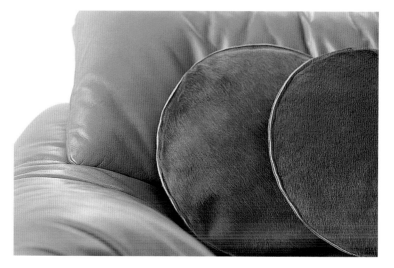

protected by a rug or runner, or by rearranging furniture at times, to expose different parts.

If you use a hard floor such as wood, tiles, or stone, you may want to soften the overall appearance by adding a decorative oriental flatweave mat or rug, such as a kelim or dhurrie. (Remember to attach a nonslip backing to the rug.)

Another popular way to cover a large wooden floor is with a substantial square or rectangle of carpet. This will cover the majority of the floor, but leave a rim of wood exposed around the edge of the room.

Curtains and cushions

The fabric used on curtains does not need to be as durable as that for upholstery. However, lightweight curtain fabrics usually need to be interlined and lined, and even heavier ones hang and drape more easily if they have a light backing or cotton lining.

Scatter cushions can be round, square, rolled, or even triangular. They are decorative, fun elements that can be made from leftovers of material, which links them to the other furnishing fabrics in the room. Alternatively, they can be made in dramatic, contrasting colors and patterns.

Felt rug and floor cushion

Materials

¼in (6mm) felt in three colors
(6½ x 6½ ft/2 x 2m of each
color is sufficient for the rug,
but be sure you also have
enough to cover your cushion,
if required)
Black tapestry wool
Nonslip backing strips (optional)
Cushion pad
Hook and eye fastenings

Tools

Soft pencil
Metal rule or set square
Sharp scissors
Tailor's chalk
Hole puncher
Darning needle

Felt is an increasingly popular furnishing material. It has many advantages, as it is naturally eco-friendly (made from boiled scraps of wool), warm, and does not fray when cut. Felt is not often considered as a flooring material, but ¼in (6mm) thick industrial felt is ideal as it is warm, durable, and soft underfoot. This patchwork-style rug is stitched together using a traditional blanket stitch. It is important to use a non-slip padding if the rug is to be used on wooden or laminated flooring.

Making the squares

1 Mark out three squares of each of the different colored felts, using a pencil and metal rule or set square to be sure they are identical sizes (we have made ours 1½ft (50cm).

2 Cut out each of the felt squares carefully, using a pair of sharp scissors.

3 Mark the position of the stitching holes at ½in (1cm) intervals along all of

Measure each felt square using a pencil and set square to make sure they are all the same size.

Using a pair of sharp scissors, carefully cut out each of the different colored felt squares.

Know your materials

Because of the thickness of the felt used in this project, it is essential to punch holes in the material before sewing. We have joined the squares of felt with a simple overstitch that, when pulled firmly, butts the two pieces of felt together tightly. This is simply formed by passing the needle from one piece of felt and into the other (see picture bottom right). Traditional blanket stitch has been used to bind the edges and give them a neat, finished appearance. This is formed by passing the needle through the fabric then under the loose thread (see picture bottom left, page 185).

the sides of each piece of felt, using a soft pencil or tailor's chalk. Check carefully that the holes will line up.

4 Use a hole puncher set on its smallest hole setting to cut out the holes you have marked on each piece of felt. (The felt is too thick to be pierced with a darning needle.)

Stitching the squares together

5 Thread a darning needle with a double thickness of black tapestry wool. Sew the squares together using a simple overstitch, making sure that they butt together closely. Alternate the colors of the squares in order to build up the required checkerboard pattern over the surface of the rug.

6 When all the squares have been joined together, use a blanket stitch to finish off the outside edges of the rug. Join the wool with a neat knot on the underside of the rug, otherwise it will eventually work its way undone. Then position self-adhesive, non-slip backing strips onto

With a soft pencil, mark out the position of the holes on each piece of felt.

Use a hole puncher set on its smallest setting to cut out the holes marked on each piece of felt.

Use a double thickness of black tapestry wool to overstitch each of the squares together.

the back of the rug if it is going to be placed on a hard surface, as it would be difficult to walk on without slipping otherwise.

Making the floor cushion

7 Use the same technique to make the coordinating large floor cushion. It is very simple to do this—first, cover a large cushion pad with two squares of felt, and then join them together securely using the blanket stitch once again. You should then make a slit down the center of one side of the cushion using a sharp pair of scissors.

8 On either side of the slit sew on hook and eye fastenings using a darning needle.

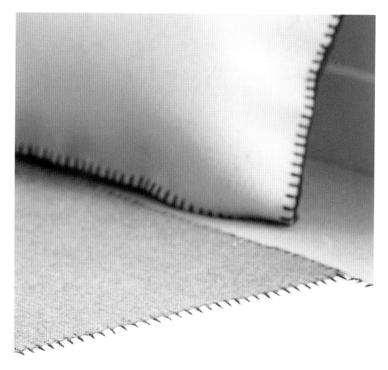

Finish off the outside edges of the rug by stitching blanket stitch all the way round.

Once you have made the basic cushion, use scissors to cut down the middle of one square.

On the other side of the opening, sew on a number of hook and eye fastenings.

Alternative

If your style is more opulent than the simple, understated look of felt, adapt the design to use luxurious fabric with beautiful glass bead trims. Affordable beaded trimmings are now available in fabrics departments, and work well alongside rich velvets and silks.

To make an opulent patchwork throw, cut out six equal-size velvet squares, with a ½in (1cm) seam allowance all the way round. Press and then pin them together before machine-stitching them. Cut a piece of silk or satin backing fabric and a lightweight lining fabric to the same dimensions as the velvet top section. Sandwich the layers with the right side facing in. Place the bead trim between the layers, lining up the flat edge of the trim with the raw fabric edges. Carefully pin it in place so that when it is turned right side out only the beads are visible. Machine-stitch all the layers together, leaving enough of an opening to turn the throw the right side out. Hand-stitch this closed using slipstitch.

Lighting your
living room

The lighting in the living room should be variable and flexible so that during the daytime task or reading lights can be focused for close work, while at night decorative and ambient lighting may be used to create a relaxing mood and atmosphere.

Effective lighting

The real skill of lighting design is to have a good balance so that the light can be adjusted to suit every action or event that takes place under its beams. The color and finish on walls, floors, and furniture will also have an effect on the lighting you need in a room. For

Types of lighting

Background or ambient lighting is a substitute for natural light, providing a general level of visibility. On its own, this type of lighting is fairly uninspiring.

Task or work lighting has specifically directed beams that provide a localized light in a prescribed area where an activity such as reading takes place.

Accent lighting is used to highlight color, texture, or objects. It can range from a pinhole, fine beam to a broad spot. Decorative lighting covers anything that is attractive but not necessarily useful.

example, in a room with white walls and few pictures or additional wall decoration, plain, light carpets and natural or neutral upholstery, a lot of light will be reflected, so fewer and less high-strength lights will be required. However, if a room has dark walls, a heavy, rich carpet and heavy, upholstered furniture, then more light fixtures will be needed, as each of these dark-colored items will absorb a certain amount of the natural light. Matte finishes also tend to absorb light, while shiny ones reflect it.

Planning your lighting

You need a central or main light that illuminates the room when you first enter it. In a traditional setting this is usually a pendant light. In modern homes, however, this is often replaced with a number of recessed ceiling spotlights or wall lights.

In a living room a general scheme usually includes three or

Above: By opening up the roof and installing laminated glass panels, the amount of natural light in this room has more than doubled.

Above: Classic plaster uplighters can be painted to blend in with the color of the wall. Church candles provide additional decorative lighting.

Above right: One small wall light might get lost in the center of a wall, unlike this group of three.

four levels of lighting. The first is general ambient light, which is provided by the pendant and other elements such as wall lights. These can also be wired to a dimmer switch so that the level or brightness can be lowered to alter the atmosphere of the room.

In order to choose other levels of lighting, you need to identify specific areas of use in the room. Task lighting may be required if there is a table or a desk, or close to the CD and TV so that you can see the controls. It will also be needed near chairs and sofas, where newspapers and books are read, or knitting or sewing occurs.

You may also want to include accent lighting to highlight a feature or collection, such as a picture, glass, or particular plant. These accent fittings can vary from a specific, wall-mounted picture light to a recessed, ceiling spotlight that has its beam directed onto the chosen object.

The adjustable spotlight gives a broad spread of light to the immediate area, but draws the eye to its focus. A strip light or picture light runs along the top of a picture and casts an even light from top to bottom, illuminating the whole of the picture. Another option is a specialized framing light with adjustable shutters that train the beam of light exactly onto the picture.

Architectural features, such as decorative arches, pillars, or a series of beams, can also be

"painted" with light. Halogen spotlights or eyeball downlighters pick out the feature and can be effective if the ambient lighting is dimmed lower than the spot.

Using light as a disguise

Although light is usually seen as a way of illuminating things and making them easily visible, it can also be used to disguise areas and, surprisingly enough, to make a room seem more spacious.

By placing larger pieces of furniture away from the walls and locating a couple of incandescent uplighters behind them, the light will reflect off the walls and make the place look larger. You can also focus light away from an area that you don't want to be seen, leaving it in shadow and making it retreat into the background.

Display and
storage

Different sizes and types of objects should be treated in various ways to suit their purposes. It is best to store useful, but not necessarily attractive, items out of sight or in an orderly way, while interesting and decorative pieces should be grouped attractively and given prominence.

Storage choices

In a living space storage is important, as it helps to keep order and to make movement around the room easy. Bookcases, freestanding or built-in, are the most usual way to contain books, CDs, videos, and general household artefacts. Open shelves give the easiest access, but this is also the most dust-prone arrangement. Shelves contained in cupboards, whether glass- or wood-fronted, will keep their contents cleaner for longer.

The secret to success in clutter management is to edit the things you possess to a controllable number, selecting those you really need or want, and then allotting them to a specific space or area. Throw or give the rest away.

Simple shelving systems

Modern storage is usually practical as well as aesthetically pleasing. Even shelves can be of interest in their own right.

Purpose-built and contemporary shelves often appear to hang magically in the air, although they are in fact attached to the wall by concealed pegs and brackets. The most basic, ready-made shelving

Above: This wall-mounted CD rack is very striking, but also displays the CDs in such a way that they are easy to identify, remove, and return.

Specialized shelves

As well as single or purpose-built shelves, there are also more specialized modular and flexible systems, which can be bought from good furniture and office-storage suppliers. Many have fine metal frames with adjustable brackets and shelves, but will come with additional features such as angled display shelves, where a flat object, such as a book or plate, can be supported but easily seen on a shelf that is raised at the back. Other options, such as cabinet and roll-front enclosures, are also available. This type of system is usually attached to the wall by brackets and screws so it is securely fastened.

When planning a set of built-in shelves, calculate the distance between them carefully, because once they are in place they are there for good. For example, if a mid-height shelf is to support a TV or hifi system, measure the depth and height of the piece of equipment, and allot the appropriate amount of space. Also, look

systems have open, usually pre-fixed, shelves, and are made of cheap wood such as pine, which can be painted or stained. Adjustable shelves with support brackets that slot into regularly spaced niches in the uprights are also available.

As well as shelving systems, you can buy single shelves with individual supports such as gallow brackets. These are triangular wooden supports that are screwed into the wall and the base of the shelf with a cross support between the two right-angled legs. Another single shelf option is

the steel shelf bracket that consists of two metal legs at a right angle to each other. These strong metal brackets are screwed into the wall and the base of the shelf.

Alcove supports are lengths of wood, preferably with a sculpted or finished front end, that are screwed into the wall with a glass or wood shelf resting on top. Finally, you can make the support invisible by using a wooden or laminated shelf that is grooved or drilled along the back surface. This hollow section slips over dowels or fastened supports into the wall.

at your collection of books and artefacts, and see if they fall into height categories so that you can allocate two narrow shelves for small softcover books, and one taller shelf for hardcover glossy art books.

Another popular modular system comes in cubes. These wooden cubes can be empty, with one shelf, two shelves, three drawers, or a door. You select the number of cubes you need to fill your area and then pick the arrangement of storage you want, so tailor-making your own system. This style of unit is usually connected across the back so that the units are interlocked, and will form a single, freestanding block, but for safety, especially if you have an uneven or irregular floor surface, you may also want to secure them to a wall.

Displaying objects

Some of the shelves in your room will probably house small objects and photographs, arranged in a set-piece display. These items should be carefully chosen, as they are going to be in such a prominent position.

When arranging items, you should also think about height and depth—try to avoid having everything at the same level, as this can appear monotonous. A group can be placed so that a taller item is to the back, with a mid-height and small item in front. This sort of display could include a plate propped up against the wall, with a bottle in front and a little dish or bowl in the foreground. Above all, you should try to avoid clutter—don't let your shelves become places where general household mail, matchboxes, and unframed photographs build up, as they will detract from the display items and can make the area look messy.

Decorative shelves

Shelves need not be dull—they can be beautiful architectural features. They can be cut and arranged to form a shape, such as a pyramid, or be sculptures in their own right.

Shelves can be painted the same color as the wall so that they almost disappear, or painted in a vibrant, contrasting color so that they become a definite feature. Polished or varnished wood can also be used, and the wood can be chosen to highlight or emphasize any wood elsewhere in the room.

You can also embellish shelves with a fringe, panel, or cutout, attached to the front edge of the shelf. Another choice is a beaten metal strip, such as copper.

Concealing or decorating radiators

Radiators are rarely elegant or attractive, so they are best disguised. Radiators are often placed under windows and, if the window is long and elegant and the radiator small and painted the same color as the wall, the window will be the eye-catching feature and the radiator hardly noticeable. At night curtains may also be drawn over the radiator.

On the other hand, if the radiator is in a prominent position, you may want to disguise it. Do this by boxing the top and sides using MDF or wood. The front should not be completely obscured, so that heat can still flow, so choose an open-mesh or decorative fret-cut panel.

Storage systems can also make wonderful room dividers. A set of freestanding shelves can provide a screen between one part of a room and another without permanently blocking it off.

Open shelves will also allow light to pass through them from one side of a room to another, so maintaining an open and airy feel. Conversely, a shelving system with a solid back will provide a dense screen, which will make a space feel more enclosed and private. Bear in mind, however, that unless the shelving unit reaches right up to the ceiling, sounds from each area will still carry.

Practical considerations

When deciding on the type of storage for your room, try to identify what belongs where. In the case of a living room, this will depend of the amount of space available and the allocation of tasks to the room (see Planning your space, pages 149). If it is a multipurpose room, you will need practical elements such as bookcases or shelves and cupboards, but you may also be able to introduce decorative storage, for example an antique wooden box or chest, a decorative chest of drawers, or a console table with drawers. Consider

TV cabinets

For those who find the presence of a large black TV screen offensive or distracting, there are purpose-built cabinets and tables that will conceal the box when it is not in use. Behind the doors there is usually a sliding shelf on which the TV rests, and beneath are shelves for storing tapes and videos.

Another option is a deep chest, like an old-fashioned blanket box or traveling chest. This oblong box can house a concealed lift, which is operated by remote control.

You could use a console or side table with a lower shelf. Place your TV on the shelf, and conceal it with a cloth that hangs to floor level.

what your shelves will be supporting—lightweight objects only need light shelves, but heavier things will need robust shelves and secure fastenings.

Try to keep things that you use frequently to hand, and store other items that are used occasionally in a less accessible area,

Above: The niches in this decorative display unit are painted in bright colors to create a feature.

Right: These deep boxes slot neatly under the coffee table, but keep magazines and books close to hand.

Left: The different-color interiors of this storage system, and the objects within, form several small pictures or points of interest. The concealed lighting also highlights objects such as the glass balls and the pyramid.

or even in another room, or the attic. For example, place video and DVD storage next to the TV, and CD racks near their player. If the living area is a place for plants and displays, but may also be a space for children to play in, it can be worth providing some higher-level shelves or storage so that fragile or breakable objects are placed out of the reach of small hands.

Think about subdividing storage to fit objects into a container of an appropriate size. For example, if you are putting a number of small things into a drawer, consider subdividing the space so that you have several small compartments, each containing one or two things that are easily accessible, rather than a jumble of objects.

Living-room accessories

Accessories are the finishing touches that bring personality and individuality to a room. In a living room these small items all add up to create a complete interior, and should be selected for their individual merit, as well as their contribution to the overall effect. The choice of accessories will be influenced by your chosen color and theme, but there may also be architectural limitations to consider, for example, small windows and a deep sill may point you in the direction of shades rather than curtains, a large expanse of wall may call for decorative, wall-mounted lights, and a dark or rich-colored room will require more light than a light-colored, bright, and sunny room. Even practical aspects such as radiators, door handles, and light switches should be thought through, as these will all contribute to the general appearance of the room. Radiators, for example, need not be ugly or dominant. There are many discreet, low-level radiators to choose from, and if you already have an large, featureless style, then one can be boxed and disguised.

Clockwise from top left:

An ornate lampshade made from porcupine quills creates an unusual pattern and coloring when electric light passes through it.

A mantelpiece is often a place where cards, mail, and general paperwork accumulate—try to choose just a few, special pieces for display. The mantel and fireplace are usually the focal point of a living room, and the first place that someone entering the room will look at.

In a room with a low ceiling a neat, close-fitting lightshade like this will provide light, but not restrict head room.

This magazine storage is made out of leather. Although unusual, it still provides ample space to keep magazines and other papers tidy.

If you have small windows, a well-tailored set of shades will be more space-effective than a pleated curtain.

The lighting in this living room has been carefully planned to focus on this magnificent statue.

Door and cupboard handles should not be overlooked, because the sum of these small details is significant.

Dimmer switches can be used to lower the lighting and change the mood of the room. It is a good idea to cover all light switches with a protective shield that can be wiped clean easily.

Textured fabric can add a luxurious finishing touch to your living area.

Bookshelves are a neat storage solution, but can also become an attractive feature in a living room.

Pieces of craft or artwork should be displayed to look their best. Here, the grain of the wood shelf supporting this bowl accentuates its shape and texture.

Photographs that have been mounted and framed in a similar way can be arranged together on a wall.

This twisted-glass lamp base has a plain, pleated shade, which does not distract from its intrinsic beauty.

A whimsical plain- and colored-glass chandelier adds an opulent touch.

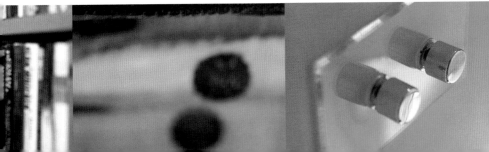

Bedrooms

Planning your bedroom

We spend a third of our lives in bed, and so the bedroom is an important part of the house and should be a space where you feel comfortable and can retreat to after a busy day. Above all, it needs to be warm, inviting, relaxing, and quiet.

Below: Wood paneling such as this will provide a certain amount of sound insulation for your bedroom.

Below right: As well as creating a tranquil scheme for your room, be sure that it is located in a quiet part of the home.

Opposite: The leather-paneled wall acts as a screen for the bathroom, and also doubles as a very attractive headboard.

Planning your space

The quality and quantity of sleep that you get has a profound effect on the way that you function, both physically and mentally. During periods of deep sleep the body restores and heals itself. Sleep also affects the body's ability to process and store carbohydrates, as well as regulate hormone levels. And during the day the spine is compressed by gravity, but at night it is given the chance to recover. So it is important that the room where you rest at night is designed to encourage good sleep.

The bed is one of the most important pieces of furniture in the home, and so the general advice given is to spend as much as you can afford on a good-quality bed (see Choosing the right bed, pages 210–14). And don't think that a bed is for life—you should replace it every eight to ten years.

Above: If the best position for your bed is close to the door, then a screen can provide a useful shield to create privacy.

To be sure of a quiet space, you may need to install double-glazing, double doors, or other forms of sound insulation. Double-glazing will muffle exterior noise, while double doors help to reduce noise by creating a small lobby or barrier between you and the outer elements. Sound insulation between you and a lower area can be improved with good padding beneath a carpet, or with insulation boards or cork tiles.

Finding the right location

Almost more important than the amount of sleep you have is the quality of it, so make sure that you are not disturbed unnecessarily. If you are able, locate your bedroom at the back or on the quietest side of the building, away from traffic noise.

If you are in an apartment block, check out what rooms are above and below you. Investigate the ground floor of your building—you may have moved away from traffic noise at the front, to have repositioned yourself above the kitchens of a restaurant or nightclub, where activity carries on until the small hours of the morning, or begins at daybreak.

An effective bedroom layout

More often than not, it is the shape and configuration of the space that dictates how the bedroom is laid out, and particularly where the bed can be set. If you have a window in the room, it is pleasant to have it at the foot or side of the bed so that you can look out at the sky or view beyond, but avoid sleeping with your head directly under a window because you may be subjected to drafts of cold air while you are asleep, which can cause stiffness in the neck and shoulders.

The door to the room will also influence where the bed is. Try to allow adequate space for the door to open and for the person entering the room to have a clear margin to turn around, without walking straight into the bed. Some people prefer to place their bed behind a door so that it is hidden or shielded from view. This is because a bed is the most personal and intimate piece of furniture in the home, and one that some people prefer to keep as private as possible.

The position of cupboard or wardrobe doors will also have to be considered, and if the wardrobe is built-in, then the location of the bed will have to be fitted around it. There should be enough space for the wardrobe door or doors to open and give adequate access to the contents, without having constantly to move other pieces of furniture or battle with the bed.

Creating the right environment

Once you have decided on the layout of the room, there are other important considerations, such as good ventilation and maintaining the right temperature. There is a tendency to make the bedroom too warm, as people feel that this

Left: This clever sliding wall panel has been covered in fabric to link with the rest of the room. It can be pulled across to conceal the storage when access is not needed.

is a place where they are naked or only lightly clothed, but an overheated bedroom may cause the sleeper to dehydrate. The ideal temperature for a bedroom is 55–60°F (13–15°C), though it should be slightly warmer for children and older people.

A humidifier helps to keep a little moisture in the air, especially during the height of the summer. You don't need an expensive humidifying machine, just a good-size, shallow bowl of water, with a reasonable surface area. Wash

the bowl and replace the water every day, so it does not become stagnant. Although it is best to sleep in a well-ventilated room, do be careful to avoid drafts.

It is also beneficial to air the bedroom each day by opening the window and door to get a flow or circulation going. If you live in the city or close to the road, leave a washable cotton sheer or voile curtain over the window while it is open, to help reduce the amount of smog and grime that will inevitably come in through

the window. Bedclothes should be turned back each morning so that the bed can be well ventilated.

Bedroom flooring

Floor coverings in a bedroom are important because they help to muffle noise, and also because they usually come in contact with bare skin. Wool carpets are the softest and warmest underfoot, but if you suffer from allergies or are dust-sensitive, a carpet can be a place that harbors fine particles and produces fluff.

Wooden floors are quite warm on bare skin, but need to be well sealed to prevent splinters. Wood is also easy to clean. To soften the area around the bed you can use a rug or mat made from cotton or other washable fibers. Stone is

not usually a good bedroom floor covering, as it is hard and, unless underheated, also cold.

Color and style

The bedroom is often the room where people indulge in decorating fantasies, choosing a favorite color or theme, something with rich-colored 19th century overtones or a Zen-like, cool space.

If a husband and wife, partners, or young children share a bedroom, then it may also be a place where a compromise has to be reached regarding color and style, so that the room is neither overpoweringly feminine nor too masculine. Many people prefer to keep the decoration of the bedroom simple, so that it is easy to clean and

Positioning pictures and mirrors

If a mirror is to be used for applying makeup and for checking clothing, then it should be positioned so that it benefits from a source of natural light.

Some people find it disturbing to have a mirror directly opposite or over the foot of the bed because it reflects their image, and shadow play makes them think that there is someone else in the room. But in a small space a large mirror can help to reflect light from a window and make the room seem larger.

range of the spectrum. Warm, soft yellow, watery blue, or pale green are all worth considering.

Yellow is a sunny color, which is cheerful and heartening on winter mornings. Choose your tone of yellow carefully—one with a paler, white base can be more comfortable than one with a red/orange emphasis, which might make you feel overheated. Some sludgy yellows with green overtones also look slightly grubby in low electric lighting, which is not an inspiring or appealing sight in a bedroom.

Some people find blue cool, but it is the color of natural elements (water and the sky), and it is said to be a color that can aid relaxation. Cool blues can be warmed by a touch of red, taking them to the lavender side of the color wheel, or with the addition of accessories and bed throws that are decorated with patterns that include various warmer shades.

Green is said to be a color of rejuvenation and growth, and the right shades can be bright and fresh. But be wary of teaming it with its contrast color of red in a bedroom, as these colors are diametrically opposed, and in certain strengths and shades can appear to fight or clash, which is neither calming nor relaxing.

At-a-glance color guide

Light pastel colors are good for bedrooms because they are relaxing and calming. Yellow is a warm color at night, but sunny and bright in the morning. Blue can be cool and refreshing, but may need elements of pink or lavender to prevent it from making a room seem cold.

Green is associated with renewal, and it can be invigorating to wake up to in the morning. Red is a bold color that is rarely used in a bedroom because it can make a room feel very claustrophobic.

maintain. Swags and frills tend to be dust stores, and a plethora of knickknacks and decorations just adds to the burden of cleaning the room.

Clear space is also more therapeutic and relaxing than a cluttered room. A bedroom should be comfortable and an enjoyable place to be, but not a dump for unwanted collections of clothes, shoes, and books. Well-placed and plentiful storage is extremely necessary in a bedroom (see Display and storage, pages 233–7).

Using color

Good colors for bedrooms are those from the neutral and pastel

Soft almond or pale mint green can be used successfully with wooden bedroom furniture, as green and brown have a natural earthy affinity. These colors together can be used to create a pleasant and tranquil room.

Potent, strong colors may be used to create a bedroom with impact. You can create an interesting scheme using one wall of strong color or pattern and then decorating the rest of the room in a soft, plain color. The wall that is often chosen to make a feature of is the one behind the bedhead. This is because the color creates an impact on entering the room and highlights the bed, which is the main feature and purpose of the space.

The other advantage of putting strong color or pattern behind the bedhead is that you don't see it when you are in the bed, unless you deliberately turn your head round. In this way the color and fun are there, but when you are lying on the bed or are in it,

Above: This basement bedroom is painted a bright, warm, vibrant color because there is little access to natural light.

Opposite page: This young girl's bedroom has soft decorative touches, such as the painted wardrobe, and is not overtly childish, making it a comfortable and enjoyable room for an adolescent too.

Above: This young girl's bedroom is warm and comforting, with soft pastel-colored walls with a delicate print, which is repeated in the curtain at the small window above.

Opposite: This skylight is not overlooked, so there is no need to add a curtain or screen unless you prefer total darkness in your bedroom. The use of a mirror also reflects the natural light and makes this compact top-floor room feel more spacious. The neutral colors give it a relaxed feel.

unwinding or going to sleep, your eyes focus on the soft, plain color that has been used on the other walls.

Using fabrics to create mood

Light and decorative fabrics such as toile de Jouy can be attractive in a bedroom. These prints are generally in red, blue, or gray, and on a white or off-white background. They depict cameo scenes and views—many are inspired by 18th-century pastoral paintings, but modern interpretations can also be found.

When using fabrics in a bedroom, try to keep the words "fresh and simple" in mind. If you are eager to have a multifloral material or dense pattern, restrict it to curtains and perhaps a bed cover, or maybe a single chair or cushion, but avoid teaming it with a floral or similarly busy wallpaper. If you cover every surface with a dense pattern, the room will appear overcrowded, and stifling.

Secondary uses

In an ideal world the bedroom would be a single, dedicated sleeping space, but in reality, and particularly in metropolitan living, the bedroom may need to double up and be used as an exercise

facility, dressing room, and clothes storage area, or even a place to study or work in. It would also be great if every child could have a large playroom and garden den, but modern homes rarely provide this luxury.

Instead, space often has to be found within their bedrooms. Whether in an adult or children's bedroom, making the secondary function fit in around the main one will require careful planning. For example, in one-room or studio apartments it may be worth considering a foldaway bed that pivots back against the wall. This sort of flip-up bed is generally housed in a purpose-built cupboard, so that when it is not in use its presence in the room is unnoticed. Other options are foldaway sofa beds and futons.

Another solution that works well in tall, high-ceilinged rooms, and provides a dedicated bedroom space, is the sleeping platform. This is a purpose-built mezzanine level, which needs only to be the width of the bed plus a few feet (about a meter) around it. This can be installed against an end wall, leaving the floor space underneath free for use as an office or living area. With sleeping platforms, it is important to have enough head room above to make them comfortable. To save more

Containing a work area

A specially devised cabinet or cupboard is one way of containing your work area. This type of cupboard is deep and opens in half—one side contains shelves for storing files and paperwork, and the other forms a desk with a computer. When it is not in use, one half folds over the other to conceal the contents.

A deep wall cupboard can also be kitted out in the same way, with a desk shelf or platform on a slide or pivot base so that it can be pulled out on a runner. The shelf may be folded back and closed up out of sight in the cupboard door when work time is over.

Above right: Timeless pieces, such as this brass bed, look good in a traditional setting. The cool blue used in the room has been warmed up by the brass fixtures.

space on the lower level, a sleeping platform may be cantilevered or supported on brackets, negating the need for pillars. This sort of structure should be devised by an engineer or architect.

In children's rooms space can be invented by the installation of a platform bed with a play area underneath it. Of course, this is only suitable for older children, who are able to climb a ladder. By raising the height of the bed to the level of the upper bunk of a

bunk bed, a desk or den area can be created underneath. The newly reclaimed floor area can house a desk or workstation, with a chair. To save more space, the desk can be built-in against a wall and a set of shelves constructed to one side, for storing books, crayons and other items (see Display and storage, pages 233–7).

Elsewhere in this underbed zone there could be a curtain so that the lower area can be screened off from the rest of the

room. A couple of floor cushions could be introduced, as these take up less space than rigid chairs and can be easily stacked one on top of another when not in use. Whether the space is used for play or study, your child will love having such a unique room.

Another option is to raise the floor level by building a row of deep steps up to a bed platform. This does not need to be so high off the ground as the other option, because the room underneath will be used for general storage rather than a built-in desk.

By raising the bed to about 3ft (90cm) off the floor, you will gain copious amounts of storage underneath. The access to the bed is by two or three long, but shallow, steps. These steps can, when not needed for access to the bed, be softened with cushions, and be used for sitting. The space under the steps, accessed by doors in the side, will provide valuable storage.

Above: This child's bedroom has been carefully planned to fulfill changing needs. The fabric around the bed can be pulled across while the room is used as a play area during the day. And as the child gets older, a quiet study area will be needed. The desk will provide that, but for now, it is a display area for the child's doll house.

Furnishings and
textiles

The golden rule for a relaxing and calming bedroom is to keep the furnishings and decoration simple. The cleaner and more accessible the space, the more enjoyable it will be to live in. Natural, soft, and absorbent fabrics are ideal.

Choosing the right bed

The major piece of furniture in a bedroom is, of course, the bed. On average, we spend a third of our lives in bed, so it is vital that you try out plenty and then buy the one that is right for you. There are those who strongly advocate a firm mattress for a good night's sleep, but that may not be the best type for you, especially if you already suffer from aches and pains.

What you really need is a bed that offers the right support for your spine, while allowing the hips and shoulders to lie comfortably in their natural curvature. Your spine should form a shallow S shape when you lie flat, and a straight, horizontal line when you lie on your side. Use a pillow, neither too thick nor too thin, that supports the nape of the neck correctly and aligns the head.

It is also advisable to raise the bed or mattress off the floor, to enable adequate air circulation

around the whole bed. Also, sleeping on the floor puts you closer to dust and fluff and can make it more difficult to get in and out of bed.

The standard bed available for purchase today comes in three main parts—the mattress, the base, and the set of headboard and footboard.

Mattresses

On the surface most mattresses look the same, but there are a number of different interior constructions on offer. Foam mattresses are made from different layers and densities of material that "give" when a person lies on the surface. This type of mattress is best suited to a slatted base.

Above: The walls of this Scandinavian-style bedroom have been covered, above chair rail height, with a fresh, blue-and-white gingham material, which creates a soft and cosy environment.

Opposite: This traditional-style bed is raised off the floor, which ensures all-round air circulation.

Above: This tone-on-tone scheme is lifted by textures of waffle and linen.

Right: These bedcover and cushions are quilted. Fabric can be quilted by sewing along the lines or motifs of a printed pattern.

Far right: White bedclothes are not boring. The details make it special.

The most popular type of mattress on the market today is the pocket-sprung. A good bed will have a high number of tight-packed springs, as many as 1,500 in a double, which offers great individual support. Pocket-sprung beds don't have completely flat surfaces—there is a slight undulation—so the bed molds itself to the body shape.

Futons, originally Japanese mattresses used for sleeping on the floor or low wooden platforms, are another bed option. The traditional futon is unsprung and offers a firm place of rest. It is a space-saving option because it can be rolled up after a night's sleep and stored in a box or cupboard.

Base options

The base of a bed is usually a divan or slatted. Some old-fashioned beds have a frame with springs, but these are rarely found at modern retailers.

The divan base is the most popular type. It is a box-shaped construction with a slightly padded top. It is generally upholstered in the same fabric as the mattress, and is fitted with casters for mobility. Some even include deep drawers, which are useful for storing spare bedding. A divan base generally comes without a headboard or footboard, but these can be bought separately and added as necessary.

Slat bases have flexible slats made from laminated wood and supported on a frame. These offer a certain amount of "give," and in some systems the tension can be adjusted for firmer/softer support. A slatted base is recommended for foam mattresses.

When buying a mattress and base, make sure that you try the two together before purchasing, to be sure that they are compatible.

Bed frames and boards

The most traditional bed dressing is the four-poster. This dates back to the time when curtains were hung around the bed so that they could be drawn to keep the cold at bay. Now, in the days of heating systems, the curtains have a purely decorative purpose. The traditional four-poster has turned wooden posts and a frame over the top. The back panel is sometimes hung with a thick or tapestry-style material between the two posts at the bedhead. Then a canopy is placed over the top and curtains are draped around the side.

This ornate and heavy dressing has, in recent years, been refined and simplified into a simple, plain, wooden frame over which a single length of cotton voile is

draped. In country-style bedrooms, gingham and printed fabrics may be used on the voile.

The simplest dressing option is the covered headboard that can be attached, with long screws and washers, directly into the divan base. When choosing a headboard, whether it is fabric-covered, wood, or metal, find a style that is best suited to your overall decorative scheme. If your room is to be simple and Zen-like, then a natural cherrywood, paneled, or rail-topped headboard, or a waxed pine surround would be in keeping with the overall mood. On the other hand, if you are opting for a scheme that is more decorative and colorful, then a padded headboard, covered in a bright fabric with contrasting piping of decorative quilting, is a good option.

There is also the contemporary padded cushion or long tabard arrangement with tab or tie tops, which are hung from a rod attached to the wall to make a buffer between your head and the wall (see Removable bed head tabard hangings, pages 216–19).

Tall people often prefer to have a bed without a footboard so that they are not restricted by it, but for many traditional styles of bed surrounds, such as those wrought from iron, wood, and

Adjustable beds

A fairly recent introduction to the mass market is the adjustable bed. Adjustable beds are usually operated electrically, and in the case of a double-width bed there are two single mattresses and bases so that individual arrangements can be made for each sleeper.

The adjustable bed allows you to raise the head of the bed, or the foot, or both ends at the same time. By raising the head it can be more comfortable for reading or drinking, and raising the feet slightly may help people who have digestive or circulatory problems.

and tendril, Art Nouveau decorations. Many can be custom-built to your specific design by a blacksmith or forge owner.

Bedclothes

Dressing the bed is also an extremely important decorative element. There is such a wide choice of bedclothes that it is often difficult to choose what you want. Changing your bedclothes can also be a simple, but very effective way of ringing the seasonal differences in a room, keeping deep colors for winter, and white or lighter colors for the summer. There are many reversible duvet covers and pillow sets on the market today that are designed specifically to help create this very type of mood change.

Looking after your mattress

Mattresses should be replaced every 10 years because they will have deteriorated as much as 75 percent. Many need to be turned over regularly to spread the wear and tear, and to give springs a change so that they can rebalance.

A mattress protector is also important. This can be a simple calico or cotton cover that is pulled on over the mattress's own ticking cover and can easily be removed for regular washing. There are also special dust-mite protective covers that people with eczema and asthma find particularly helpful.

copper, matching head- and footboards are part of the effect.

Although there are many antique bedsteads to be found in specialized stores, they tend to come in smaller sizes and may require custom-built mattresses and bases. There are, however, many modern copies of these traditional designs. These brand new versions are made in contemporary bed sizes, and will most likely be coated or treated to make them rust-resistant and, in the case of brass bed frames, tarnish-resistant.

Traditional materials are also used to create modern steel and iron bedsteads. These can be simple, following traditional wooden designs, or they can be more ornate and fanciful, with frond

Although colored and patterned bedclothes have been popular since the 1960s, classic, white, crisp cotton bedclothes have been a perennial favorite and suit every scheme and style, from simple to ornate. White bedclothes do not have to be boringly plain—the small details are what make them special. For example piping, broderie anglaise trim, a self-pattern, or a monogram will all lift the appearance of a white, linen-covered bed.

A range of pillows and cushions can make a bed attractive and contribute to the overall decoration of the room. There are many different shapes and sizes—some pillows are large and square, others long and rectangular. The old-fashioned bolster is a long, cylindrical pillow, which was traditionally placed across the top edge of the bed, providing an angled support for a second pillow. Try experimenting with various shapes of pillows to find an arrangement that suits your bed.

You can also use different-colored pillowcases or slips to emphasize a scheme in a room. For example, you could use a dark shade on large square pillows in the background, and a paler cover for the oblong pillow in the foreground.

Curtains and shades

Curtains and shades are a great way of pulling the overall color scheme in the bedroom together. When choosing the shade, look at the fabrics that have been used elsewhere in the room, such as the bedclothes or cushions, and try to find a tone that will complement them.

Make sure that the style of curtains you choose fits with your decorative scheme. Light sheer voile curtains work well in a contemporary bedroom, while heavy, rich-colored curtains, complete with swags and cascades, create an opulent ambience that would complement a traditional, period scheme.

Above: It is important that the fabrics that you choose for your curtains and bedclothes are complementary. Here, simple white cushions work well with neutral curtains that have a colorful trim.

Far left: Neutral furnishings, such as this lamp, work well next to simple, understated bedclothes.

Left: A cushion echoes the trim and fabric of the quilt.

Removable bedhead tabard hangings

Materials

39ft (12m) natural heavy-weight canvas
Cotton thread to match
Gray silk embroidery thread
Nine large mother-of-pearl buttons
5ft (1.5m) length of 2in (5cm) diameter bamboo

Tools

Sewing machine
(or needle and thread
for hand-sewing)
Calligraphy book
Photocopier or computer
Tracing paper
Soft pencil
Embroidery hoop
Needle
Tailor's chalk
Set square
Tape measure
Utility knife or stitch ripper

Calico tabard hangings sit comfortably in a modern interior, and also provide useful storage space for bedtime reading matter. Adding embroidered monograms gives a personal touch to a utilitarian bed. We used strong, heavyweight canvas, which was the ideal width to fit our bed. Basic sewing skills are needed to secure the storage slots, then chunky bamboo is slotted through channels at the bottom of the tabards to weigh it down into place. Mother-of-pearl buttons provide a decorative touch and secure the tabards over the bedpost.

Preparing the fabric

1 Cut three lengths of heavy-weight canvas to fit the drop between your bedpost and mattress. Allow half a drop extra on one piece for storage slots and about 1in (2cm) hem allowance on each end. Press and hem. Fold two of the lengths of fabric in half and position these over the bedpost. Choose some initials from a calligraphy book

Transfer the monogram onto the fabric using tracing paper and a soft pencil.

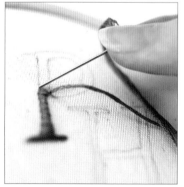

Use satin stitch and contrasting thread to form the letters of the monogram pattern.

Know your materials

Canvas is a strong, utilitarian material that is available in a number of different weights, which makes it suitable for many different uses. Heavyweight canvas is available in widths suitable for re-covering deckchairs with prefinished edges. It can be found in various striped colorways as well as the natural color used here. Its main advantage in this project is its strength, as it can easily support the weight of books and magazines. It is readily found in large department stores and at scenic (theatrical) suppliers.

and enlarge them on a photocopier, or size and print them on a computer. Trace the initials onto a piece of tracing paper, selecting those you need to form the required monogram pattern.

Sewing the monograms

2 Transfer the monograms of your choice onto the tabards using a soft pencil (see picture bottom left, page 216).

3 Secure an embroidery hoop in place over the monograms, and use satin stitch to form the letters (see picture bottom right, page 216). Choose a color that complements your bedroom scheme.

Making the pockets

4 Take the third piece of fabric and fold the front section of fabric forward to form a loop, and pin in place. With the tailor's chalk and a set square mark out two channels, using a folded magazine as a guide. Pin in place, then sew.

5 Use a couple of softcover books or magazines to measure the required depth for the top pockets. Pin the fabric in place, then sew using a medium-length straight stitch.

Hanging the tabards

6 Drape the fabric loosely over the headboard, making sure that all pieces are level, then mark four equidistant points

Use a magazine to measure the size of the looped pocket, and then pin in place.

Make sure that you leave enough room to store most books in the bottom pocket.

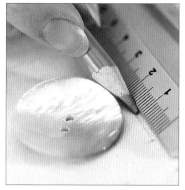

Measure down from the pole for the position of the buttonholes and mark with tailor's chalk.

across the top of the fabric, 1½ in (4cm) down from the rod. Measure the buttons and mark the positions of the buttonholes with tailor's chalk.

7 Machine-sew the button holes or, if you prefer to hand-sew them, cut horizontal slits that are slightly smaller than your chosen buttons. As a finishing touch, neaten the edges with a button-hole stitch.

8 Pin both ends of the stitching and then slit open the button hole with a sharp utility knife or stitch ripper.

9 Stitch the buttons on the insides of the tabards, secure, and slot the bamboo into place.

It is easiest to use a sewing machine to make the buttonholes for the hangings.

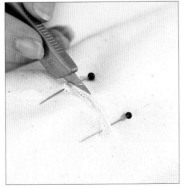

Pin both ends of the stitching and use a sharp utility knife carefully to slit open the buttonholes.

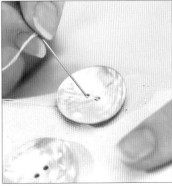

Stitch the buttons securely in place before hanging the storage tabard on the wall.

Alternative

Canvas is also an ideal material to make sturdy hanging storage from, as it can be folded up when not in use. The shelves are made from thick cardboard covered in canvas. These are stitched to each side panel, giving a concertina effect. It is essential to measure your hanging space before you begin, and to consider the dimensions of the items you wish to store so that you make your unit to the correct size.

Cut two equal-size side panels, press, and hem with a sewing machine. Decide on the number of shelves you require—don't forget the top and bottom pieces. Cut these all from sturdy cardboard using a utility knife and set square. Cut pieces of canvas to cover each, and machine-stitch in place. Mark the position of each shelf in tailor's chalk on the inside of each side panel. Machine-stitch in place, then add two flaps to the top of the unit with sturdy Velcro fastenings that fit over the wardrobe or hanging rail. Machine-stitch the top and bottom panels in place.

Cork headboard with decorative niches

This simple, minimal headboard is designed to look as if it is a built-in piece of furniture. The dimensions are dictated by the size of the sheets of plywood, which come in 4 x 8ft (1.25 x 2.5m) sheets, making it perfect for use behind a futon bed. The cork covering is an ideal surface for pinning up mementos, while the shallow niches hold bedtime essentials like alarm clocks. The open sides of the headboard are ideal for storing magazines. Due to its height and weight it requires careful handling, and should be firmly secured to the wall using mirror plates.

Materials

2in² (5cm²) square-section dressed wood cut to the following sizes: 4 lengths of 8ft (2.5m), 5 lengths of 3ft 10in (1.1m)
Wood glue
Wood screws
2 sheets of ¼in (6mm) thick plywood
Cork tile adhesive
Cork tiles
White wood wash
Quick-grip adhesive
Satin acrylic varnish

Tools

Pencil
Set square
Handsaw
Chisel
C-clamp
Electric drill
Jigsaw
Metal rule
Utility knife
Abrasive paper
Miter saw

Making the framework

1 Begin by marking up the half-lap joints on the wood in order to make the framework. To form the center, use one length of 8ft (2.5m) long wood. Use a pencil and set square to mark the positions of five equal-spaced horizontals (remember to take the thickness of the wood into consideration when doing this). Use a

Using a chisel, remove the wood so that you end up with a U-shape notch.

Apply a layer of glue into each notch and then slot the half-lap joints together.

Know your materials

Miter cutters and saws are useful tools that enable you to cut a perfect 45-degree angle, which is essential for neat frame-making joints. If you do not want to buy a miter saw they can be rented on a daily basis from all good rental stores. Alternatively, you could use a more primitive miter block, which consists of a U-shape trough made from wood or plastic, with precut 45-degree slots. Your wood can be placed in the trough, and then the slots can be used to guide a handsaw to cut through at the required angle.

handsaw to make two parallel cuts halfway through the thickness of the wood. Then use a sharp chisel to remove the waste wood, leaving a U-shape notch. Do the same to three of the 3ft 10in (1.1m) lengths, laying them across the center vertical and marking the corresponding notch.

2 With all the half-lap joints cut, spread a layer of wood glue in the notches before slotting them together (see picture bottom right, page 221). Grip each joint in turn in a C-clamp, drill a hole, and then screw in place, making sure that the heads of the screws are countersunk below the surface. Fix the surrounding pieces in place using simple butt joints.

3 Lay the framework onto each sheet of plywood in turn, and mark the positions of the wood on it using a pencil. Clamp the marked side of the plywood onto the front of the frame, and drill through the thickness of the plywood into the wood frame using a wood bit. Use countersunk screws to attach the plywood to the frame.

Marking the niches

4 Mark the positions of the cut-out square niches on the remaining piece of plywood using a pencil and set square. Make sure that each niche will sit just above a strip of wood, which will provide the shelf.

Drill through the plywood into the wood frame and hold it in place using screws.

Mark the positions of the cut-out square niches on the remaining piece of plywood.

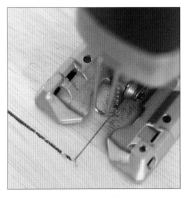

Using a jigsaw, carefully cut out the niche squares from the plywood sheet.

5 Cut out the niches from the plywood sheet using a jigsaw. Attach the sheet to the front of the frame, screwing it into the wood with countersink screws.

Applying cork tiles

6 Spread adhesive over the front piece of plywood and lay tiles. Cut where necessary with a metal ruler and utility knife.

7 Lightly sand the cork tiles, then paint with a couple of coats of white wood wash.

8 Finish the edges of the niches and the headboard by cutting an L-shape trim with a miter saw. Attach this with quick-grip adhesive, and hold in place with a C-clamp until set. Apply varnish.

Glue down the cork tiles over the whole surface of the front piece of plywood.

Lightly sand, and then paint over the cork tiles using two layers of white wood wash.

Hold the L shape trimming around the niches and headboard in place using a C-clamp.

Alternative

If you prefer a softer, tailored look, then why not create a padded headboard instead? Keep the dimensions tall and square to be sure of a contemporary look. Upholstering a headboard in soft suede or leather is the ultimate in luxury, and it will last for years, but for a budget version try mock suede or moleskin in a subtle color.

Decide on the size for your headboard. Get your lumber merchants to cut two pieces of ½in (1cm) thick MDF, then sand the edges lightly. Get two firm pieces of thick foam cut to the same size as the MDF boards, then stick them in place using strong white adhesive. Cut two pieces of fabric large enough to cover the foam-covered boards. Use a staple gun at the back to anchor the fabric cover in place, pulling it tightly over the foam as you do this. Staple opposite sides at the same time so that you achieve a good, even tension. Attach the boards to the wall just above the mattress, using mirror plates to fasten them.

Framed linen shades with panels

Materials

½in² (1.2cm²) section
dressed wood
Wood glue
Brad nails
White latex (acrylic)
Natural linen or similar-
weight material
Linen or linen-look ribbon
in two different widths
and colors
Pins
Fabric bonding
Fabric glue

Tools

Tape measure
Miter saw
Tack hammer
C-clamp
Paintbrush
Scissors
Iron
Staple gun
Hinges or sliding door kit

These panel shades are a great tailored alternative to fussy, frilly window treatments. Natural linen is sheer enough to let plenty of light in, while still maintaining privacy. We have added a woven-linen, ribbon-cross motif that is attached by a no-sew bonding material. Fastened on a light wooden framework, the shades can be made to fill any size of window. To mount them we used a sliding mechanism, but for a window level with the wall, attach them with hinges to the frame and a hook and eye fastening.

Making the frame

1 Work out the size of frames you will need to make by measuring your window accurately. Next, cut the wood to make the frames using a miter saw. Apply wood glue to the mitered pieces, then fasten them in place using brad nails and a tack hammer. Clamp them using a C-clamp until the glue is firmly set. Repeat the process in all four corners of each frame, leaving them overnight to set.

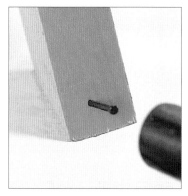

Glue the miters together using wood glue, and then secure them with brad nails.

When the frames have been constructed, paint over them with white latex (acrylic).

Know your materials

Fabric bonding consists of a thin material and backing paper in sheet or tape form that has been impregnated with fabric glue. It is used in sewing and dressmaking as a quick way to hem a garment or apply an appliqué patch without actually sewing. It comes in a variety of different widths and strengths suitable for bonding different weights of material. The glue is activated by pressing the fabric with a warm iron, then the backing paper is peeled away. The bond is made by sandwiching the two layers of fabric together and pressing them, again with a warm iron.

2 Paint over the surface of the frames with a coat of white latex (acrylic) paint (see picture bottom right, page 226).

Preparing the panels

3 Cut panels of linen material that will be large enough to stretch around the frames. Next, cut the lengths of your widest ribbon and arrange them so that you form a cross on each panel. Add narrower ribbon over the top

to form a border. Use pins to hold all the ribbon in place while you turn it over.

4 Press lengths of fabric bonding onto the back of the ribbon, following the manufacturer's instructions.

5 Spread the linen panels on a large, flat surface, such as a dining-room table, that has been protected with a heatproof cloth, and press the ribbon trim in place. The fabric bonding will make it stick to the linen.

6 Stretch the linen panels tight over each frame, folding the raw edges under. Staple these in place, making sure the fabric is pulled tight in each direction.

Make a cross pattern with the two sizes of ribbon, and pin the two layers together.

Turn all the ribbon over and press fabric bonding onto the backs of each piece.

Put the ribbon back in place on the linen and press it into its final position.

7 Use a non-staining fabric glue to fix the ribbon trim around the edges of both frames, so that it hides the staples and produces a neat finish. (We also added a border of ribbon to frame the panels. This is optional but adds to the effect.)

Attaching the panels

8 Attach your linen panels to the window frames in the most suitable way. If you want the panels to swing open, screw hinges to the sides of the panels and attach the hinges to the window frame. For panels that slide to the side use a sliding door kit, which consists of a channel fixed to the wall or ceiling. Then attach wheels or runners to each panel.

Staple the linen onto the frame using a staple gun. Make sure that the material is pulled tight.

Hide any staples by gluing on ribbon trim around the edges of the panels.

Attach the panels to your window using an appropriate method. One way is to use hinges.

Alternative

If you prefer a simpler window treatment, make a pull-up shade. These shades are less structured than Roman shades; they are gently gathered. They look particularly effective made of a soft, natural fabric and hung unlined so that the light can filter through them.

Measure and cut a piece of fabric approximately 4in (10cm) larger all round than the dimensions of your window. Turn over the edges, press, and hem with a sewing machine. Machine-stitch a channel at the top of the fabric and feed in a wooden strip the same width as the shade. Hand-stitch to enclose it at each end. Stitch three vertical rows of small brass rings at regular intervals of about 1ft (30cm) along the back of the shade. Attach three brass screw eyes along the back of the wood. Feed a length of cord through the screw eyes, then along the rings. When pulled, this will raise and lower the shade. Attach the wood with L brackets to a second strip just above the window.

Lighting your
bedroom

Lighting in a bedroom should be on two levels—a general central light or wall lights that illuminate the whole room, and small bedside lights that can be used for reading. Remember to position the main light switch beside the bed so you can turn off all the lights without having to get out of bed.

Planning your lighting

The lighting that you use in a bedroom can play a fundamental part in creating a relaxing atmosphere. For general points about lighting design, see Effective lighting on page 187.

Bedroom lighting needs to work on two levels. First, you need to have an efficient ambient lighting system. This needs to be powerful enough for you to see clearly when selecting clothes or applying makeup. Second, the bedroom is the room where you wind down and read before you go to sleep. As such, your use of task and decorative lighting is key.

Ambient lighting

In most bedrooms ambient lighting is provided by a pendant or by a series of recessed lights in the wall or ceiling. The decoration of

Right: Floor-level lighting can provide a stylish effect in a minimalist, contemporary bedroom.

Left: An adjustable lamp attached to a bed-head gives light to read by.

Below right: A decorative Devoré velvet shade softens the light.

Below left: This light is attached to the wall next to the bed, saving space on a bedside cabinet.

these central lights can be as ornate or as simple as you wish. Chandeliers and pretty, decorative shades work well within a traditional scheme, while recessed ceiling lights complement the contemporary bedroom.

When planning the wiring of these lights, make sure you have switches by the door and the bed, so that you can illuminate the room as you enter, but also turn off all the lights in the room without having to get out of bed.

To make a bedroom a really relaxing place to be in, you may also want to add a dimmer switch so that the main light can be reduced to just a subtle glow. This type of arrangement can also be beneficial in a baby or small child's room, so that just enough

light remains to provide comfort, and ease of access for an adult, without disturbing a child's sleep.

Task lighting

The bedside light can be in the form of a traditional ceramic or wooden base and shade, a wall-

mounted adjustable lamp, or a concealed light over the bed-head. You can also have a light with a baffle that focuses the light on one side of the bed so that a partner sleeping on the other side will not be disturbed by the beam.

A dressing table needs its own light source positioned so that the light is not seen directly in the mirror, as this will dazzle and make it difficult for the viewer to see, yet the light should be targeted so that it illuminates the person who is using it.

Display and
storage

The more efficiently your wardrobe is arranged, the easier it will be for you to see what is there and select your clothes. Bundles of sweaters stuffed at the back of a shelf, and odd shoes hidden under the bed slow down the process of dressing, and make it difficult, rather than pleasurable.

Storage furniture

Effective storage in your bedroom is essential to keep it tidy and inviting. When planning your bedroom, consider what storage option would be most suitable to meet your requirements.

Wardrobes and cupboards

Division of wardrobe space is important—keep one section for long coats and dresses, but subdivide the rest of your hanging space into two levels to double the capacity. Shirts and skirts can go in one half, and jackets and half-folded pants in the other.

Wardrobes come in a variety of styles and shapes. The most common these days is the built-in wardrobe or prefabricated built-in wardrobe, which stretches across one wall or is built into niches on either side of a chimney breast. The freestanding wardrobes now available are usually either the traditional, heavy, wooden closet style, or the MDF variety.

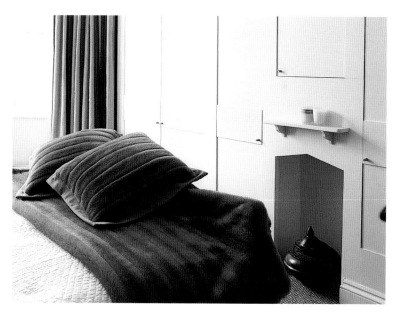

If space in the bedroom is limited, then you could use a metal rod fastened to the wall or on its own supports, with a fabric curtain to cover the clothes and prevent dust from gathering on them. Sliding doors also work well on wardrobes in a small room, where there may not be enough room to open hinged doors fully.

Above: This wall of wardrobes was built around a fireplace. The shelves above the fireplace are less deep, but are still perfect for smaller items, such as T-shirts or knitwear.

Left: A walk-in wardrobe combines hanging and storage space with a dressing room.

Opposite page: This wall-mounted bedside table takes up a minimal amount of space.

space, then use a bright, fun fabric to reflect the child's interests.

Chests of drawers

The other main area of storage in a bedroom is usually a chest of drawers. Drawers can benefit from being subdivided so that things are kept in separate niches instead of in a jumble. Small items such as socks and pantyhose can easily be rolled up into a ball and slotted into individual sections of a drawer divider.

When planning your shelf storage, think carefully. Some people choose a few big, deep shelves, but they would be better with more narrow shelves, as you tend to end up with two piles of clothes with a deep shelf. This means that the ones at the back are difficult to get at without removing everything in front. Narrow shelves allow the clothes to be positioned in accessible stacks.

Bedside tables

A bedside table or tables are also practical. These can be

Above: Built-in wardrobes can be tailored to fit in and around even the most awkward spaces. The interiors can also be arranged to suit your clothes and accessories.

On the other hand, if space is not a problem, divide off a section of your bedroom and create a walk-in wardrobe. You can install directional, recessed spotlights into the ceiling so that the light is good and everything is visible.

In a child's bedroom the divides between hangers and shelves can be smaller because children's clothes need less space. A recess could be fitted with a deep drawer at the base for shoes and boots, a couple of narrow shelves for small sweaters, T-shirts, and shirts, and then a hanging space incorporated above for jackets and shirts. If you use curtains instead of doors to cover this freestanding units, or in some cases are an integral part of a headboard. As the bedroom is a place for relaxing, books, a radio, and CD player may be placed on these tables, along with a telephone and bedside light. Then there are all the things that may be needed—a box of tissues, an alarm clock, a glass of water.

This essential night-time equipment can build up and up until it eventually overflows onto the floor or under the bed. Therefore you should try to make sure that your bedside table is commodious enough to house all the things that you need. Look for something with shelves or a cupboard underneath so that there is plenty of storage for different-size objects.

To ease the pressure on the limited space of a bedside table, you could use a wall light instead of a table lamp—something with an adjustable head or arm so that the light can be positioned for reading. If you have a tabard cover for your bed-head (see pages 216–19), you could also sew pockets at the edge to hold small, light, useful objects, such as tissues and a pocket alarm clock.

Additional storage items

If your room is spacious, you may like to add a blanket box or chaise to the end of the bed. The blanket box provides more storage, and is also a useful place to lay clothes and sit on.

An easy or occasional chair, whether it is a small armchair or a more genteel style, such as a slipper chair, can also be an asset in a bedroom. As well as being attractive to look at, it is useful when you want to sit down.

Storage solutions

Another consideration in bedroom storage is the diversity of size of things that are kept there. Items range from earrings to overcoats, and from flimsy lingerie to boots and shoes. Each requires special containers to suit its size and shape.

Seasonal storage

Most storage in the bedroom revolves around seasonal changes, between the spring/summer and fall/winter divide of clothes and bedclothes. Most space will be needed in summer, when bulky duvets, overcoats, down jackets, and thick sweaters are not in use.

The simplest way, once they have been dry-cleaned or laundered, is to zip them up into large plastic storage bags and put them at the top of your wardrobe or in drawers in the base of your bed. You can also buy storage boxes on wheels that are specifically designed to slip easily under the bed.

Shoes and boots

Boots and shoes take up space, and are awkward to store unless placed in a specially designed container. You can buy or make hanging shoe pockets. These have a banner-shaped backing, with rows of deep pockets sewn on the front. Each pocket is long and deep enough to hold a pair of shoes.

Another alternative is a shoe rack or drawer that can be stored in the lower part of the wardrobe. Shoe racks come in two main styles—a metal version has upright loops onto which the shoes are slotted so that the toe of the shoe points up and the heel down. The second style is made of wood and is a simple, narrow, two-shelf construction onto which the shoes are lined in pairs. Another possibility is to store your shoes in bags or shoe boxes—label these on the outside for easy identification.

Boots are usually best stored with boot trees. Another option is to hang them from coat hangers with clips at the end. The weight of the base of the boot helps to pull the boot straight.

Scented liners

Both wardrobes and drawers can benefit from the introduction of scented liners. In wardrobes, especially where men's clothes are stored, the woody, slightly musky aroma of cedar blocks can be most attractive. These can also be slotted among shoes and boxes at the base of the wardrobe.

Liners are decorative paper sheets, impregnated with scent, that are placed at the base of a drawer to gradually release their scent and keep clothes resting on top of them lightly perfumed. Some people also put bars of good-quality soap in drawers to perfume the contents.

Jewelry and neckties

Jewelry is generally small and delicate, so it needs to be stored extremely carefully to avoid any damage. Long chains or necklaces may be best arranged in curls or circles in a deep box, or hanging from a coat hanger. Earrings should be stored in pairs. You can buy boxes that are subdivided into small compartments, and these are ideal. Otherwise, visit a jewelry wholesaler or jewelry store, where you can buy specific earring boxes.

Neckties and belts can be hung on small brackets or racks

fastened to the inside of a wardrobe door, again keeping them in groups and subdividing them into colors so that they are easy to select and remove when you are dressing.

Cosmetics and toiletries

As well as clothes storage, there will be a certain amount of space needed for cosmetics, hairbrushes, hairdrier, and other toiletries. A collection of little bottles and pots may be best stored on a tray or in a small box that is kept in a cupboard or dressing table. The tray or box will enable them to be lifted out together easily.

A few decorative bottles and attractive pieces can be left on show, but remember that perfume is adversely affected by exposure to direct sunlight. Therefore, even though the bottle may look pretty on your dressing table, its contents will go off if it is left out in the bright sunlight for too long.

If you have an en-suite bathroom, a certain amount of cosmetics and toiletries can be stored and used in there. However, for putting on your makeup you may prefer to use the bedroom where a mirror can be located adjacent to a window, in order to benefit from the daylight.

Decorative storage

Large boxes that may be used for storing blankets and thick sweaters can be made to look more attractive and more an integral part of the room's scheme if you cover them so that they coordinate. If you are wallpapering the room, you could simply use excess paper to cover the boxes. Otherwise, simple, inexpensive lining paper is a plain alternative.

For a more ornate finish you could staple or glue on remnants of material, such as pieces of left-over curtain material or upholstery. For a really simple finish, you could paint the boxes the same color as the walls, or cover them with a few layers of gloss enamel paint to make them look like a lacquer chest or container.

Top: This cupboard has narrow shelves for neat rows of shoes.

Above: Perfume bottles are attractive items to display.

Opposite page: These are specifically designed shoe drawers in a bedroom cupboard.

Bedroom accessories

The bedroom is a place where many people indulge their decorating dreams, but it is also a personal space where you relax and unwind, so it should be comfortable and well-organized. Apart from the larger items, such as the bed, and general storage, it is the small touches that will add to the intimacy and coziness. If there is space, a chaise longue, day bed, or chair and footstool can be added so that you can sit or recline comfortably without actually having to get into bed. A blanket box or ottoman, with storage in the base, may also be placed at the foot of the bed and be used for laying down clothes, or sitting on when doing up boots or shoes. Window dressings also play an important role—they should be dense enough to provide privacy and darkness to help you sleep, but decorative and attractive so that when they are pulled back during daylight they are a feature. Whether plain or ornate, the fastenings and valance should be treated as part of the overall design, and complement the fabric and style of the dressing beneath.

Clockwise from top left:

On this straight cornice, a motif has been picked out from the dominant fabric in the room and painted onto the corner to complement the curtains.

An oriental, embroidered door hanging has been used to soften and decorate the mantel in this bedroom.

A simple decorative scheme with neutral colors and natural fabrics can be relaxing and calming.

This appliquéd cushion brings together several shades of pink used in the room.

A bedside lamp is an ideal task light for reading in bed. Additional ambient lighting, such as this candle, can be used to create a relaxing atmosphere.

A simple, opaque, white canvas blind obscures the view in this minimalist bedroom.

Here, scented cedar blocks in a small sachet are hung around the neck of a coat hanger. Their subtle scent will permeate the whole wardrobe.

Cosmetic items, such as this perfume bottle and matching glass pot, can also double as bedroom ornaments.

Use scented paper to line any shelves that store clothing. This will keep it fresh, and will also add a pleasing but subtle aroma.

When in doubt, choose plain simple, white bedclothes, as you can never go wrong with them.

This tight metal wire provides an easy, no-sew method for hanging lightweight curtains.

Don't forget the smaller details—by choosing decorative knobs for your cupboards and drawers, you can lift and unify the whole scheme.

A paper bag filled with dried herbs, such as lavender, can scent your clothes. Alternatively, you could fill it with mothballs.

Well-designed storage is vital in a bedroom. This cupboard has neat compartments for hanging items, as well as storing folded clothes and accessories.

Dining rooms

Planning your
dining room

These days few homes have a separate dining room—the space tends to be part of another, for example, the kitchen or living room. This duality of spaces means that the decoration of one will be influenced by the other, so schemes for these areas must be planned carefully to suit both.

Above: Tall, folding doors create an elegant divide between the modern kitchen and a classic dining room.

Left: An arch creates a passageway between dining room and kitchen.

Opposite: The colors of the spacious dining room and the adjacent kitchen complement each other, so that there is no visual barrier between them.

Planning
your space

The role of the dining room is continually being usurped by the kitchen, where a table caters for the needs of both scattered and regular family mealtimes.

The advantage of a detached dining room is that it can be prepared in advance, and after the meal the door can be closed, and the debris forgotten until later. It is also removed from the clatter and preparation in the kitchen, and provides a change of venue and ambience from the living room.

The separate dining room dates back to the 18th century, when eating and drinking were taken seriously, so the dining room was considered of great importance and status. Today, entertaining is still an enjoyable way of spending time with friends, but there is little formality, and the explosion of interest in the more casual styles of foreign cooking and barbecues makes a separate or grand dining room a little out of place.

Delineating the dining area

The modern dining room is most likely to be part of an open-plan main living area, or an adjunct of the kitchen. In both cases, the location and type of lighting will play an important part in altering the mood, so that there is a change of ambience between a family breakfast, watching TV, or an evening meal with friends. In addition, the table setting style and the overall décor of the room will also be influential.

A change of flooring may also help to delineate the food preparation part of the room from the entertaining section. In the kitchen, the floor should be durable and practical, so stone,

Protecting your dining table

You can buy lightly padded table protection by the yard or meter in most good furnishings stores. This has an insulation layer that prevents heat from damaging the varnish or finish, and prevents dents or marks being made by heavy pots or knives. Over this you could put a plasticized or vinyl-coated cloth for day-to-day use.

linoleum, or terra-cotta tiles are ideal, whereas in the dining area the floor could be warmer, welcoming and stylish, so wood or a high-quality, polished limestone, perhaps with a rug or kelim, would be appropriate.

In many kitchens, a section of work area—an island or length of units and worktop—creates an actual, physical break between the two areas. This works well and creates the impression of having a distance between the dining and food preparation zones of the room.

The dining table

The configuration and layout of the dining space should allow for a certain amount of flexibility, so that a family of four will be comfortable having lunch there, but a dinner party for eight will feel equally at home. An extending table will help to accommodate this, whether there are separate leaves to be inserted, or adjustable flaps that fold down.

There are some ingenious round table designs that enlarge by the addition of segments, like putting pieces into an orange.

A simpler method is to have a larger disc, made in an inexpensive material such as MDF or chipboard, that clips on top of the smaller table and can be disguised by a round tablecloth. The larger disc can be hinged in the center so that it may be folded in two and stored in a cupboard, under a bed, or in a garage, until it is required.

Seating arrangements

Dining-room seating is an important consideration. It is one thing perching on the edge of a wooden stool when you are gulping down breakfast, but quite another to be expected to sit through a long dinner party on a hard stool with no back support.

Dining chairs should have a back to provide some bracing for the diner, and if made of wood or metal, a cushion is important. You can also dress chairs up to give them a more formal appearance by adding a tabard or slip cover (see box, page 248, and pages 255–9).

Another option is to build a well-upholstered window seat or

Above: A low wall separates the dining and kitchen area from the seating space beyond.

bench-style arrangement along a wall. This is ideal for children and enables you to seat more people than you could in separate seats. The table can be placed in front of the window seat, with extra chairs lined up around the edges.

Color and style

When considering what colors or style options to use in a dining room, look at the other functions that take place in the space, and also how natural light and artificial light will affect the color and décor at different times of day.

Using color

If you have a separate dining room, you may like to look at richer, darker, more dramatic tones. Dining rooms are most often used at night, so you can afford to indulge in a real splurge of jewel shades.

Dark red, rich emerald green, and even chocolate brown can look wonderful under muted electric light and candles. Even minimalist and contemporary schemes can include a panel or single wall of these rich colors, to spice up a simple setting.

For a living/dining area choose a scheme that is suitable to both day- and night-time living. Again, table dressings and lighting can help transform a dining area, but

the wall color and floor covering should be compatible to both functions. If in doubt, choose a neutral or plain scheme, and then add details such as pictures, table lamps, and patterned cushions.

For a kitchen/dining arrangement the emphasis should be on practicality—fabrics and dressings should be easy to remove and washable. In general, stick to light colors, which enhance a feeling of cleanliness and productivity.

At-a-glance color guide

Eating room red is a traditional color for dining room walls—it is a rich, period color and looks opulent in candle or electric light. Chocolate brown, which has an element of red in its composition, is also a luxurious color against which crisp, white linen and sparkling glassware look good. However, these rich, lavish colors lose something of their intensity in daylight, so are best used in evening-only rooms.

Choose a darker tone of the same color for the dining area because this will create a division, but retain a link between these parts of the room. Or paint the kitchen in a single, pale color and then incorporate this color into the dining area in conjunction with a darker tone of the same color, or a paint effect combining the two shades.

There are certain colors that have an affinity with food, and others that don't work so well. Deep purple is a color that is seldom found in kitchens or dining rooms, and the sludgy shades of olive green, mouse brown, and mid-gray are also rarely seen. They may appear as part of a pattern or in a worktop material such as slate or granite,

Above: This open space is divided into separate rooms, but the wide-open doorways give the impression of being a single space.

Left: The way you dress the dining table is as important as the decoration of the room. It should echo the style of the meal being served, whether it is formal or informal.

Opposite page: This dining area is part of a family kitchen, yet the high-back, upholstered dining chairs and chandelier give it a distinct identity.

High-back, padded dining chairs are comfortable, but can be covered to make them a feature. The most simple dressing is a long panel of fabric, the width of the back and base of the chair. This drapes over the front and down the back of the chair, and is held in place with simple ties at the top and base of the seat back. More tailored covers with skirts that cover the legs are also popular. These can be held in place by bright buttons or contrasting ties of cord or tape.

Loose covers such as these can also be used for high-backed wooden chairs to make them more decorative.

but in quantity and on their own they can give an impression of grubbiness.

Even though you may vary the floor covering from one area to another, and even dress up plain walls in the dining section, it is advisable to keep the ceiling in a uniform, plain color, providing continuity and reflected light.

Style and furnishings

As well as linking shared spaces with color, it is advisable to keep to a similar style of furnishings. If the kitchen is futuristic in steel and glass, then the dining area should have complementary elements to reflect that look. If the sitting area of the room is in a neoclassical style, then the dining area should follow suit with columns, pilasters, and furniture in a similar vein. But, if you have a separate dining area in a room by itself, then you can choose whatever style you think is most suitable.

Above left: This dining area is at the front of this house, overlooking the street. However, clever use of half shutters and crisp, white linen curtains means that the view is obscured but natural light can still come into the room.

Right: This dining room, with rich, black walls and bead-fringed curtains, is designed for evening entertainment. This scheme glows in artificial light, and the mood created is opulent and decadent.

Tiled tabletop with limed driftwood edging

Materials

1/3in (9mm) exterior-grade
plywood for the base
Planks of wood slightly thicker
than your tiles
Wooden trim deep enough to
cover the plank wood and edge
Liming wax
White glue
Panel adhesive
Screws
Tile adhesive
Small "stone" ceramic tiles
Sandstone grout
Brad nails

Tools

Tape measure and pencil
Set square
Handsaw
Miter saw
Blowtorch
Fine steel wool
Soft cloth
C-clamp
Electric drill
Notched spreader
Level
Flexible grout spreader

This tabletop can be teamed with the legs of your choice and used as a dining, coffee or even outdoor table. Its tiled surface makes it practical to care for, as well as heat-resistant. We used ceramic tiles, which mimic more expensive sandstone or marble. Their irregular edges give them a handmade appearance, and blend well with the driftwood finish of the wooden edging. To give new planks a weathered finish, we first raised the grain of the wood using a blowtorch, then toned down the effect with white liming wax. The wax protects the surface, too.

Calculating the framework

1 Sketch out the dimensions of your table, making sure that you will not need to cut any tiles. This will give you the measurements for the plywood base and the lengths of plank, which will form the frame. Use a set square or the edge of a hand-saw to mark the 45-degree corner angles, and use the miter saw to

Measure the size of the table, marking the 45-degree corner angles before cutting.

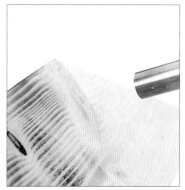

With a blowtorch, scorch the surface of the plank frame until the patterns in the grain show.

Know your tools

When using a blowtorch, light it with care, following the manufacturer's instructions. Always wear heavy-duty gloves and a protective eye mask. To get the hang of the scorching method, practice on scrap wood so you can see how long it takes to raise the grain without burning the wood.

Always use a notched spreader for the adhesive. This provides a grooved bed of adhesive, which grips the tiles better than a flat surface can.

Flexible spreaders are used once the tiles have stuck firmly to the adhesive to force the grout into spaces between the tiles and remove excess.

cut out your wood to form the four pieces for the frame.

Preparing the frame

2 Gradually scorch the surface of the plank frame using a blowtorch on a low setting. The patterns in the grain will emerge gradually as the surface scorches (see picture bottom right, page 250). Make sure that you don't forget to do the sides of the frame, too.

3 Apply liming wax to the surface of the wood using fine steel wool, working it well into the grain. Allow this to dry, then polish the surface with a soft cloth to remove any excess liming wax, and to make sure that you create a neat finish.

4 Seal the surface of the plywood with a coat of diluted white glue, and allow this to dry for approximately half an hour. Anchor the frame in place on the plywood base using panel adhesive. Clamp the frame in place with a C-clamp until it sets, and then drill a hole through the back of each corner and put a screw in place to make sure that you have created a very firm fastening.

Preparing the surface

5 Apply a thick layer of tile adhesive to the plywood, using a notched spreader. Cover the surface up to a height that will make sure that the tiles will all sit level with the surface of the frame.

Apply liming wax to the surface of the wood using steel wool. Work it into the grain.

Glue the frame and plywood base together, clamp them, and drive in screws in the corners.

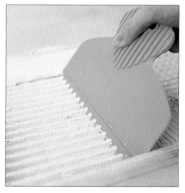

Apply an even layer of tile adhesive to the surface of the plywood, which will be tiled.

Laying the tiles

6 Embed the tiles firmly into the adhesive, checking regularly with a level to be sure that you achieve a level surface. Then make sure that you allow the tiles to set overnight.

7 Use a flexible spreader to work the grout well into the tiled surface, making sure that there are no gaps. Allow this to set, then polish off the excess with a soft cloth.

8 Scorch and lime-wax the flat edge trim before mitering it to cover the edge of the table. Stick in place using a thick layer of panel adhesive. Position small brad nails at regular intervals for an extra-firm fastening.

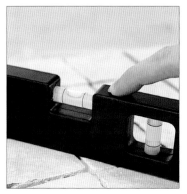

Lay the tiles in place, and use a level to check you are achieving an even surface.

Grout over the surface of the tiles, making sure that you fill in all the gaps.

Glue the scorched and limed trim to the sides of the tabletop to finish it off.

Alternative

To make a tiled table for outdoor use, buying a ready-made metal frame is the best option. Many small metalworking companies will be happy to make a table base to your dimensions. To apply an intricate design to it you should use the indirect mosaic method.

Get your supplier to cut you a piece of exterior-grade plywood to fit snugly within the table frame. Seal both sides with white glue diluted one part glue to two parts water. Use colored pencils and a piece of graph paper to plan your design, working out the exact number of tesserae needed. Cut a piece of strong brown paper to the size of your tabletop, and scale up and transfer your design onto it. Glue individual tesserae, grooved side up, onto the paper. Spread tile adhesive onto the plywood surface. Carefully lift the paper and apply to the tabletop, paper side up. Allow to dry before wetting the paper in order to peel it away from the surface. Finally, grout around the tiles.

Suedette dining chair cover

Any straight-backed dining chair can be instantly transformed with a simple slip cover. For a really luxurious look we have used a chocolate brown suedette, which is an imitation suede. Suedette is far more economical than the real thing, is easy to cut and sew, and will not fray. The trick to getting a really good fit is to make a calico or paper toile, or pattern, first. The leather thong lacing allows the material to be adjusted around the chair legs, and also minimizes the amount of sewing involved. Decorative punching along the skirt and delightful bead trims provide a final flourish.

Materials

Calico or newspaper to make toile
Pins
Suedette (around 5ft/1.5m)
Cardboard
Eyelet kit (consists of eyelet punch and riveter)
13ft (4m) leather thong
Beads to trim

Tools

Scissors
Tape measure
Pinking shears
Sewing machine (or needle and thread for hand-sewing)
Pencil
Hole puncher
Tailor's chalk pencil

Making a template

1 Begin by making the toile or pattern for the cover. Drape the calico or newspaper over the chair and use scissors, a tape measure, and pins to cut and form the shape of the cover. For a snug, tailored fit, one long piece should be folded over to cover the front and back of the chair back. The patterns for the seat and skirt can then be formed by using additional pieces of calico or newspaper.

2 Remove the paper or calico pattern from the chair and pin the pattern onto the suedette. Cut the pattern out of the material using pinking shears. Leave just over 1in (2cm) allowance all the way round, in case you have to make any necessary final adjustments.

Lay the template over the suedette and cut out the material using pinking shears.

3 Turn the fabric inside out and pin it onto the chair, marking

Know your materials

Making a paper pattern or calico toile is useful because it allows you to make slight adjustments as necessary on a cheap material, before committing yourself to cutting the final, more expensive material. If you have never cut a pattern before, practice by cutting and pinning a cheap calico toile over a simple shape, such as a footstool or cushion. This will help you get a feel for the technique. You should soon be able to cut an accurate pattern with the right seam allowances, which will mean you are confident enough to move on to work on the proper fabric.

the position of the seams along the sides of the seat and back using pins.

Sewing the cover

4 Working either by hand or using a sewing machine, sew the pieces of the cover together using a short straight stitch. Then press the fabric while it is still inside out, using a cool iron. Turn the suedette cover back the right side out and place it over the back of the chair to check the fit again. Make sure that the flaps meet neatly. Use scissors to trim any excess fabric as necessary.

Creating a pattern

5 Make a pattern of carefully measured holes with a pencil

on a piece of thin cardboard, and then use a hole puncher set on different settings to punch out the design (see the picture bottom left, page 258). Use the cardboard as a template, placing it on the suedette. Mark the design on each flap using a tailor's chalk pencil.

Once the fabric is pinned on the chair, mark the position of the seams using pins again.

Sew the pieces of suedette together using a short straight stitch, by hand or machine.

Once you have a template, mark your design onto the fabric with a tailor's chalk pencil.

6 Turn the suedette over and use the hole puncher set on several different-size settings to punch out the design on the suedette skirt.

Lacing the skirt

7 Using the tailor's pencil, mark six eyelet positions on each side of the skirt at just under 1in (2cm) intervals. Punch these out with the hole puncher. Thread lengths of leather thong through the holes to lace the skirt together.

8 Cut the ends of the thongs to length so that the thongs will hang below the cover but not reach the floor. Thread a silver bead onto each one, tying knots to secure the beads in place.

Punch out the design on the skirt using the various sizes on your hole puncher.

Punch holes along the sides of the skirt, and then lace them together with leather thongs.

Place a silver bead at the end of each leather thong, and secure it by tying a knot.

Alternative

If you prefer a more traditional look, then why not adapt the pattern to add stylish, covered buttons that fasten along the side of the chair? Covered buttons come in two parts: you simply cover the front piece in your choice of fabric before snapping the back in place.

Measure your chair and cut the fabric following the steps given in the main project, but add a slightly larger seam allowance. Then cut two additional pieces of fabric that will form side flaps to cover the back of the chair. Pin together inside out. Machine-stitch the pieces together, hem the back piece neatly, and then turn the cover right side out. Position the cover in place over the chair, and carefully work out the positions of the buttons, making sure that when done up they will provide a snug fit. Hand-stitch them along the side of the cover. Stitch small loops of elastic in the corresponding positions along the back flap. Slip the buttons through the loops to secure the cover in place.

Cotton curtains
with raffia motif

Materials

Cotton muslin or voile fabric
(you could use ready-made
muslin curtains)
Ribbon
Pins
Coarse green jute string
Raffia
Pearl buttons
Green ribbon

Tools

Tape measure
Scissors
Sewing machine (or needle and
thread if hand-sewing)
Tailor's pencil
Metal rule
Darning needle

These simple curtains are the ideal way to dress a dining-room window that overlooks a garden, linking inside and out. You can either make your own panels from scratch, following the steps below, or start with ready-made curtain panels,and then just simply customize them. We used coarse string and raffia for the embroidered flowers, which have a naïve quality and add a pleasing, textural dimension to the panels. Finishing them off with ribbon tabs is one of the simplest ways to suspend them from a rod.

Creating the curtains

1 Measure the drop from your curtain rod to the floor, and add about 1in (2cm) for a hem allowance. Cut the cotton to form panels.

2 Cut lengths of ribbon to fit the top of the panels, then cut another eight 4in (10cm) lengths of ribbon per panel for the loops to go over the rod. Pin these pieces at intervals under the long length of ribbon.

3 Sew the ribbons top and bottom in order to be sure that they are attached in place securely. Next, create a hem along the bottom of each of the panels by using a straight stitch (can be done by machine).

Positioning the flowers

4 Use a tailor's pencil and metal rule lightly to mark out the position of the flower stems on each curtain panel.

Sewing the stems

5 Next, thread a darning needle with a length of coarse green string and sew along each of the stems, using a large running stitch.

Making the flowers

6 Form the flowers using a length of raffia, which should be threaded onto a darning needle. Sew large loops of raffia to form the petals of the flowers. Finish each of them off by knotting the raffia neatly on the

Hem the bottom of each panel by using a straight stitch, working by hand or on a machine.

Mark out the position of each of the stems on the cut panels using a tailor's pencil.

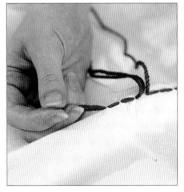

Sew along the stems with coarse green string, using a large running stitch and darning needle.

Know your materials

Cotton is a natural fabric, which is available in a variety of different weights. There is a comprehensive range of plain and patterned finsihes available, and patchwork and most quilting suppliers will often offer a range of space-dyed cotton fabrics.

Muslin is a fine, soft cotton fabric with a fairly open weave, which gives it a relatively gauzy appearance—this material is ideal if you want to make curtains that let plenty of light into the room. If you want to use an even more sheer fabric, choose from organza, voile, and chiffon.

reverse of the fabric. This will make sure that the flowers keep their shape.

7 Then sew a pearl button in the center of each flower head to complete the design. If you want to use this type of design in a children's room, there are many alternatives—for example, you could customize it by using colored pompoms instead of buttons. Brightly colored raffia flowers and colored ribbon tab tops would also work well.

Petals are made by sewing large loops of raffia and securing them with a knot at the back.

Sew a pearl button in the center of each flower head to complete the design.

Alternative

For a colorful alternative you could always try dip-dying your piece of fabric. To do this, mix dye powder and fixer in a bucket, stirring well. Dip the ends of the curtain panels into the dye bucket and secure the top (on a washing line, for example). Leave in the dye for the manufacturer's recommended time. You will see that the dye begins to travel up the fibers of the fabric. Remove from the dye bucket and rinse under running water until the water runs clear. Leave until it is completely dry.

Another method you could try is tie-and-dye. This is a technique that involves tying small bunches of fabric tight with string. When dipped in the dye, the string acts as a barrier to it, so that the areas covered by the string do not get dyed. For a simple pattern of small circles, try tying small coins at regular intervals over the fabric. Dye, then hang on a washing line to dry before untying all the coins to reveal the pattern.

Occasional and small
space dining

Small and occasional dining areas are a feature of many homes. Although the lack of space can be restricting, careful planning and the use of furniture and fixtures designed to cope with such problems can make the best of what is available.

Design features

There are some design features that you can incorporate into your home that will enable you to make the most of the space that you have available.

Breakfast bar

This type of arrangement can be slotted in around other functions, for example, a peninsula worktop may also double up as a breakfast bar or occasional dining area. A worktop-only island unit can be covered with a cloth or mats to create a central dining point.

Make sure when planning this type of arrangement that you leave enough overhang on the work surface so that the diner may pull their seat up under the worktop and sit with bent knees. It is also advisable to locate this type of eating area away from dishwashers and clothes washers.

Breakfast bars or raised-shelf dining areas are best finished with rounded edges rather than angular ones. It is more comfortable for the diner to sit close to a

round edge rather than jutting, angular corners, and if people bump into them, they will be less likely to hurt themselves.

Effective table designs

There are certain types of occasional-dining furniture that are also very useful in small dining areas, because they fold or stack away so that the maximum

amount of floor space is available when the dining facility is not required. A clever system is a faux top drawer. This has a fake front panel that slips neatly into a standard unit of drawers, but when pulled out it opens up into a tabletop or dining surface (see box on page 267).

As well as the extending drawer table, there are standard foldaway tables, either semicircular or

Above: The overhang of the surface of the unit in the foreground creates a breakfast bar, which is used in conjunction with stylish high stools.

Opposite: Tall stools that can be pulled up beside an island unit to make a casual dining space work well in this colorful family kitchen.

Above: The bright, striped dining chairs surround a table for formal dining, but a row of stools tucked under the glass ledge is ideal for perching on for informal occasions. The use of glass surfaces and shelves makes the whole area look bright and spacious.

square, which are usually hinged to the wall and have an adjustable leg underneath that can be pulled around and fastened in place for stability. When you have finished, the leg is folded back and the table is dropped flat against the wall. A similar arrangement can also be connected to the end of a section of worktop that has free space around it, possibly at the side of a passageway or entrance.

Tabletops can also be supported on hinges or a pulley so that they are raised and concealed in a cupboard, but then dropped and supported on a foldaway leg when needed. Another option is a wide, fixed shelf at the bottom of a row of shallower shelves. The narrower shelves above can be used to store books and china, but the wider shelf at the bottom is at a height to accommodate people eating. This works well along a flat wall, but can also be used in a corner. Corners can be awkward spaces to use, but can have triangular shelves installed to provide storage.

Chairs

Seating in small-space dining areas is often on high stools. These should have padded, sculpted, or at least pliable seats and backs, and, most important, a foot bar or rest. The main problem with sitting on a high stool is that you have nowhere to rest your feet, unless there is an integral foot bar, or a bar is run along the lower section of the facing units.

The lower tables and surfaces will also require chairs. Again, the foldaway and stacking designs can be neatly stored but easily brought in to use.

Making your dining space look bigger

In small dining areas, you need to plan carefully in order to make the space feel larger and with more room than it really is. There are several tricks of the trade that will enable you to do this without too much work.

Using mirrors

A mirror can be effective because it reflects light and offers a feeling of space beyond, rather than a solid, definite wall. Mirrors can be set into panels in doors, giving them a less dense and solid appearance.

However, a mirror must be treated with care, not only because it will shatter if a chair or the corner of a table is smashed against it, but also because too much mirror can make a small room become disorienting. Mirrors on opposite walls will create a continuous repetition of images, which can have a dizzy and muddling effect, as well as giving a room something of a fairground or circus appearance.

Using glass

Another practical surface in a small dining area is glass because, like mirror, it does not appear solid or defining. Glass shelves, made from laminated and tempered glass, can be used along a wall without making the space feel smaller, although what you stack or display on the shelves should be selected to emphasize this effect, rather than conceal it. Glass, light-colored china and ceramics, and pale wooden objects are best, rather than row upon row of books, which will be heavy in weight and give a dark and solid appearance.

Using color

Pale colors will also help you to impart a feeling of space in a small dining area, so look for fresh, light colors such as

Multi-level systems

In a very small kitchen you can devise a two- or three-level system of worktop and dining area that will maximize the available space. By using different levels within the same perimeters, you can increase the available space. For example, the main level is the cooktop or food preparation level, which should be at a height that an adult can comfortably work at standing up. On the other side of this unit, a breakfast bar or dining shelf can be installed at a level a little lower than the cooktop, so that it functions for people sitting. A third raised area, at a level above the cooktop height, could be used for coffee pot, toaster, and things needed by the seated diner.

yellow, cream, beige, blue, and almond green. Avoid dense and ornately printed fabrics, and for window dressings a neat shade may save valuable inches (or centimeters) over a heavy, pleated curtain.

Floors and ceilings should be in pale colors, and you can rarely go wrong with a white ceiling and pale wood floors or pale stone tiles, both of which

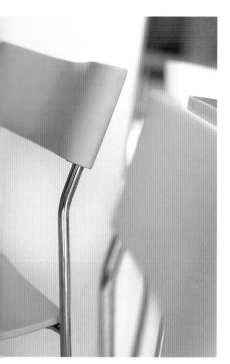

Above: For more leisurely dining, chairs with supportive backs are preferable to stools.

Opposite: This extension has not only enlarged the kitchen area and made room for a separate dining space, but it has also increased the amount of natural light in the main room.

will help add to the feeling of spaciousness. If the floor and ceiling are dark, it can make them feel closer and create a boxy and claustrophobic environment in a small space.

Clutter will also fill in the limited area you have, so pare down the amount of things you have on show. However, a balance must be found, as a room devoid of objects or decoration will be boring and bland. A few carefully selected decorative objects will enhance, but not overpower the room.

Playing with light

Lighting can also help make a small space seem larger. Small corner floor lamps can be placed in the corners of a room so that the beam shines directly up the wall from the floor, emphasizing the height of the space as well as illuminating the corners of the room, making them appear bright and defined.

A light placed over the middle of a centrally positioned table will also draw attention to the center of the room, and if the rest of the room is subdued, this will create a feeling of greater space as well as concentrate the focus on what is going on immediately in front of the diners, rather than what lies behind them.

Building extensions

In some cases, it may be possible to extend a small room to create a dining space. For example, if you have a side return from a yard, alley, or pathway, you could push out the exterior wall to incorporate this space. In situations such as this, it is often difficult to incorporate side windows into the scheme, as building code regulations may not allow them if it is felt that the side windows will overlook a neighboring property. Also, the view may not be worth the expense of installing a window. In these cases, a glass roof or panel can be the answer.

A sloping or arched glass roof, made of toughened panels, will allow light to flood into the dining area during the day, and at night provide an interesting celestial ceiling to the room. Two factors that will have to be considered in this type of extension are ventilation and screening. The glass roof will not only allow natural light to penetrate the room, but also the sun. During the summer it may become incredibly hot, so louvers or a window section in the roof will allow air to circulate and help counteract the problem. The sun will also fade fabrics, and canvas blinds or wood louvers may be the best option.

Display and
storage

Display and storage in a dining area may, in some cases, be one and the same thing, because useful items can also be beautiful. To keep the right emphasis, the pieces kept on show should be selected for their decorative appearance, rather than their utilitarian qualities.

Storage tip

You may find it useful to line the shelves or cupboards with paper to protect them from pots and pans. Use plain white or off-white lining paper to provide a removable and slightly absorbent base, so that when the time comes to clean them you simply replace the paper.

The paper will also create a soft layer on which upturned wine glasses can be stored. You will be less likely to knock and chip the glasses against the hard surface of the shelf if you have a buffer layer of tidy, lined paper.

Right: When planning your dining-room storage, be sure that you have enough shelf space to keep all the items you may want near the table.

Opposite: A simple, three-shelf dresser-top structure, placed above a boxed radiator, provides an attractive display unit.

Organizing your storage

The amount of storage that you need to allow for in your dining room depends on the layout of your home, whether you have a separate room for the purpose, or whether it forms part of the kitchen or living area.

In the kitchen/dining area storage is paramount, not only to contain the ingredients and crockery, but also to keep equipment and utensils under control. A cluttered kitchen will overwhelm a simple dining area, so it is best to keep kitchen surfaces as clear as possible—this will also provide more space on which to work.

If space is limited, then you may need to store table linen and tableware in your living/dining room. It is particularly important to keep such items out of sight, otherwise the living and relaxing area is in danger of becoming

linked with the kitchen. While it is acceptable to have glass, bowls, jugs, and other attractive china on display in the kitchen/dining area, a living area is mainly for entertainment and relaxation.

Storing dining equipment

Storage for dining-related items needs to be subdivided. Allocate a shelf for linens, tablecloths, and napkins, and another shelf for heat-resistant mats, table-napkin rings, and coasters. Cutlery is best kept in a subdivided drawer with separate divisions for knives, forks, and spoons. If the cutlery is of good quality, perhaps silver plated or with a raised design on the handles, then the partitions should be lined with felt to avoid the surfaces of the pieces becoming scratched.

A traditional canteen is another option. This is a box divided into specific areas to hold individual knives and forks. With knives, the blades slot into a niche at the top of the box, and the handle rests in a slightly wider container at the bottom. There are also specific holders for forks and spoons.

Decorating storage units

Storage in a dining room does not have to be dull. You can decorate

storage units to make them an integral part of your scheme.

Decorating cupboards

The front of a cupboard is like a blank canvas, and can be decorated in subtle or ornate ways. Simple moldings can be used to create a panel, or the doors themselves could be painted in different colors. Alternatively, you could transform the doors with a decoupage arrangement of black-and-white photocopies, postcards, insets made from panels of self-adhesive paper, or sheets of manuscript music.

Making a plate rack

A plate rack consists of an oblong, box-like frame with corresponding pairs of dowel rods $5/8$in (1.75cm) in diameter, which are attached at either side.

The distance between the rods (from front to back) should be sufficient to hold a plate or saucer (approximately $1^1/2$in/3–4cm), and the length between the two sides needs to be wide enough to accommodate a dinner plate of about 1ft (30cm) diameter.

such as newspaper and brown paper, can be cut into an attractive fringe or edge, and have the advantage of being easy and inexpensive to replace.

In a contemporary setting, the nose of the shelf can be covered with a strip of copper or other fine metal. Thin copper sheets can be cut into narrow strips, beaten over the edge, and held in place with tacks. The metal border can be left plain as a simple highlight strip, or punched to create a pattern or simple motif.

Display storage

Storage in a dining room can be made into a display feature. It is important to choose items that complement the design and decoration of your dining area.

Storing plates

In an informal or rustic-style dining area, plates can be displayed on a dresser or plate rack. In some homes a narrow shelf, with a groove or recess on the upper side, is sited around the top of the room. Plates can be arranged on this ledge and displayed at an angle, with the lower edge resting in the niche of the shelf and the back of the plate against the wall.

Some people hang decorative ceramic plates, serving dishes, or parts of old dinner services on

Above: This cupboard has an automatic interior light so that when the door is open the interior is lit up, which makes it easier to locate the item you are looking for.

Opposite: A wooden cube wine rack can be tailored to slot in to most gaps between units.

Another choice is a fabric panel. In traditional kitchens, the material most often used was a simple checkered cotton, but linen tea cloths can be just as effective.

Dressing shelves

In a country-style dining room, simple, wall-mounted shelves can become the decorative focal point of the room. A length of deep border lace can be pinned to the front edge of the shelf, or plain white paper cut in a simple zigzag pattern can also look charming. Even more mundane materials, the wall instead of conventional artworks. To create a more contemporary look, colored glass plates, chargers, or large, decorative platters could be used.

Storing other utensils

Collections on dressers can be a mixture of various styles, colors, and shapes, or themed. Some people collect a certain type of china, such as teapots or egg cups, and others a particular pattern or decoration of tableware, or even a particular designer's work.

The arrangement of china on dressers can also be informal, made up of a haphazard collection of sizes and styles. To get the full benefit of the pieces, taller objects should be kept at the back and smaller items in front.

Drinking glasses and glassware are most practically stored in cupboards. If you want them to be admired, have doors with glass insets, but without the protection of an enclosed space they will quickly lose their shine and become dull with dust and atmospheric pollutants. Glass is at its best when brilliant and polished.

Storing food

Fresh fruit and vegetables can be arranged to create an appropriate and attractive display. For example, in summer a glass bowl full of

zesty lemons and limes will allude to freshness and piquancy, in the fall a glass or silver stand filled with dark red and green grapes gives a hint of opulence, and a cream bowl of globe artichokes can provide an interesting and alternative table center in the winter, when flowers are less readily available.

Storing bottles and glassware

There are a number of types of wine racks available (see box, right). Only limited amounts of wine should be kept in the dining room, because the room is liable to be warm, which isn't good for wine, and also because the bottles gather dust. A small display of a couple of dozen bottles can look

Choosing a wine rack

Wine racks are useful in a dining room or kitchen, but generally only to store red wines that are best served at room temperature. Bottles can be contained in wooden racks consisting of individual boxes in a grid-like formation, or in a cheaper accordion construction, which provides diamond-shape niches to place bottles in. Terra-cotta stacking grids are also good, especially for white wine, as they tend to be cool, and can be cooled even more by pouring a little icy water over the surface. Plastic wine racks, like bottle crates, are also available from good stores.

Reducing shelf height

Big, deep shelves are fine for storing large items such as coffee pots and glass fruit bowls, but for smaller or flatter pieces, such as saucers, plates, and cups, a deep shelf can make them more difficult to access and leave a lot of wasted space.

Reduce shelf height either by fitting another shelf between, or by hanging plastic-coated shelf dividers from the upper shelf. These clip over the nose of the upper shelf and hang beneath. Note, however, that these temporary shelves are not designed to support heavy weights.

Opposite: The narrow shelving unit creates a division between the kitchen/dining and sitting areas, and is an ideal place to display decorative objects. The low dividing wall is a perfect resting place for dishes, plates, and cutlery, rather than cluttering up the limited amount of work surfaces in the kitchen.

attractive and can be slotted in neatly below a console or side table, the bottom shelves of a bookcase, or even in a disused chimney. Good wines and those stored for any time should be kept in a temperature-controlled environment, such as a cellar.

Other types of alcohol, such as spirits and liqueurs, may also be stored and displayed. Again, keep a few well-chosen bottles on show, rather than a huge range.

Decorative or attractively shaped, clear-glass bottles with clear or colored contents can be made into a feature if a subtle shaft of light is directed or focused on them. Likewise, glass decanters may also be arranged as ornaments.

Another place to display drinks and bottles is on a trolley so that they can be easily wheeled from one area to another. This is especially useful if you are serving drinks before dinner in the living room, but want to provide liqueurs or refresh glasses during dinner in the dining area. There are many types of trolleys available from the classic, beech-laminate Alvar Aalto model, to metal and wood designs. Choose one that is lightweight, easy to maneuver, and in keeping with the rest of your furniture and the room decorations.

Decorative display

Display in a dining room does not always have to be practical. In fact, you can create a decorative display feature that is the centerpiece of your scheme.

Minimal decorative displays

In a contemporary setting, displays should be orderly, in keeping with the surroundings. There is an oriental custom where the prized artefacts and artistic possessions of the household are stored in a chest. Each item is taken out in turn and displayed alone for a period of time, so that its full beauty can be admired.

In a situation such as this, the few items that are put on show must be of high quality and of real interest, because there is little else to draw the attention or eye away.

Display backgrounds

The background against which a display is set is important. For example, in a rich- or deep-colored room light colors, black-and-white prints or photographs, gilt frames, and mirrors will stand out very successfully. But if you put a pastel or subtle-colored watercolor painting in a pale frame on a neutral or similar-

colored wall, it will not be accent-
ed. In the same way, a display of
cream items against a cream wall
will also be lost.

Against a plain or palely decorated background, displays and
arrangements can be used to
bring in highlights and stronger

accents of color. For example, in a
simple, off-white rustic dining
room it can be a nice idea to
create an arrangement of old,
hand-blown glassware and simple
terra-cotta bowls. The glassware
will provide a green tint, and the
bowls a brownish hue.

These items can also inspire a
table setting with a decorative
linen cloth, white china, silver
cutlery, and rich green napkins,
and the mood can be changed
with a bunch of yellow flowers, a
pale yellow cotton cloth, and
green and white napkins.

Exotic wallhanging with tassels

Materials

Enough fabric to cover your walls
Gold thread
Bead trim
Pins
Contrasting organza for pockets
Gold mirror trims
Wood strips
Brass hanging rings (used for picture-framing)
Brass picture nails or hooks
Paste gems or tassels

Tools

Scissors
Sewing machine
Paper
Iron
Hacksaw
Awl
Hammer

It is quick and easy to transform a neutral dining room using hanging fabric panels, which give parties an added sense of occasion. We used a semi-sheer sari fabric here because of its vibrant color. Contrasting pockets of sheer organza with iridescent bead trimming can be used to hold menu cards or fragrant spices. You could vary the designs to suit different occasions—for example, use gingham and pockets filled with colorful candy for children's parties, or velvet with fur trimming at Christmas.

Preparing the material

1 Cut the material into panel lengths that will fit your room size (do not try to span one long wall with a single panel, as it is far easier to hang several side by side). Thread your sewing machine with gold metallic thread —you may need to adjust the tension and use the manufacturer's recommended needle size for metallic thread. Fold the border over on itself top and bottom,

Using gold thread, fold the border over on itself, and sew along to form a channel.

Using a paper template, cut out three squares of organza per panel, allowing for a hem.

Know your materials

Saris are excellent value for money, when used to decorate a home, as a single one provides around 33ft (10m) of good-quality fabric. They also come in stunning colors. They can be purchased from Indian and Asian fabric merchants, but are increasingly available in large furnishing stores, too. Many saris have ornate, woven metallic borders, which add extra interest to the material and can be used as a feature in your design.

Saris make great lightweight curtains, simply draped or clipped onto a rod. For extra privacy, and to soften the light, use them with a shade.

press, then sew along the length to form a channel. Pin the bead trim in place under the top channel, tucking the binding under the flap of fabric. Then sew a second line of stitches in order to secure it into position.

2 Use paper to make a square pattern, then cut three squares of organza per panel, allowing $1/2$ in (1cm) hem allowance each side (see picture

bottom right, page 276). Press with a cool iron.

Decorating the pockets

3 Cut lengths of bead trim to fit around the squares that will make up the pockets, and then pin the trim in place.

4 Sew the bead trim onto the pockets (you will need to position the machine foot on the left or right setting to avoid crushing the beads). Pin the pockets in place at equal intervals on the fabric panels, then sew them on to secure.

5 Sew gold mirror trims onto the center of each pocket by hand.

Pin the bead trim in place around the top of each of the organza squares.

Sew the trim in place on the pockets, taking care that you do not damage the beading.

Now hand-sew the gold mirror trims or other ornaments onto the center of each square.

Attaching panels to the wall

6 Cut the flat wood strips to the correct length with a hacksaw, and feed them into the channels at the top and the bottom of your fabric panels. Hand-stitch the channels closed.

7 Use an awl to make small holes that drive through the fabric right into the wood strips. Then carefully screw brass rings so that they sit along the top of each of the panels.

8 Attach the panels to the wall using small brass picture nails or picture hooks, which you can either decorate with tassels (as we have), or glue paste gems into the center of each one.

Feed your wood strips through the channels at the top and bottom of your panels.

Use an awl to make holes in the top of the fabric, then screw brass rings along the edge.

Use picture hooks to attach the panels to the wall. These can then be decorated.

Alternative

If you prefer to create a more per-manent fabric wall covering, there are various methods to choose from. It is possible to buy textile wallcoverings from specialized wallpaper suppliers. They are fairly expensive but durable, which means that they are often used in commercial interiors. Suitable fab-rics include those with heavy weaves like jutes, or slubbed linens with a high natural-fiber content. They consist of a textured fabric surface with a paper backing, which is hung in a similar way to standard wallpaper.

Another choice is to fix slim wood strips along the top and bottom of the wall. The fabric should then be stretched tight and stapled, or tacked top and bottom onto the wood. Each width of fabric should be overlapped slightly so that no gaps appear. Canvas or fabric with a high natural-fiber content is an ideal choice for this, and when stretched, it can be sprayed lightly with water, to cause it to shrink tight.

Lighting your
dining room

Lighting a dining room requires several levels of illumination, and ideally a dimmer switch so that the intensity of light can be fine-tuned to create the ambience for different occasions. The focus should be on the table, and the light must be distributed so diners can see each other.

Creating a mood

For general points about lighting design, see Effective lighting on page 187. In dining areas, lighting plays an important role in creating the right mood. For breakfast time the light needs to be bright and invigorating to get sleepy people going. In the summer, natural light is best, so windows should have dressings that can be pulled well back to allow the light to pour through. In the winter, artificial light takes the place of natural, so it is best to allow curtains and shades to block out the dark and cold.

Lighting for different occasions

A central light over the table can help to focus attention on eating, and will illuminate the food and related items on the surface. Wall lights may also help to bring up

Right: Light passing through this segmented lampshade creates a swirling pattern on the ceiling.

the overall level of light in the room. Breakfast and lunchtime should not need much artificial light, apart from during a very dull day, when lights can be used to boost the amount of light present in the room.

A retractable center light over a table is a great way of changing the feel of a mealtime according to your needs. If the light is pulled up close to the ceiling the spread of light is wide, covering most of the table with a fan of

Above: These Chinese ceramic bowls, with patterns created by grains of rice, make an attractive table decoration when they are lit up with candles.

Right: In a large room a chandelier, such as this one with its ornate iron structure, can be a focal point and help to reduce the feeling of height and distance in the room.

illumination. On the other hand, if the light is pulled down closer to the table the beam will be concentrated on a smaller area, making the atmosphere more intimate, ideal for a dinner party.

Dimmer switches are another useful way of changing the mood of a room. For breakfast and family mealtimes the light should be bright and clear, so that the food and utensils are clearly visible. However, for smart lunch parties in the fall and early spring, or an evening meal for adults, the lights can be dimmed to a low level. They can also be augmented by candlelight and low-level wall lights to create the desired atmosphere.

Reflected lights

In a dining situation, reflected light is subtle and attractive. This can be achieved in a number of ways, the most obvious being with a mirror. If you have one over a mantelpiece or on the wall behind a console or side table, you can arrange a group of candles so that the flames are reflected in it. This doubles the impact of the light from the flames, and also creates an interesting feature.

Candles can be used in wall sconces too. These are wall-mounted candle holders with a back plate that was originally used to prevent fat and wax from splashing on the walls, as well as increasing the efficiency of the light. The back panel of a sconce is usually made from polished metal, copper, brass, or steel, and is sometimes made of a shaped piece of glass or mirror.

Plain glass can also reflect a certain amount of light. If you place a small table lamp or candle in front of a window at night, the polished surface of the window will reflect light back into the room. The darkness outside will also make the light stand out.

Light shades

The shades you use on the lights will influence the level of

light that comes through them. If you choose a yellow-tinted glass shade, then the light will assume a golden hue, while a white shade may mute the strength of light slightly, but in general will still be bright and clear. A dense shade will restrict the flow of light through the sides and concentrate the flow directly down.

If the base of the shade is open, as in a standard, coolie-hat-shape shade, then the light will shine out of the base, and a small amount through the narrow top, in an increasingly wide triangular pool. A tubular shade will direct the beam in a downward direction, while a round or ball shade will not create a direct beam at all—the light will be emitted through the sides of the shade and will create a soft, overall glow, although there will be an opening at the top of the shade to accommodate the light fiixture, and to allow heat to escape.

Light bulbs generate heat and therefore will increase the ambient room temperature during the course of an evening. Light bulbs should never be in direct contact with a shade or covering because, as they heat up during use, they may cause the material in contact with them to burn or melt.

Using candles

Great care should be taken when using candles, especially in glass containers, because they may overheat and shatter, so only use containers that are specifically designed to hold candles and are wide enough not to be in direct contact with the flame. Never leave a naked flame unattended in a room. Scented candles are best avoided in a dining room or eating space, because their perfume may interfere with the aroma of the food. The senses of taste and smell are close-linked, and sweet perfume and savory aromas may conflict and make the food unappetizing.

Dining area accessories

Accessories for the dining area really revolve around the tabletop, and will reflect the type of dining, and maybe even the food that is being served. For casual meals the dressing can be less formal—maybe bowls for pasta or noodles, a knife and fork, a side dish for salad, and glasses for water and wine. Mats can be used instead of a cloth, and colorful napkins are fun and functional. For more formal entertaining, however, the table is likely to be set with a cloth and a full complement of cutlery; crisp, white napkins; and several glasses for water and various types of wine. The addition of candles, flowers, and other table decorations will depend on the amount of space you have on the tabletop, and the time of day when you are entertaining. All these things will add to creating that special sense of occasion. Seating around a dining table should be chosen for its comfort as well as appearance—a rigid and upright chair with little or no back support will make diners restless during the meal, whereas a padded seat and flexible back will help them to relax and enjoy their time with you.

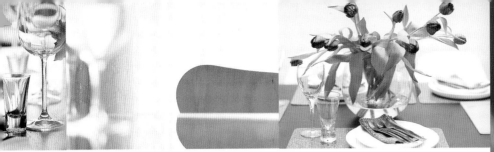

Clockwise from top left:

Decanting mineral water from plastic containers into decorative, colored glass bottles will add to the attractive appearance of your table.

Trays are useful for carrying items to and from a table.

Various sizes and shapes of glasses are appropriate for different wines and other drinks.

Table surfaces such as glass and wood may need to be protected from sharp blades and hot dishes, otherwise they could get marked and damaged.

Don't make a table center decoration so big that people sitting opposite have to strain to see each other, or find it difficult to hold a conversation.

The other furniture in a dining room is as important as the table—think about coordinating the materials they are made from, as well as using the same handles on all storage items.

This voile envelope contains the cutlery for a single place setting. It can be a useful way of allocating cutlery for a buffet party, so that each guest has his or her own special container to pick up.

In a more informal dining area, perhaps one that is off a kitchen, stools and a breakfast bar work well for everyday eating.

Don't forget to think carefully about every aspect of your dining area—even light switches can be chosen as decorative embellishments.

A small plant, such as this cactus, can be made more dramatic and have larger impact if set in an outsize bowl.

Think about the type of seating that will suit your dining space—stools are an effective way of making the most of limited space.

This table setting has modern elements—leather mats and napkin rings—yet still has a classical feel.

A gilded Moroccan tea glass makes a perfect holder for a night-light candle.

Candelabra add a touch of romance and glamor for evening dining.

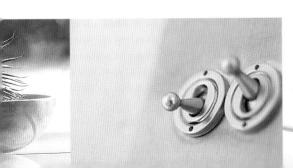

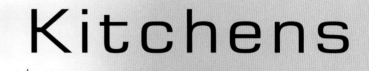

Kitchens

Planning your
kitchen

The kitchen is the heart of the home—it is where people tend to congregate, have coffee, and chat, but it is also where food is prepared, stored, and cooked. Standards of hygiene in a kitchen should be rigorous, and safety is a factor that must be taken into consideration, both in planning and decorating your kitchen.

Opposite: This small kitchen makes the most of all available space. The sliding panel at the back of the room connects to the living room.

Below right: There is easy access between the different working areas of the kitchen, and the island unit provides plenty of work surface.

Planning your space

The role of the kitchen has changed in the last thirty years. It used to be a room with just one function, but it now often has to be multifunctional, serving as office and dining area.

Whether you are designing a kitchen from scratch, altering, or adapting an existing one, it is best to be aware of the basic rules. The most important of these is that you should always take professional advice and help with plumbing and electric wiring.

Kitchen layouts

Galley kitchens are long, usually narrow, passage-like spaces where work surfaces and units are lined up along opposite walls, as in the galley of a ship.

Island kitchens are generally found in large rooms, where a central block of units and worktop has been installed to make it easier to create the work triangle. The block of units is referred to as the island, because it sits alone on the floor area and is not attached to any other section of worktop or units.

Left: Here, the upper units are long and narrow, which makes the room seem taller. The glass fronts stop the units from being too heavy.

Opposite: These stylish kitchen cupboards are tailored to follow the line of the opening that leads from the kitchen to the dining room.

Opposite, below: Where wall space is at a premium these open shelves are effective.

Appliances

When choosing appliances, you should be guided by the amount of space you have, and the way that you eat and entertain. If you are mainly a take-out eater, then you probably won't make much use of a semi-professional range. If you live alone and have a dishwasher, then a double sink with integral waste-disposal outlet and double drainer may be beyond your needs.

The work triangle

It takes time and effort to create a well-designed layout for a kitchen. Each one is unique in shape and size, and will also have its own variety of problems that have to be solved. The standard rule to use as a starting point is to be sure that you create the work triangle. This maps out the three main working areas in a kitchen—the sink, range, and refrigerator. These areas should be sited at the points of an imaginary triangle so that you work efficiently and effectively between each point during the preparation of a meal.

Beside each point on the triangle it is best to have a worktop.

This work triangle should not be interrupted by the main traffic thoroughfare, so don't position it between two main doorways. The space between each point should be easily accessible, and they should not be too far apart. If the distances between the refrigerator and cooking and washing surfaces are substantial, and you cater for a large family or regularly entertain lots of people, you may find a trolley useful to bridge the gap. A butcher's block or island is another option.

It is also wise to keep the refrigerator/freezer and range apart because, although both white goods are already insulated, the heat emitted by a high-temperature oven may affect the freeze-and-chill mechanisms and efficiency of the cooler machines.

There are recognized bodies who regulate the work of the main trades. Many of these bodies or associations award credited operators with a symbol or association membership, which guarantees that they have attained certain standards.

Check that the craftsperson or operator you are employing for any job has such support, and confirm their accreditation with the association.

Storage considerations

When planning your storage, take into consideration the doors on the units and appliances. Allow plenty of space for each one to open, and to be sure you have easy access to the inner depths.

Make sure that you allocate suitable storage beside each element of the kitchen. By the refrigerator/freezer you could, for example, have storage for fresh fruit and vegetables in wicker drawers or racks. By the dishwasher cupboards to stack china and drawers for cutlery and glass may be useful (see Display and storage, pages 300–2).

Built-in or freestanding?

There are two basic types of kitchen units, built-in or free-standing. You can choose either, or go for a combination of both. The built-in kitchen generally gives a more tailored appearance, while freestanding ones allow more versatility and variety.

In small kitchens, built-in units can be structured to make the most of all the limited space available. Freestanding units usually look best in a large kitchen. Here, a dresser can be placed along one wall, and a collection of cabinets can be used to create a variety of working areas. Freestanding furniture can be a good option if you live in rented accommodation, as you can then take the units and fixtures with you when you move.

Freestanding schemes allow you more time to accumulate the various pieces you want. With this type of kitchen, you can freely add to it as and when your budget

Right: One of the advantages of a built-in kitchen is that you can have cupboards specially made to fit the space available, such as the narrow corner units in this kitchen.

Opposite page: This single-sheet, steel backsplash is easy to wipe and polish because it has a continuous smooth surface.

permits, and when you come across an attractive piece. A built-in kitchen, on the other hand, is usually bought and installed in one go, so you need to be sure that you have the money to pay for it all at once, or commit to an instalment payment scheme.

You may decide that you want a combination of built-in and free-standing furniture. It is usually best to make sure that the areas where the larger machines or

major plumbing is involved are built in. For example, items such as a wall-mounted oven and the sink need to be in a stable unit to support the plumbing and waste points. However, general storage and a table/worktop area can easily be freestanding.

Installing your kitchen

Unless you are a real home-improvement enthusiast, leave the installation of a kitchen to

craftspeople. The process is often fraught with problems and requires technical knowledge.

Consult the electrician, plumber, and unit installer before they start, and make sure that each knows what the other is up to. If they work individually, rather than being employed by the same company, try to get them to work out a timetable so that they don't get in each other's way, and work in a logical order.

When installing a kitchen, you should do all the groundwork first, and then add decoration. This is because the wiring and ducting for pipes and vents are best done before any flooring or tiles are put in place. Get the range, exhaust fan and hood,

cooktop, sink, and heaters plumbed and wired in before you paint and tile. The refrigerator/freezer can be put in later, as it only requires a power socket and, sometimes, a water inlet.

Most built-in units have a base plinth, which can be put in place after the flooring has been laid. The plinth fits between the base of the unit and covers the adjustable legs that support most base units.

Filling the gaps

Very few kitchens are perfectly symmetrical and able to accommodate a precise number of regular-size units. The basic units are base- and wall-mounted and come in standard sizes, but most manufacturers produce fill-in units

Keeping your kitchen safe

Make sure that you always have a fire blanket and a small, handheld fire extinguisher near the cooktop and oven. Also install a smoke detector or alarm in an area away from the main cooking facilities.

If children have access to a kitchen, install door-fastening devices on cupboards. Attach guard rails around cooktops and cookers and, if possible, a safety gate across the door.

Don't keep sharp knives in a cutlery drawer. Wall-mounted magnetic bars are a good idea. A knife block keeps knives in order, with blades covered.

such as broom cupboards and wine racks, which can be used to complete a scheme.

Most of the standard, factory-made units have a chipboard, plywood, or MDF carcass with a melamine-resin or similar facing on the side. Drawers and door fronts can be made of a wide variety of finishes, and are attached to standard carcasses. Inside the carcasses you can have a fixed shelf, or variable shelves that can be moved up and down. Corner

units have a number of special fixtures, including swing shelves that pivot around a central pole—these allow the full depth of the corner to be used. Some units come with a single drawer, while others have a complete set that runs from top to bottom.

Styles of decoration

Once the practicalities have been sorted out, you can turn your mind to color and decoration.

There are various styles of kitchen to choose from, so you need to think carefully about the look you want to create, and how this fits with the various roles your kitchen needs to be able to fulfill.

Domestic-professional kitchens

The domestic-professional style of kitchen is modeled on the steel-clad industrial kitchens of professional chefs. In its ultimate form the scheme is white, steel, and clinical, but it is easily adapted to a domestic setting by using color, wood, and softer elements.

The primary pieces of equipment are the industrial-inspired range, large refrigerator/freezer, and clean, long expanses of work surface. This is a kitchen for eager cooks. The professional oven usually has double the capacity of the standard appliance, and you can add a plate-warming cabinet and eye-level grill.

Left: One way of softening the industrial look is to introduce wood, such as this work surface.

Right: This kitchen is typical of the domestic-professional style—its focal point is the large, steel-clad cooktop and industrial-style vent. Raising the solid unit on tall legs makes it appear less dominant, because there is space and light beneath.

To go with these large and serious pieces of equipment you need an equally large refrigerator, again steel-clad. Large, American-inspired designs are now available on the retail market.

To link these steel-clad machines, the work surface and backsplash of the kitchen is often made of steel as well. This type of worktop usually has to be custom-built, and is ideally made from a single steel sheet so that there are no unsightly lumps or joints in the middle of a run of working area.

This style of kitchen is very durable and longlasting, due to its industrial background. The domestic versions of these appliances are not made to such high-mass catering specifications, but they are still tough and will therefore also have a long and productive life in the average domestic kitchen.

Using such a large amount of steel in a room can make it feel cold and hollow, so it is important to balance this by introducing natural elements. An occasional warm wood-unit front, wooden flooring, or a panel of color will help. The colors you choose should work with the coolness of the steel so blues, soft shades of lavender, and even orange can look good. The flooring can be wooden, but if you want to keep strictly to the industrial feel, look at polished cement, gray slate or stone, or textured, industrial rubber sheets for your flooring.

If this style of kitchen is part of a kitchen/dining room, try to avoid too many soft and fluffy elements in the dining area. Echo the clean, uncluttered lines of the kitchen, and use similar colors. Simple geometric patterns will complement the modern, no-nonsense look of the kitchen section of the room.

Above: The apron-front sink and lever faucets are typical of a country-style kitchen.

Left: This metal-clad kitchen has a sleek, modern style.

Simple, modern kitchens

A less severe version of the domestic-professional kitchen is the simple, modern style. This creates a light and airy surrounding with color and space. It is still streamlined, but has a certain softness to it. Here, the layout is practical and functional, but elements of color are encouraged. The doors of the units are generally plain, or have a minor panel detail, but they are dressed with interesting and functional knobs

or handles and a colorful laminate or finish. The flooring may also be colorful but washable—for example, a linoleum in a complementary shade to the unit doors, which incorporates a patterned layout of checkerboard tiles, or a laser-cut overall pattern, may be used.

This style can be based on a palette of two or three colors, or two colors and a lighter or darker tone of one of them.

If you are in any doubt when you are first devising a scheme, you should start by keeping it very simple. You can always add more decorative elements later, but if you put too much in to start with, then it will be much more difficult to subtract any of it later. Simple is usually best.

Country style

Another look that is popular is the country style. Even in city-center homes there are kitchens that look as though they have doors that open out onto green pastures, rather than a six-lane highway. The rural idyll provides inspiration for a number of interpretations. For example, folk style incorporates tongue-and-groove paneling, brick or flagstone floors, the dominant, enameled, old-fashiojned range with a shelf or fire surround, and plenty of

At-a-glance color guide

Kitchens are best decorated in light, fresh colors on the walls—secondary color can be introduced in units and soft furnishings.

The domestic-professional kitchen (see pages 294–6) is usually white with plenty of stainless steel, but to soften this look for the home, add elements of wood and some splashes of color such as orange or blue.

The simple, modern kitchen (see left) can incorporate a scheme of two colors as well as tonal variations of each of the main colors.

The country-style kitchen (see left) generally mixes white or cream with pea-green, sky blue, cherry red, or sunflower yellow, unless you go for a Mediterranean scheme, where terra-cotta takes the place of the white, and lavender blue and olive green become the complementary colors.

Traditional style (see page 299) often mixes wood with slate, stone, glass, and ceramics, and revolves around a natural color palette, rather than fashionable colors.

utensils, crockery, and other items on show.

Country style can be pared down to a neater, more spartan Shaker or Scandinavian interpretation, or taken to Mediterranean climes, where the walls are roughly plastered and painted. White teamed with cobalt blue accessories follows a Greek influence, while terra-cotta and bright, handpainted plates evoke Italian or Spanish settings.

Two areas that are usually constant in the country genre are the range and sink. The oven is often an enamel-fronted range cooker, and dominates a wall of the room. The sink should be a deep, oblong, white-ceramic apron-front sink. With this type of sink you may also go for the old-fashioned style of faucets.

The color schemes you choose for the kitchen should complement the genre of country style that you have chosen. Cooler shades such as gray, muted green, and pale gray-blue indicate a more Scandinavian approach. Stronger tones, such as deep green-blue or oxblood red mixed with warm cherrywood, and a leaning toward the neat and tidy, indicate a Shaker-style kitchen. A more cluttered and colorful range of inspirational pictures, with a cottage garden feel and a diverse

range of colors, is in the English rural vein. Terra-cotta mixed with either green, red, yellow, or strong blue will hint at more distant shores and the warmth of the Mediterranean lands.

For a contemporary take on this old-fashioned style, and to avoid creating a pastiche, extract the elements that you like best and work around them. For example, warm colors and textures, especially those like the adobe walls of traditional south American homes, will suggest heat. Instead of putting your bottles of olive oil in the cupboard, leave them on a shelf. Pots of fresh basil and oregano on the window sill will provide a subtle hint, and some nice, clear-glass storage jars with various dried pastas will also allude to their country of origin.

Traditional kitchens

The last style is the traditional kitchen, which relies mainly on a longstanding, tried and tested formula. In its purest form this is a working kitchen like the semi-professional, but instead of taking stainless steel as its main feature, wood is dominant. The wood can be natural, painted, or even stained, and is mixed with other established materials and finishes, such as ceramic tiles. Slate, stone, and glass are also present.

In some cases, wood is simulated with modern materials and finishes to create a traditional appearance. MDF units can be routed to create a faux tongue and groove, and paintwork may be rubbed down in areas where, over time, signs of wear would naturally appear.

The basic traditional kitchen is once again a simply decorated room, but it is up to you to accessorize and embellish. However,

Above: A Scandinavian country setting—the main material is wood.

Opposite: Bright colors in a kitchen work well to soften the sometimes clinical look of modern design.

although this type of kitchen is meant to feel lived in, you should never let the amount of accessories you have get to a level where they begin to interfere with the functionality of the room.

Display and
storage

In a kitchen, storage should be allocated so that the items are close to the place where they will be used most often. For example, keep spices near the cooktop, where they will be shaken into dishes, and spatulas and wooden spoons near the work surface, where you stir ingredients.

Storing and displaying kitchen equipment

Kitchen cupboards are important areas for storing equipment, pots and pans as well as canned foods and drygoods, but there are also many display opportunities around the kitchen. A well-planned kitchen makes the most of these opportunities.

Storing utensils

In most kitchens, a number of frequently used utensils are kept out so that they are always to hand, so this inadvertently leads them to being on display. The way in which these things are contained or shown will depend on the style and decoration of kitchen that you have chosen, but here are a few suggestions. Spatulas, wooden spoons, and light wooden utensils can easily be kept upright in a glass, ceramic, or metal container that is positioned on a worktop.

Poles or rods and butchers' hooks are popular hanging options. You can use a wooden pole in a country or traditionally decorated kitchen, or steel in a more contemporary one. Butchers' hooks are S-shaped, made of

Storing pots and pans

Care should be taking when storing pots and pans. If you stack frying or shallow pans on top of one another, fold a double thickness of kitchen towel and place it between the two to prevent damage to the enamel or non-stick surface of the lower pan. Before storing woks and cast-iron pots, dry them thoroughly and brush over the surface lightly with cooking oil.

Opposite page: Butcher's hooks are used to hang steel utensils close to the cooktop, where they are used.

Right: Plates can be neatly stored away inside a drawer. Wooden dowels prevent the plates from moving around and getting broken.

Below right: Frequently used and stylish equipment can become part of your display.

steel, and come in two sizes—the large is big enough to support pots and pans, while the smaller size is ideal for hanging spoons, spatulas and whisks from.

When hanging heavier items, make sure that the rod is strong enough to support the weight. If you use a long rod that is holding heavy weights, then you may need to fasten a couple of extra support brackets to the wall or ceiling, along the rod.

If you want an alternative to a rod, then you can use a chain, which should be made of a strong metal with good-size links. The chain can be hung horizontally between two points, or cut in lengths that are individually hung and allowed to fall vertically.

Storage containers and units

Storage jars need not always be shut away in a cupboard. Think about displaying them on a shelf to add a decorative feature, and also to allow easy access to the items stored within them, such as tea, coffee, and sugar. Give such jars a sense of unity by choosing a matching set, such as steel and glass, or white ceramic containers. Glass containers are extremely good for display, as they show the contents from top to bottom.

Traditional wicker and reed baskets are fine for general storage, but they do tend to hide most of their contents behind their dense sides, so you should really only use baskets in cases

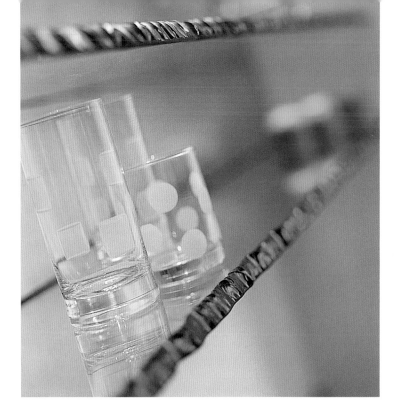

espresso coffee maker and a kettle are also fashionable kitchen equipment today.

The rule with this sort of kitchen accessory is that it should be both useful and beautiful. If you are leaving it on display, then make sure that you choose the nicest shape, the best finish and also the one that has the most interesting lines, because it will become part of the overall look of the kitchen.

Storing and displaying food

Fresh fruit and vegetables can bring a pleasant splash of color to a kitchen, and will also be a con-stantly changing embellishment as you replace what you have eaten from the display. To display fruit and vegetables well, look at open-weave metal baskets, which allow the fruit to show through and also breathe, and glass bowl containers. The disadvantage with glass bowls is that they restrict the airflow to the lower fruits, which means that they will ripen and rot much more quickly. Make sure that you use fruit and veg-etables within a few days, before they start to wrinkle or go moldy.

where you don't mind concealing from view whatever is contained within them.

Plate racks can be fitted inside a cupboard or on the wall over the work surface. These enable you to slot washed, flat tableware in between the sections in order to leave it there to dry (see Storing plates, page 272–3).

Displaying equipment

Although the clean worktop approach is advocated in modern kitchens, a few useful pieces of equipment can be left on show on the worktop to soften the edges

and provide the feeling of a lived-in space.

Salt and pepper mills are often placed on an open shelf so that they are easily accessible, because they are in constant use. Mills come in a variety of shapes and sizes, but a matching pair of chrome, glass, or wood pieces will look very appealing in any kitchen. Choose a pair that will go with your overall color scheme.

Classic pieces of equipment, such as the Philippe Starck Alessi juice squeezer, a cafetière, or French coffee percolator, are common show pieces. A compact

Wall writing paint effect

Painted lettering is a cheap and effective way of adding wit and humor to a wall. Writing in a foreign language always looks far more stylish than your mother tongue, and will also add a touch of glamor and mystery to something as mundane as a recipe. The writing is achieved by using cotton swabs and wet acrylic scumble glaze. If you are confident of your own handwriting style you can work freehand but for a neater, more controlled look use an overhead projector.

Materials

Pale blue latex (acrylic) for your base coat
Acetate projector paper
Acrylic scumble glaze in slate blue
Cotton swabs
Satin acrylic varnish

Tools

Paintbrush or roller
Computer
Marker pen
Soft-bristle brush
Overhead projector
Varnish brush

Preparing the surface

1 Apply the pale blue base coat to the wall with a brush or roller and leave it to dry.

Creating the acetate

2 Type out your chosen recipe on a computer using a suitable font, and print it out on acetate paper. Choose the font carefully so that it will look decorative without being overly fussy. Alternatively, you can handwrite onto the acetate using permanent marker pen, which is what we did here.

Apply the pale blue base coat over the whole wall, using a brush, or roller if you prefer.

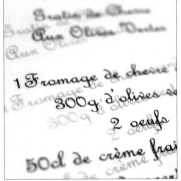

Type your recipe and print it out onto acetate paper, or write directly onto the acetate.

Transferring the recipe

3 Use a broad, soft brush to apply the scumble glaze to the prepared wall, using easy, random strokes.

4 Place the acetate sheet on the projector and adjust it so that the recipe fills the required wall space. Overhead projectors can be rented from most good tool rental firms. Work quickly, writing in the glaze with a cotton swab. Take a fresh swab as soon as the one you are using becomes clogged.

5 Once the writing has completely dried, protect the recipe wall by applying a coat of satin acrylic varnish, using a varnish brush.

With a broad, soft-bristle brush, apply the scumble glaze in random strokes to the wall.

With the writing on the acetate projecting onto the wall, write in the glaze with a cotton swab.

Once the writing is completely dry, protect the wall with a coat of satin acrylic varnish.

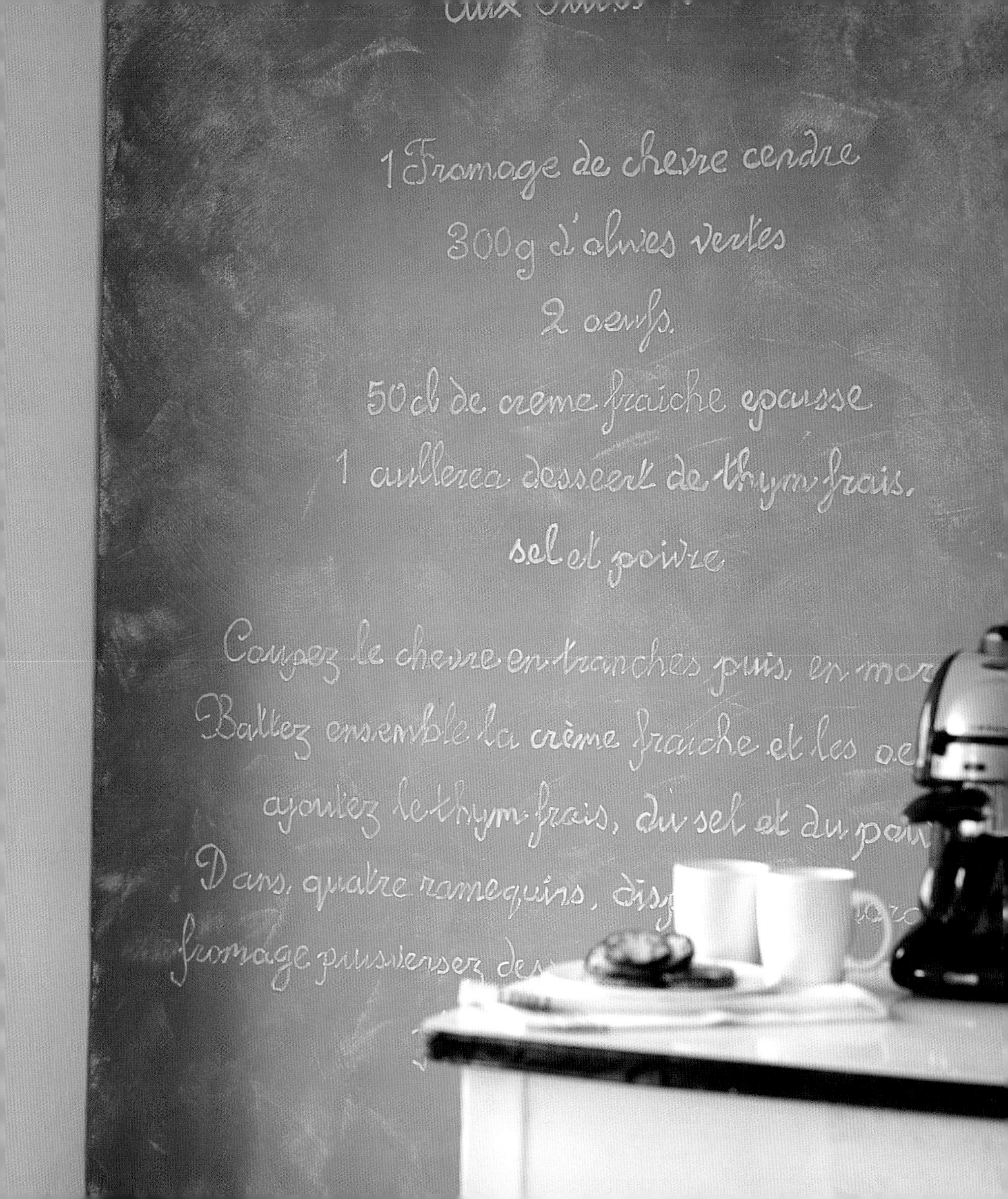

1 fromage de chèvre cendré

300g d'olives vertes

2 oeufs.

50cl de crème fraîche épaisse

1 cuillère à dessert de thym frais.

sel et poivre

Coupez le chèvre en tranches puis en mor

Battez ensemble la crème fraîche et les oe

ajoutez le thym frais, du sel et du poiv

Dans quatre ramequins, disp

fromage puis versez des

Wood veneer kitchen cabinets

Materials

Wood veneer
Contact adhesive
Mineral spirits
Yacht varnish
Knobs or handles of
your choice
Screws

Tools

Flexible sanding block
Pencil
Metal rule
Sharp utility knife
Adhesive spreader
Pile of books or
something similar
Cloth
Fine-grit silicon
carbide paper
Varnish brush
Drill and wood bit
Screwdriver

If you are fed up with your existing kitchen units or have inherited units that are not to your taste, you can modernize them in a number of ways. A simple way of giving plain flat doors a quick facelift is to stick thin wood veneer over the melamine-resin surface. The doors will look as if they are solid wood, and there is a huge variety of different veneers available.

Preparing the doors

1 Clean each melamine-resin door well to remove any grease and grime. Use a flexible sanding block to key the surface.

Cutting the veneer

2 Place each door face down on the sheet of veneer and, using a pencil, draw around the doors to mark their outlines on it.

3 Carefully cut out the veneer using a metal rule and a sharp utility knife (see picture bottom left, page 308). Handle the veneer with care—it is brittle and is easily marked.

Once you have cleaned the surface of the doors, use a sanding block to create a key.

Place each door in turn on top of the veneer, and draw around it with a pencil.

Know your materials

The best way to attach veneer panels is to use contact adhesive. This is a very pungent glue that should be used in a well-ventilated space. (Always wear a face mask for extra protection against fumes.)

Spread a thin layer evenly on each surface to be stuck, as the bond is instantly formed between the two layers. This means repositioning is impossible, so take care when placing the veneer on the door. Once stuck, apply even pressure over the whole surface to stop areas rising or bubbling—use heavy books or magazines, and leave for the manufacturer's recommended drying time.

Attaching the veneer

4 Spread a thin, even layer of contact adhesive over the front of one door and the back of its corresponding veneer, and allow to dry until just touch-dry. Carefully lower the veneer into place over the door. Accuracy is very important at this point, as the glue forms an instant bond, making it difficult to reposition the veneer. When in place, cover with a cloth to avoid marking the surface, and weigh the veneer down evenly with piles of books.

Finishing touches

5 When the front of the door is dry, cut thin lengths of veneer that are slightly wider than the sides of the doors. Spread both the door side and thin strip with glue, and stick the first one in place. Use a sharp utility knife to trim away the excess for a perfect fit (it is a good idea to use a new blade for each cut). Wipe away any residue of glue with a cloth dipped in a little mineral spirits, as it will mark the finish if left. Continue this process until you have covered all the doors.

Use a metal rule and sharp utility knife to carefully cut out the various pieces of veneer.

Cover the door and back of the veneer with contact adhesive, using an adhesive spreader.

Create thin strips of veneer to cover the door sides. Glue, stick in place, and trim to size.

6 Sand the veneer using fine-grit silicon carbide paper for a super-smooth finish, and wipe it down with a little mineral spirits (do not use water as this will cause the veneer to swell). Use a clean varnish brush to apply a thin layer of yacht varnish over the surface and sides of each door. Allow them to dry, and then sand lightly with silicon carbide paper before adding another two coats of varnish for an extra-hard finish.

7 Mark the position of your knobs or handles, then drill using a wood bit.

8 Screw the knobs in place. Hang the doors back up, and tighten the hinges.

Once you have created a smooth finish, apply a thin layer of yacht varnish to the veneer.

Mark the positions for your knobs or handles and drill the holes using a wood drill bit.

Screw all your chosen knobs into position on the doors before rehanging them.

Alternative

For a more industrial look, you can use a similar technique to cover existing cabinets in sheet metal. This is not inexpensive, and should only be considered if your cabinets are of high quality, and are still in good condition. For a really professional finish, it is best to take your cabinet doors to a specialized metal supplier who will be able to wrap the cabinet doors in thin metal sheet, to give a perfectly smooth finish. If you want to have a go at doing it yourself, get your choice of sheet metal cut to fit the front of the cabinet doors. A solid metal sheet can be stuck in place using contact adhesive applied to both surfaces. It should be weighed down until dry. If you have chosen a pierced design this method will not work, so you should use small tacks or screws to secure the metal sheets along the edges of the cabinet doors instead. Make sure that the metal you have chosen is rust-resistant—if in doubt, seal with clear lacquer varnish. Finish with knobs or handles.

Glass backsplash with tile design

Tempered glass provides a good alternative to tiles for a backsplash in a kitchen or bathroom. Glass suppliers can cut glass to your measurements and bevel or polish the edges to make it safe to handle. Ask for the glass to be drilled so that you can secure it in place. You can back the glass with the design of your choice. Here, we used a checkered aluminum leaf design.

Materials

Length of predrilled, tempered glass
Lining paper
Water-base gold size
Sheets of aluminum transfer leaf
Fine steel wool
Clear wax polish
Blue latex (acrylic) paint
Wall plugs
Mirror screws

Tools

Soft cloth
Scissors
Set square
Pencil
Small paintbrush
Drill
Masonry bit
Screwdriver

Preparing the glass

1 Clean the piece of glass thoroughly to be sure that there are no greasy marks on it, then polish with a soft cloth.

same size as the backsplash. Mark a grid of squares about the size of kitchen tiles with a set square and pencil. Make sure that there are no cuts in the design.

Designing the backing

2 Using a pair of scissors, cut a length of lining paper the

3 Place the glass backsplash carefully over the grid, making sure that all the edges line up exactly. Use the grid as a guide,

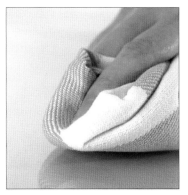

Clean the glass to remove all greasy marks and fingerprints, then gently polish with a soft cloth.

Using a paintbrush, apply a thin layer of water-base size over alternate squares on the glass.

Know your materials

Glass provides a hygienic, easy-to-clean alternative to tiles in both kitchens and bathrooms. Although it needs to be handled with care, glass is also extremely resilient when used correctly. A good glazier should be able to recommend the correct thickness for your project, and cut and drill it to the size that you require.

All interior glass must adhere to a safety code to prove that it is tempered for use in the home. It is important to ask for glass that has a polished or beveled edge, as this process removes any sharp edges.

and use a medium-small paintbrush to apply a thin layer of water-base size over each alternate square.

4 Allow the size to dry for the recommended time until it becomes clear. If necessary, cut the aluminum transfer leaf to the required size with a pair of sharp scissors. Apply the sheet of aluminum transfer leaf carefully to the size on the glass squares, making sure that it lines up exactly with the square that you have already marked on the lining paper.

Applying the transfer leaf

5 Rub the back of the sheet of aluminum transfer leaf carefully—you must make sure that it adheres firmly to the water-base size. Then gently peel off the backing paper, making sure that you leave the aluminum transfer leaf in place.

6 Dip a small piece of fine steel wool in a little clear wax polish, and use it to rub the aluminum transfer leaf gently. This action will lift away small areas of the transfer leaf, and will allow some of the backing to show through.

Apply a sheet of aluminum transfer leaf to the lining paper, making sure it adheres to the size.

Peel back the lining paper carefully, making sure that the transfer leaf remains in position.

With a piece of fine steel wool dipped in clear wax, rub the transfer leaf.

7 Using a small paintbrush, apply the blue latex (acrylic) paint over the back of each square of the aluminum leaf, and then allow the paint to dry.

Fixing the backsplash

8 Position the glass against the wall, and use a pencil to mark the drilling point. Use a masonry bit to drill a hole, and fill with a wall plug suitable for your wall. Screw the backsplash in place using a mirror screw with a chrome cap.

Paint the back of the transfer leaf with some blue latex (acrylic), and allow to dry.

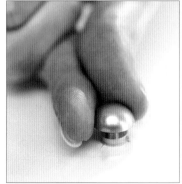

Finish by screwing the glass backsplash to the wall using mirror screws with chrome caps.

Alternative

To create a traditional tiled back-splash, you could use irregular, broken tiles or small mosaic tesserae cut with tile nippers to form organic patterns. You will need to start with a completely smooth, clean wall. Plan your design first by producing a sketch with colored pencils on graph paper. Use the direct mosaic method, which involves transferring your design directly onto the wall in pencil. Apply waterproof tile adhesive, buttering it onto the back of each tessera or tile fragment to build up the design one piece at a time. You will find it easiest to start by sticking down the pieces that form the outlines of the shapes, then fill in large blocks of color around them. Place whole tesserae first, then use tile nippers to cut smaller shapes to fit the design.

Using broken tiles or pieces of china is a good way to achieve a design on a budget. Place them in a strong plastic bag, or wrap them in a tea towel, and break them up with a hammer.

Recycled slate and zinc noticeboard

Materials

Slate roof shingles
Plywood
Abrasive paper
Slate gray paint
Sheet of galvanized metal
Contact adhesive
Screws
Roofing nails
Chalk
Kitchen string
Magnets

Tools

Pencil
Metal rule
Jigsaw
Medium paintbrush
Electric drill
Screwdriver
Tile adhesive spreader
Pair of gloves
Piece of wood
Small hammer

This stylish and useful noticeboard exploits the beautiful weathered finish of old roofing shingles, which make an ideal chalk board frame. Within the frame there is a zinc panel onto which postcards, recipes, invitations, and other stray pieces of paper can easily be attached with magnets. Let the roof shingles dictate the size of your noticeboard, so you don't have to cut them.

Measuring the frame

1 Work out the dimensions of the frame by laying out the slate roof shingles on the piece of plywood. With a pencil, draw around the shingles as a guide, then, using a long metal rule, measure $1/2$in (1cm) in and mark the frame.

2 Cut out the frame carefully with a jigsaw, and then sand with a piece of abrasive paper to remove any rough edges.

Painting the frame

3 Using a medium-size paintbrush, paint the entire frame with a couple of coats of slate

To measure the size of the frame, place the tiles on the plywood and then draw around them.

Using a jigsaw, carefully cut out the frame, then gently sand to get rid of any rough edges.

Know your tools

Power tools make most projects quicker and easier. If you do not own any, then it is a good idea to borrow them from a friend or rent them from a tool rental store. This will help you to get a feel for them before you invest in tools of your own. The most useful power tools are the jigsaw and screwdriver/drill.

Jigsaws have detachable blades that can cut various materials with accuracy. It is advisable to wear eye protection and a dust mask.

A combination electric screwdriver and drill is a dual-purpose tool. Detachable drill bits make holes of various sizes in different materials, and screwdriver bits can also be attached for speedy screwing. Pick a model that has a reverse action so you can unscrew with ease, too.

gray paint and allow to dry for a couple of hours.

4 Once the paint is dry, turn the frame over and place the sheet of galvanized metal over the hole —it should be large enough to overlap the edges of the hole by about 1in (2cm). Drill and then countersink a hole in each corner, and screw in place.

5 Using a tile adhesive spreader, spread some contact adhesive onto the front of the frame and also onto the back of the slate shingles. When using contact adhesive, always make sure you use gloves to protect your hands. Allow the adhesive to partially dry (it needs to be sticky in order to carry out the next step).

Paint the plywood frame with a couple of coats of slate gray paint, and allow to dry completely.

Using a screwdriver, screw the sheet of galvanized metal firmly in place.

Assembling the frame

6 When the adhesive is sticky, position the slate shingles onto the frame and press firmly in place with a piece of wood. Wear gloves to do this. Allow the adhesive to dry, then use a small hammer to tap a roofing nail through the holes in each shingle.

7 Attach a large piece of white or colored chalk to a medium piece of kitchen string or twine, and then tie the string around one of the roofing nails to secure in place.

8 The frame is now ready to be used. Using magnets of your choice, position postcards, recipe cards, pictures, and any other pieces of paper onto the frame.

Apply some contact adhesive to the back of the frame and the slate shingles, and allow to dry.

As soon as the adhesive is sticky, position the slate shingles on the frame and press in place.

With the shingles in place, tap a nail through the holes to attach them securely to the frame.

Alternative

As an alternative, you could create a stencil design on your kitchen noticeboard. In this dramatic piece, the elements of air, earth, and water are represented by doves, grapes, and fish. To make this, choose an appropriate size of ¹/₂in (12mm) MDF board. Use a mini roller and tray to apply two coats of blackboard paint or black flat latex. Leave to dry. Stencil a flock of doves at the top of the board. Place a grape-leaf stencil in the top left-hand corner. Stencil a bunch of grapes underneath and repeat two-thirds of the way down the board, then create the shoal of fish. To protect the pattern, gently brush on a coat of acrylic dead flat varnish using a nylon decorating brush. If you want to use different colors, experiment with variations in pearlized colors, such as jades, pinks, and silvers.

Lighting your kitchen

Task lighting that illuminates the work surfaces of a kitchen is a top priority—after all, this is the place where you will pour hot liquids and use sharp knives. But the kitchen may also be used as a dining area, so a softer, more ambient level of lighting will also be required.

Natural and artificial light

It is extremely important to provide effective lighting in every part of the kitchen. For general points about lighting design, see Effective lighting, page 187.

Using natural light

It used to be a rule that kitchen designers invariably put the sink in front of a window so that the person washing up had something to look out on, but with the advent of the dishwasher this is no longer a priority. Daylight is still a prized commodity, because its access and flow are usually restricted by wall-mounted units and machines. To get around this, an increasing number of people are putting vinyl or glass roof panels and windows in the

Right: A large window can be an asset in a kitchen because it allows plenty of natural light in. An adjustable shade will help soften the light if it is too bright.

Above: Fiberoptic lighting set into the glass work surface and lower edge of the cabinets gives a constant level of light over the whole area.

kitchen ceiling. This is a perfect solution in an extension or single-storey dwelling.

In an apartment block or house with upper levels over the kitchen it is often not possible to carry out this sort of improvement, so other choices have to be explored. Shiny surfaces are good at reflecting light, but they can be hard to keep in good condition. Pale and white-based colors will help, as will tidy worktops. By keeping clutter to a minimum, you will make your room appear lighter.

Window treatments can also contribute. Choose shades or

sheer curtains that can be pulled back, rather than heavy window dressings, which restrict light and may also be a haven for grime.

Artificial light

An overall ambient light is use-ful—when first entering the kitchen, it will give you a general view and be adequate for a simple assignment. To work within the kitchen you will need task lights that focus a steady and even beam of light on the work surface.

Task lighting is usually posi-tioned under the lower edge of wall-mounted units, and should run the length of the unit in order to allow the light to be distributed across the whole lower surface.

Spotlights or recessed ceiling lights provide a good level of light over large areas such as an island or cooktop area. This type of light needs to be carefully positioned and angled to avoid the beam casting a shadow of the person over the work area. Pendant lighting is also a useful addition if placed over an eating area.

Light fixtures, switches, and accessories

Under-unit lights are often small strip lights. Fluorescent tubes were once the main source of light here, but now mains-voltage halogen tubes are more popular.

For pendant and wall lights, it is best to avoid shades that are delicate and fragile, because they are difficult to clean, while metal, enamel, glass, and ceramic can be easily washed down.

If the kitchen is a large room or a kitchen/dining space, it may be worth having two or three different circuits of lights with individual switches. Then you can turn off the main kitchen lights but leave an ambient lighting level in the dining area. It is also a good idea to have a switch by the main door that turns off all the lights.

Left: This lighting feature at the base of an island unit faces toward the dining area and creates an unusual display in the evening.

Below: The linear lighting along the side walls illuminates the worktop from both sides, rather than from directly overhead. This type of lighting will mean that you can avoid casting shadows over food while you work.

Kitchen accessories

These are mainly practical pieces of equipment that are constantly on display in a kitchen. This could be because they are frequently used and need to be easily accessed, or because they are bulky, heavy, and difficult to store and retrieve. Where possible, keep kitchen accessories off the worktops, as they will restrict the amount of surface you have to work on, and may also become splattered with ingredients when you are preparing food. Store your utensils and equipment in good working order so that they are always ready for use. If items are left out long-term, cover them with a cotton cloth or washable cover to protect the working parts from general kitchen grease and condensation. Small items such as knives should be kept in a knife block or on a wall-mounted magnetic strip, as leaving sharp knives in drawers can be dangerous. Wooden spoons and spatulas can be kept in a ceramic or metal holder, with the handles down and the ladle or paddle section up so that it is easy to identify each one.

Clockwise from top left:

Retro-style products, such as these chrome pieces, look as though they are vintage, but are in fact manufactured to the highest modern standards.

Traditional wooden chopping boards are still very popular. You should have separate ones for cutting different types of food such as raw red meats, chicken, onions, garlic, and fruit, so that tastes, aromas, and enzymes don't transfer.

Clean, sparkling glassware is attractive and may be left on display, but be aware that it could become smudged and marked if left too close to a range.

Items that are in daily use, such as a toaster, may be left on the work surface for easy access.

Lever faucets are very easy to turn on when you have sticky hands.

It is best to keep all your knives in a wooden knife block, out of harm's way.

Stainless-steel utensils can be hung from a simple rack near to where they will be used.

This old butcher's block has seen many years of use, but is still a welcome addition and feature in most styles of kitchen.

Copper pans are treasured by professional chefs because the metal conducts heat quickly, but they must be kept well polished if they are to be left on show.

A draining rack or surface is extremely useful positioned next to a sink.

Store like things with like so that you automatically know where they are. For example, place teapots beside the cups and saucers, as you will need them all at the same time.

Colored glassware adds a quite unexpected decorative element in a practical environment.

Simple handles are best in a kitchen, because they are easy to hold and pull when your hands are wet or greasy. They are also easy to wipe clean.

Pepper and salt mills do not need to look mundane. Choose one that echoes the style of your kitchen.

Bathrooms

Planning your
bathroom

The bathroom is more than just a place to carry out your daily washing and cleaning tasks—it doubles as a sanctuary of rest and relaxation into which you can withdraw after a busy day, a place in which you can unwind and pamper yourself.

Above: Unusual faucets can give a sense of style to the bathroom.

Left: Bathrooms planned on a linear scheme, so that all the main appliances run along one wall, make the best use of long, narrow spaces.

Opposite page: In an en-suite bathroom ventilation is very important so that humidity is quickly and efficiently expelled.

Planning your space

The bathroom needs to be an adaptable space, with chameleon qualities. A well-designed bathroom should be a bright, invigorating, and high-speed cleansing space in the morning, but also a calming, tranquil oasis for a soak in the bathtub later in the day. So, planning the design, layout, and decoration of a bathroom is important.

First, identify your needs. If you prefer a shower, fit a separate shower stall into the bathroom or another space, and leave the bathtub-only bathroom as a back-up or visitors' facility. If you have a limited amount of space in the bathroom, plumb the shower in over the bathtub to provide a two-in-one resource.

Where possible, try to alleviate the pressure on a single bathroom with the sole toilet by installing another toilet and a small bathroom sink elsewhere, perhaps in a hall cupboard. Sinks can be installed into bedrooms, and even self-contained shower stalls may be plumbed into an alcove or a wardrobe space in the bedroom to take more pressure off the main bathroom.

When planning the layout and design of your bathroom, first find out and locate the following

services, because the plumber is bound to ask. Where is the access to mains water and drains? What is your tank capacity, and where is it situated?

Family bathrooms or main bathrooms need to be practical and easy to maintain. They are busy rooms where steam and damp are present daily, so good ventilation is important. Ventilation can be provided by gadgets such as a panel fan, which is inserted in a window, or ducts recessed into a false ceiling—this will disperse the dampness, as well as preventing mold from growing on grout or the shower curtains.

An effective bathroom layout

The main bathroom should be planned so that there is space to move without bumping into things. The layout of traditional bathrooms is usually worked out around the largest piece of fitted furniture, the bathtub.

The bathtub is often plumbed in at the far end of the room, with its longest side running parallel to the longest wall. At the foot of the bathtub is the toilet, and beside that the sink. The sink and toilet are usually located nearest the door, as they are used most often. This linear layout provides a corridor of space in front of each item.

Safety features

Light switches need to be carefully positioned to comply with building regulation codes. Standard panel switches should be installed on the outer wall, not in the bathroom. If the switch is in the bathroom it should be activated by a string pull from a socket set into the ceiling. The lights themselves should be contained in sealed units.

Only use electrical appliances that are specifically designed for use in a bathroom, such as designated shaver sockets.

Nonslip mats and textured tape strips that adhere to the base of the bathtub are ideal for households with young children or older people. For children's safety, place medicines and cleaning agents in a wall-mounted cupboard with a childproof catch on the door.

In a square room the bathtub could be along one wall, with the toilet and sink opposite, leaving the third wall free for the door, and the fourth for storage space or a shower.

Space-saving ideas

There are two types of bathroom suite—floorstanding and wall-hung. With floorstanding units, the sink, toilet, and bidet are mounted on coordinating pedestal bases, while with wall-hung items, the fixtures are attached directly to the wall, which leaves the floor space much more clear.

Wall-hung items can make a small room feel more spacious because of the empty floor area— also you can allow for some overlap, which may just help you squeeze in an extra item. For example, a sink can overlap with the edge of the tank of the toilet, or it can edge out over the end of the bath.

The small, modern tanks now made for toilets mean that you can hide the unprepossessing water container behind a wall panel or a tongue-and-groove section, so that it is not on view. With a panel, marble slab, or any such covering, it will, however, be necessary to make a section removable to gain access to the tank.

Another option is to mount the sink on or in a cupboard, which provides extra storage space, too. The sink can rest on top of the surround or surface, or it can even be countersunk.

En-suite bathrooms

The en-suite bathroom has also risen in popularity. This linked facility provides a direct connection to the bedroom. In some older homes, people sacrifice a second bedroom or study to have the luxury of this extra bathroom, and in modern apartments and houses it is often standard in the main bedroom.

En-suite bathrooms are often linked to, or part of, a dressing room or wardrobe area, and in these cases the decorative theme can take a lead from the bedroom and continue into the bathroom, thus keeping a common or complementary color and pattern theme.

If space is at a premium, consider sliding doors instead of conventional opening doors between the bedroom and this space. Sliding doors or panels take up less space, and can be made with an opaque section at the top so that natural light from the bedroom can filter through to the bathroom, making it feel more light and spacious.

Wet rooms

Another recent trend is for wet rooms. These are small or modest-sized rooms that are completely tanked and tiled. A waterproof liner must be installed before tiling, and a gentle slope built into the floor so that the water will drain away easily through a single outlet. Wet rooms are large showers without the restrictions of doors, curtains, or panels. They can also be fitted with steam attachments so that they can double up as a steam room. In this type of setting it is common to

find a small wooden stool or built-in, tiled bench area so that the bather can relax in the warm, moist environment.

Decoration and style

A bathroom is a private space where you can indulge your fantasies and decorate in a style that gives you pleasure.

Practical decorating

Whatever style of decoration you choose, make sure that you bear in mind the practicalities of

Above: Double sinks can streamline morning preparation time for a busy working couple.

Opposite page: In a wet room you can install a bench along one wall, and then cover it with tiles.

cleaning and the main purpose of the space. A quantity of fancy or ornate decorative objects will be time-consuming to clean, and thick-pile carpet will be difficult to sweep thoroughly. There are specially designed acrylic carpets, but this is a floor

Left: A timeless, classic rolltop bath-tub, with central faucet and over-flow, here rests on a rich, blue-ceramic-tiled floor.

Opposite page: The mint-green color used here adds a fresh touch to this contemporary white and stainless steel bathroom.

Aroma and texture

The bathroom is a place where aroma and texture play an important role. Scented candles and bath oils can add to the pleasure and therapeutic effect of a bath, so choose scents associated with relaxation such as lavender, camomile, mandarin, and orange. In the mornings, shower gels with citron, bergamot, lime, rosemary, mint or pine essence will help to invigorate you.

Texture, in the form of towels, is also important next to naked skin—for a gentle, calming rubdown, use deep-pile toweling, but for a stimu-lating and speedy dry, waffle cotton or linen towels are a good choice.

covering that is best avoided for the bathroom.

Good ventilation is paramount because the fabrics stored and displayed, such as curtains, upholstered furniture, and clothes, can be ruined by steam and damp. This also applies to linen cupboards or storage where towels and bedding are kept, as warmth and damp can give rise to mildew.

Waterproof and water-resistant materials play a major role in bathroom décor. These used to focus on the standard ceramic tiles and mirror, vinyl paints, and papers, as well as reinforced glass, but some industrial materi-als have also made their way into this domestic setting.

Stainless steel is now used to form bathtubs and sinks, as well

as panels and shower trays. Polyurethane sheets, even corru-gated as in the roofing building material, can make an unusual panel for the side of a bathtub, or even a sturdy and interesting door for a shower stall.

Acrylic, fiberglass, and resin mixes are used in the construc-tion of preformed units, such as the all-in-one sink and surround, or bathtub with integral shelf or wide lip around the perimeter. Materials once regarded as cold and uncomfortable in the bath-room have also had a reprieve—radiant heat makes stone, and even marble, a viable floor cover-ing in this space.

Tiles have also developed from the plain-colored square or those with a transfer motif. Today there is a considerable interest in mosaic, whether laid randomly in a mixture of several shades of one color, or pictorially. There are metallic and iridescent finishes, tiles with insets of metal and relief patterns, and encaustic tiles with flat, matte finishes, all available in a wide variety of shapes and sizes.

Large sheets of tempered glass are now very popular as backsplashes around sinks and bathtubs. Curved, opaque glass panels are used to create shower stalls and sinks. Wood that has been specially dried and finished for

bathroom use is also gaining recognition—it has long been used in saunas and spas, because it adds a warm and earthy element to what could otherwise be a cool and clinical room.

Using color

The color scheme that you use in your bathroom is a personal choice, but blues and greens are generally regarded as appropriate watery colors, reminiscent of sea, sky, lagoons, and other aqueous features. Yellows and oranges are bright and warm, while deep

colors can be dramatic and indulgent in a bathroom setting. Although colored bathroom suites were all the rage during the 1960s and 70s, there has been a return to white ceramic, which is fresh, clean, and adaptable. White bathroomware is also safe—it will work with every color, and is compatible with every style or theme.

Indulgent-style bathrooms

Traditional indulgent bathrooms can follow a period style, with features such as a rolltop bathtub, a 19th-century sink on a pedestal with an integral decorative backsplash and shell-like soap recesses, and a high-flush toilet with wall-mounted tank. These items are all available, either as reproductions or secondhand through antiques merchants and specialized firms.

To create an indulgent traditional style, look at 19th- and early 20th-century interiors—dark wood and rich colors were in vogue then. Art Deco style, with its angular shapes and black, white, and chrome schemes, can also be attractive and opulent, or you could go back to the founding fathers of the bathing culture and study Roman references, with details such as mosaics and sunken bathtubs. Your bathroom

could also be inspired by the style of other countries and cultures. For example, Turkish and Moorish civilizations made great use of colorful and decorative ceramic tiles. Turkish steam baths are found in a number of countries, and many are decorated with blue, white, green, and brown tiles in delightful, geometric designs. Moorish tile work, patterned and colorful, can be seen in homes in southern Spain and north Africa.

Modern indulgent schemes tend to be more streamlined than traditional styles—lighting plays an important part in creating the indulgent mood, as will the accessories. The finish and fixtures should be luxurious, as the setting will be plain.

Streamline-style bathrooms

In a traditional streamlined bathroom, the basic furniture designs may still allude to an historical period. But in this case, the room will be decorated with lighter, brighter colors, and adequate storage will make sure that surfaces are left clean, uncluttered, and easy to wipe down. Additional furniture will be kept to a minimum, and the layout be designed especially to assist quick and efficient use. However, in the evening, lights can be dimmed,

candles lit, and the atmosphere will change to one of indulgence and relaxation.

The modern streamlined bathroom is almost clinical in its efficiency and minimal lines. The materials used are businesslike and utilitarian, and there are absolutely no fancy frills or floral prints. This is a place where morning ablutions are carried out

at top speed, and there may be a floor area where an exercise mat or equipment is used. In the evening, this space can be made softer by dimming lights and putting aromatherapy oils in the bathtub or steam shower, but it will retain its minimal, uncluttered appearance, creating a restful and undemanding environment in which to unwind.

Bathroom fixtures

The first elements of your bathroom that you need to plan are the fixtures. Be aware of plumbing and space limitations as you make these plans.

Bathtubs

There is a wide variety of different styles to choose from. Bathtubs are usually plumbed along one wall. If, however, your room is spacious, you may have a freestanding bathtub in the center of the room. A freestanding bathtub is luxurious, giving a feeling of opulence simply by taking up so much room. However, with a freestanding bathtub the plumbing and waste pipes must be laid under the floor, as they cannot be run along a wall.

Sunken bathtubs are an alternative. You will need to consult a professional if you plan to install this type of feature.

Jacuzzi, whirlpool, and spa baths are luxurious choices for those who like to spend many hours soaking in a bathtub. Again, these systems need to be installed by a professional.

There are also smaller than standard bathtubs—these half or Sitz baths are popular in Europe. The Sitz bath is designed so that it is short but deep, with a step or seat cast into the center. The half bath is a compromise, but with a shower overhead, it can be used as a deep shower tray or an occasional, rather than regular, bathing place.

Bathroom sinks

The sink that you choose should complement the style of bath that you select. Sinks come in a wide range of different styles, either floor- or wall-mounted. A popular shape for the contemporary bathroom is like a large bowl, which sits on a support. Sinks are also available in different materials, such as wood, which has to be treated so that it doesn't warp or bow when it comes into contact with water.

In small or second bathrooms you can use rinse sinks—these are just large enough to be used

for handwashing or rinsing teeth, but not hairwashing. There are certain styles that have an integral return or backsplash, so tiling is unnecessary.

Showers and screens

If you don't have a preformed shower stall or a shower built into a corner with two tiled walls, a static glass panel, and a glass door, then there are a number of screen options available.

For a shower over a bathtub you could choose a static screen, standard or bifold doors, or a series of sliding panels. These will be made from textured plastic or tempered glass. To make these screens watertight, there needs to be a flexible rubber seal along the bottom edge of the section that meets with the bathtub.

For a freestanding bathtub in the center of a room or a corner bathtub, a separate screen or screens makes a sensible option. The showers for these bathtubs can either be ceiling-mounted or on a stand or rod that comes up from the center of the faucet.

Another possibility is a ring, like a mosquito-net arrangement, suspended from the ceiling. Curtains are suspended from it, and the bottom edge of the plastic liner is tucked inside the edge of the bathtub so the water is contained.

There are a number of standard fixtures that can be fastened between two opposite walls, or a straight wall and an adjacent one. The basic shower rack fixture is either straight (to be attached to facing walls), or L-shape (so that it can be attached around a bathtub with access to adjacent walls).

The simplest of these fixtures is a telescopic, extendible tube with suckers at each end. You simply pull out the pole until it is the right length for the gap, lock in place, and then slide it into position on the wall—no nails or screws are required. The other option is the fixed rod, which will need to be secured with screws.

Toilets and bidets

An unlikely area for decoration, one that should not be ignored, is the toilet seat. The standard seat is a dull, plain, plastic rim protector and lid, and the classic version is of polished wood, which provides a warmer and more comfortable surface to sit on.

The current vogue is for more decorative finishes on toilet seats, and these range from gimmicks, with beer or wine labels suspended in clear, solid plastic, to photographic images, such as tropical flowers, or even materials such as marble or granite on a plastic or resin surround.

Another item of bathroom furniture, which is popular throughout Europe, is the bidet. This is an underrated piece of equipment, which can be useful in households where there are young children or elderly people who find a bath or shower too difficult. It can also provide an effective footbath for refreshing your feet at the end of a long day.

Faucets and other fixtures

In the modern bathroom the faucets and other fixtures are an

Above: Bathroom design is now focusing more on style and aesthetic appeal than just utility. This fine wood sink and elegant chrome stand are an interesting sculptural feature for a bathroom, as well as being somewhere to wash.

Opposite page: This polished slate panel acts as a backsplash, as well as a surround for the wall-mounted faucets and spout.

Top: Many contemporary bathrooms feature sinks that are styled just like bowls sitting on a tabletop or surround.

Above: The sandstone walls used here mellow the sleek look created by the stainless-steel fittings.

Opposite: Ladder-style, wall-hung radiators not only heat the bathroom, but also double as a towel rack.

important part of the overall design. They make a statement, because the rest of the fixtures and fitments, and the general decoration are usually very simple and plain.

Among contemporary designs there are many faucets that have utilitarian roots, for example, the lever. This simple metal paddle, which is connected to the spout or water faucet, has been refined from the originals found in industrial washrooms and at hospital sinks.

Faucets have also migrated away from the sink surround, and are now likely to be wall-mounted directly above the sink and accompanied by the spout, which arches gracefully at the end.

In the traditional-style bathroom, there are a number of choices for the arrangement of faucets and related hardware, but the accepted layout in this setting consists of separate hot and cold faucets with a single mixer spout, and a plug or stopper. The classic faucet design is the cross bar, which often comes with ceramic hot and cold discs.

The modern bathroom pares down this equipment and can be as minimal as a lever with an integral spout, with the waste lever included in the back of the spout arch.

In contemporary bathrooms, these fixtures are most often in chrome, but in the traditional bathroom brass is an option. These days, many reproduction brass faucets have a lacquered finish, which means that the shine on the metal stays bright and does not need to be polished.

Towel racks

Another element of bathroom fixtures is the towel rack, which now falls into the useful and beautiful category. Towel racks have gone from being a necessity to being a star feature in the bathroom, with a wide selection of attractive designs to choose from.

There is also an amazing variety of heated towel racks available. The most popular style is the wall-mounted ladder, which supplies heat and provides a place on which to hang towels. These come in a variety of colors and finishes, and have horizontal bars grouped in sections of varying widths.

Another design is the S or snake. This can be either attached to the wall so that it is fastened in position, or on brackets so that it can be swung out at a right-angle to the wall. Make sure that the towel rack is not positioned where you may brush against it while drying and burn yourself.

Framed mosaic backsplash panel

Materials

Waterproof plywood
Abrasive paper
Bonding agent
Sheets of mosaic tiles
Grout
L-shape trim
Panel adhesive
Walnut satin varnish

Tools

Metal rule
Pencil
Jigsaw
Tile adhesive
Paintbrush
Notched spreader
Sponge
Flexible spreading tool
Soft cloth
Small paintbrush
Miter cutter
C-clamp
Abrasive paper

This mosaic panel is an attractive alternative to tiled walls, and can be positioned behind a bathtub or sink, or simply hung on the wall like a picture. Any type of mosaic tile can be used—we chose an unusual, iridescent glass mosaic, which catches the light beautifully. Although the materials of the panel are quite pricey, one of its main advantages is the fact that it is portable, meaning it can be repositioned with ease. You can choose a trim to complement your design—we chose a wooden frame stained with a dark walnut varnish that offsets the pale colors of the tiles.

Preparing the panel

1 First, plan the size of the mosaic panel carefully so that you can avoid cutting any mosaic tiles. With a long metal rule and a pencil, mark out the dimensions of the panel onto a sheet of plywood, making sure you allow for a border trim all the way around the panel.

Using the mosaic tiles as a guide, mark the dimensions of the panel onto the plywood.

Using a notched spreader, spread tile adhesive evenly over the sealed sheet of plywood.

2 Cut out the panel using a jig-saw and then, using a piece of abrasive paper, sand to remove any rough edges from it.

3 Seal it with a solution of two parts bonding agent to one part water, and allow to dry.

4 Using a notched spreader, apply a layer of tile adhesive to the sealed sheet of plywood (see picture bottom right, page 340). Wear gloves when you do this.

Attaching the mosaic tiles

5 Place the sheets of tiles face-down into the adhesive, pressing them firmly to make sure that they adhere to the panel. Allow the mosaics tiles to dry overnight.

6 Use a wet sponge to thoroughly soak the paper backing of the mosaics. Allow the water to sink in for a few minutes before peeling away the backing.

7 With a flexible spreading tool, force the grout well into the gaps between the tiles. Wipe away any excess grout, then allow it to dry completely.

8 Polish the mosaic tiles with a soft cloth until they shine.

9 Using a miter cutter, cut an L-shape trim to form the frame, stick it in position with some panel adhesive, and clamp it in place until dry. Color the frame with a varnish or stain of your choice.

Know your tools

Having a set of good-quality clamps is essential for many woodworking projects, as they hold glued joints together, exerting pressure until the glue has dried enough to form a strong bond. (These clamps are most often known as C-clamps.)

The miter cutter used in this particular project is the type often used by picture framers. It allows for fine adjustments of the blade, so making sure of a perfect angled cut. Miter cutters can be bought from all home-improvement stores.

Place the mosaic tiles carefully onto the tile adhesive, and press them firmly into place.

Soak the paper backing of the tiles, then let the water sink in before peeling off the backing.

Using a flexible spreading tool, force the grout well into the gaps between the mosaic tiles.

Wipe away any grout, allow to dry, and then polish the tiles with a soft cloth until they shine.

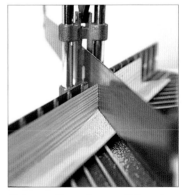

Using a miter cutter, carefully cut an L-shape trim to fit around the border of the panel.

Alternative

If you prefer to tile directly onto your bathroom wall first be sure that your wall is perfectly smooth, and that the surface has been sealed with bonding adhesive.

Mosaic tiles are usually supplied with paper or mesh backing, which enables you to work with squares of about 1ft (30cm) at a time. If you are tiling behind an existing sink, it is advisable to start in the bottom right-hand corner and work your way along and then up. If you are tiling an entire wall, then use a level wood strip tacked to the wall as a guide. Always order 10 percent more tiles than you think you need, to allow for mistakes or breakages. If you are using blends of more than one color, it is wise to mix the sheets up well to be sure of a good color mix.

When your tiles are hung and grouted, you should seal the gap between any bathroom furniture and tiles with silicone sealant. This will form a flexible watertight seal between the fixtures and the tiled surface.

Exotic fabric shower curtain

Shower curtain designs only seem to cater for lovers of shiny plastic with wacky or nautical themes—there are few that add instant glamor to your bathroom. This painted organza shower curtain is both pretty and practical, as it is backed with clear vinyl. The two materials are joined at the top, allowing you to separate them so you can shower with the plastic layer inside the bathtub or shower stall, while the delicate fabric remains dry on the outside. For added glitz, we used iridescent fabric paint to attach small glass and diamanté beads all over the surface of the fabric.

Materials

Organza fabric
Clear vinyl
Ribbon
Curtain weight
Iridescent fabric paint/glue
Small glass beads
Small diamanté gems
Curtain rings

Tools

Pins
Tailor's chalk
Metal rule
Scissors
Sewing machine (or needle and thread for hand-sewing)
Hole puncher
Riveting tool
Eyelets

Measuring the shower curtain

1 Measure the drop (this is the distance from your shower curtain pole down to the floor) and then add about 1in (2cm) to allow for the hem. Pin both materials together, making sure that the clear vinyl is on top. Next, use tailor's chalk and a long metal

Using a pair of sharp scissors, cut the material carefully along the marked straight line.

Pin the length of ribbon along the bottom of the material, and sew in place to form a channel.

Know your tools

Clear vinyl sheet is sold in fabric stores, and is often used as a table covering but is just as suitable for a shower curtain.

Organza is a lightweight material woven from metallic threads, which gives it a shimmering quality as it catches the light. It is quite slippery, making it tricky to sew. Set the tension on your machine to a setting suitable for lightweight fabrics, and use a needle designed for metallic thread. When sewing the layers of vinyl and organza, it is best to practice on some scrap pieces until you find the ideal tension settings.

rule to mark a straight line, and then cut the material to the required length using a pair of sharp scissors.

Sewing the shower curtain

2 Turn over the bottom edge of the material and press down on it to flatten it. Next, use a sewing machine set on a medium straight stitch, or a needle and thread to sew a length of ribbon along it (see picture bottom right, page 345). This will then form a channel along the bottom of the material.

3 Cut a length of curtain weight and feed this through the channel. Secure the curtain weight with a couple of small

stitches by hand at each end. Carefully trim the sides of the shower curtain.

4 Turn over the top edge of the shower curtain material and once again press down on it. Then cut another length of ribbon to fit over it. Make a sandwich of the ribbon, organza, and vinyl material, and pin them all carefully in place. Stitch along the top and bottom of them with the sewing machine set on a medium straight stitch. Alternatively, use a needle and thread.

Decorating the shower curtain

5 Using an iridescent fabric paint or glue, attach some small glass beads and diamanté

Cut a suitable length of lightweight curtain weight and thread through the ribbon channel.

Turn over the top edge of the curtain and stitch together the ribbon, organza, and vinyl.

Using an iridescent fabric glue, attach some diamanté gems and glass beads to the curtain.

gems to the organza. Because it
will come in contact with a lot of
water, make sure that the fabric
glue is waterproof.

Attaching the
shower curtain

6 Use the hole puncher to make
holes at even intervals along
the top of the curtain.

7 Using the riveting tool, fit
small eyelets into each of
these holes.

8 Thread the curtain rings
through the eyelets, and hang
the shower curtain from the
shower rod. We used rings with
decorative glass droplets here,
to provide an extra-glamorous
finishing touch.

*Make holes at even intervals along
the top of the shower curtain with
the hole puncher.*

*Use the riveting tool to fit the small
eyelets along the top of the shower
curtain.*

*Thread the curtain rings through the
eyelets, and then hang the shower
curtain from the rod.*

Alternative

Simple, recessed shower stalls with sleek glass doors look particularly effective in contemporary surroundings, where a fussy shower curtain would look out of place. Many homes have a cupboard or alcove that could be transformed into a showering area. Take advice from a reliable plumber, who will guide you through the process. Ventilation and ease of running pipes to the site are the most important things to take into consideration. It may also be worth installing a pump to increase the water pressure.

To make the area watertight you need to install a shower tray, or tile the floor area and add drainage. For the walls use conventional ceramic, mosaic or stone tiles (or consider wateproof lining panels in a number of different materials, including masonite or glass).

If you cannot find a ready-made glass door for your alcove, many bathroom manufacturers will be able to make a frame and door to your requirements.

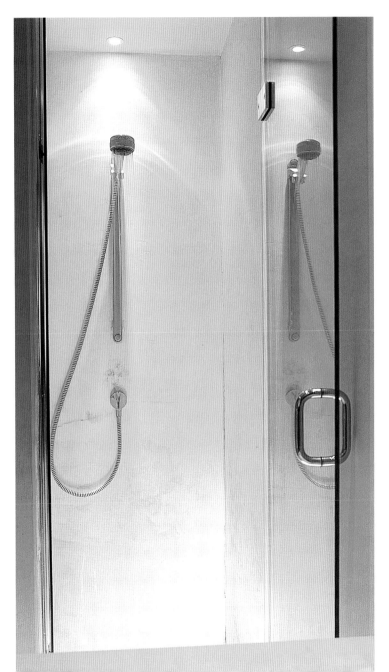

Recycled glass bead curtain

Materials

Glass beads
Strong bead wire
Crimping beads
Doweling
Silver spray paint
Wood drill bit
Two long nails
Metal washers

Tools

Pliers or scissors
Handsaw
Pencil
Drill
Tack hammer

Bead curtains make a delicate alternative to lace or voile curtains, and catch the light beautifully. Their moisture resistance makes them an ideal choice in the bathroom. We chose beautiful recycled beads in watery shades of blue and green. It is important to be sure that your wire or string is strong enough to support the weight of your beads. We used a fine-gauge, heavy-duty wire and small crimping beads to hold the glass beads in place, and hung the strands from doweling or a metal pole.

Measuring the drop

1 Measure your window or doorway to work out the exact number of bead strands that you will need for the curtain. Next, work out the necessary drop or length that each strand should be, and then cut the appropriate number of lengths of wire using your pliers or a pair of scissors.

Threading the beads

2 Use a glass bead in order to anchor the bottom of each

Cut out the number of lengths of wire that you will need with scissors or pliers.

Anchor the bottom of each length of wire with a glass bead. Secure it with a crimping bead.

Know your materials

Spray paint is available in a wide range of different colors and finishes. It is ideal for providing even paint coverage, and is often used for stenciling. Hold the can at a sufficient distance from the surface you are painting, and do not attempt to put too much paint on at any one time, or you will end up with runs and drips. Make sure the area around the item is well masked, because spray paint can travel into the smallest of areas. Use only in well-ventilated conditions, and always wear a safely mask when using it.

Thread all your beads on a piece of wire, and use a crimping bead to secure the last one.

Once you have cut the piece of doweling to length, spray it with silver spray paint.

Measure and drill holes in the doweling for the lengths of bead to be suspended from.

length of wire, threading it through a loop and then securing a crimping bead with pliers to hold it in place.

3 Thread the remaining beads in place. While doing this, you can either build up a pattern, or use them completely randomly. When you reach the end of the bead string, use a crimping bead to hold the last glass one in place.

Preparing the doweling

4 Use a handsaw to cut the doweling to the length that you require.

5 Use a spray can to apply a coat of silver paint to the doweling, and allow it to dry.

Attaching the strings

6 Mark the position of the bead strings at intervals along the strip of doweling. Grip the doweling in a vise, and drill the required holes using a wood bit.

7 Thread different-shape beads onto a slim nail, and then tap the nail into the end of the doweling with a tack hammer to form a finial. Do the same at the other end of the doweling.

8 Anchor the bead strings by feeding them through the hole in the doweling, add a metal washer, then loop the wire around a small glass bead and hold in place with a crimping bead. Fix the doweling and brackets in place on the wall.

Thread beads on a thin nail, and then hammer it into the end of the doweling as a finial.

Once the bead strings are in place, attach a metal washer and crimping bead to secure.

Alternative

When it comes to screening windows and doors, anything goes. You could combine traditional wooden slatted shades with an elaborately decorated sheer curtain to create a multilayer effect. Dress the curtain by stitching decorative beads or mirror pieces at random intervals, or attach tasseled hems along its lengths. The light will be reflected off these decorative features back into the room.

Use your imagination to come up with your own ideas when dressing windows. You could use any material that can be attached to a length of string or wire. For a hi-tech solution, try shiny compact discs threaded onto strong nylon—their shiny surface reflects colored prisms onto the walls of the room. For a whimsical, nautical look, try decorating with shells, sand dollars, and small pebbles gathered from the beach. Use a small drill bit on a low speed to drill holes in shells carefully. Use rustic garden twine to complete the look.

Lighting your
bathroom

Bathroom lighting needs to be focused on individual areas—for example, the mirror over the sink where shaving or makeup application takes place. There should also be lighting focused on a shower stall or bathtub so that you can see gels, soaps, and shampoos.

Planning your lighting

For general points about lighting design, see Effective lighting, page 187. Lighting in a bathroom needs to be located so that it focuses on the needs and moods of the person using the space. In the morning and evening, good lighting above or around the mirror is a priority for shaving, applying makeup, and cleaning.

Practical lighting

Even if there is a good-size window in the room, you will most probably need additional electric lighting. This can be provided by targeted spot or task lights on the ceiling that are directed onto the mirror in front of the sink. Make sure that these lights are directed to shine into the mirror so that it is reflected back at your face. If

Above: Here, the lighting highlights and makes a special feature of the glass sink.

Left: Lights can be placed directly over a bathtub and shower—such fixtures will need to be installed by a professional electrician.

Above: As well as a good-size normal mirror, it is useful to also have a magnifying mirror in the bathroom.

Opposite: In this small bathroom in a converted attic space, attic windows have been set into the roof to provide good natural light.

good-quality light will give an accurate color rendition and color temperature, which are important, especially if you are using the lit area to apply your makeup.

For close inspection there are magnifying mirrors that have integral surrounding lights, so that the illumination is directly positioned to shine onto the face, or section of the face that is being examined. These enlarging mirrors are wall-mounted, and the electric cables are enclosed in the casing of the arm or support.

Decorative lighting

Floor lights are increasingly popular in contemporary bathrooms. These lights are contained in sealed casing, and are used to uplight a shower stall from the outside, or in the side panels of the bathtub. They can be used in the corners of the room to emphasize height and space.

Shelf lighting is sometimes used in the bathroom. A single, long glass shelf can be used to support decorative objects, and by positioning a small light below or on either side of the shelf, you can create an effect where the shelf appears to glow.

Lighting in a shower stall is best done with ceiling-mounted spots or enclosed fitxtures, such as a nautical bulkhead light.

the light shines down too steeply, it will light your back.

A strip or row of bulbs may also run along the top and sides of the mirror so that the light is evenly distributed and regular, otherwise wall-mounted side lights with adjustable arms or heads can also be effective.

With the halo or surround of light on the edge or front of the mirror, it can be more effective to have more low-voltage lights than too many high-voltage ones, as the latter will create an intense, unflattering light that will make you look pallid. The right level of

Bathroom
storage

A variety of items and products needs to be stored in a bathroom—towels should be kept aired and dry, while bottles of shampoo and bath preparations are often slippery, soapy, and damp, and thus need to be kept separate and contained so that any drips or leaks are not allowed to travel.

Storage units

Storage can be provided either by built-in or freestanding units. Built-in units can provide storage in places such as under the sink, in linen and towel cupboards, and even under window seats. They are particularly helpful in small bathrooms, where furniture can be made to measure.

Large storage units can be subdivided into narrow shelves for smaller items, and wider ones for bulkier things. Even within deep shelves you can section the space with baskets or boxes to keep smaller objects in order.

In some bathrooms there will be a water heater, which is a bulky, rather unattractive thing. Depending on the type of heater, it may be possible to disguise it with a built-in cupboard, but check with a professional before you do, as some require venting.

If you don't have a heater and would prefer freestanding units, there are many available. These vary from modern designs, with

light wood or steel frames and glass panels, to the more traditional armoire with short legs.

Baskets are useful, but natural rattan or woven coconut-fiber types should be used for dry things, rather than wet. Baskets can be used to hold waste as well as dirty linen.

Small storage solutions

Different types of small storage solutions are needed in a bathroom to cope with the variety of items that are kept there. For example, children's bathtime toys will be wet after playtime, but can be rounded up in a net bag or

Above: In a shower, the shelves should also be constructed so that water will drain off them, rather than sit in stagnant puddles.

Opposite: Traditional bathtub racks that hold soap and sponges are still widely used.

Although glass and ceramic containers look attractive, they are not ideal materials for the bathroom, because if they break they will leave tiny, sharp shards that can be difficult to clean up. These shards are painful if stepped on in bare feet, or if one accidentally gets stuck in your finger.

Angular corners and hard edges should be avoided on storage units and furniture because they can hurt unprotected skin. It is easy to lose your balance while drying, and bump into the corner of a sink surround or bathtub enclosure, and a sharp edge will hurt more than a bull-nose or rounded edge.

Left: Baskets are useful for containing laundry and towels because they allow air to circulate around the fabrics inside.

Opposite: The glass shelves in this room are backed by the glass wall of the shower stall, and are used to display a collection of old perfume bottles. The shelves are a decorative rather than practical feature, but help to create a barrier between the bathtub and shower elements without cutting down on the flow of light from the window beyond.

similar soft, mesh container and left to drip-dry over the bathtub or sink. They are then easily retrieved for the next set of water activities.

Other items that are in frequent use, such as soap and sponges, are often damp, so should be kept on or in a holder that has a grille structure or a punched base so that the excess moisture flows away or evaporates.

A basket or tray will make a neat container for items that need to be taken out from a cupboard regularly.

Bathroom
accessories

Bathroom accessories should be functional as well as attractive. First, you will need to choose the main items, such as faucets and towel racks, which are part of the general furniture of the room, but may also be made into a feature. For instance, the style of the handles on the sink and bathtub faucets, or the structure and finish of a towel rack will have visual impact on your whole decorative scheme. Then there are the secondary accessories, such as soap dispensers or dishes, holders for tissues, cotton balls, and toothbrushes, as well as mirrors for close-up use. As a rule, try to choose small accessories that have a similar or matching finish to the rest of your scheme. Keep decorative items in the bathroom to a minimum, because they will gather dust. Try to avoid glass and fine ceramic or china containers, unless they are high up on a shelf. Plastic and metal are good, robust materials for bathrooms, but check that there is a sealant or varnish on the metal so that it doesn't tarnish or rust.

Clockwise from top left:

This is an old-fashioned style of shower lever with a white ceramic handle, which would fit into a bathroom decorated in a traditional period style.

A star-shaped shower head will give a wider area of spray than most shower heads.

This contemporary, bowl-style sink is made of colored glass to fit in with the rest of the bathroom.

Stacks of neatly folded towels can be a useful, as well as attractive, addition to a bathroom shelf.

Smooth, curved handles on drawers and shower stalls are easier to grasp when your hands are wet or slippery with body lotion or bath oil.

This modern take on the traditional bath rack has a magnifying mirror.

Ceramic and glass containers are attractive, but should be carefully positioned so that they won't be knocked over and broken by the edge of a towel or a passing hand.

Ladder-style, wall-hung radiators can be plumbed in level with the wall so that they take up minimal room.

These wall-mounted, decorative, X-shape faucets and spout are plumbed above a sink—their crisp, clean lines complement the stark but functional slate back panel.

This neat metal grid is the outlet for water in the base of a shower stall—the ridges in the tiles and a slight incline direct the water to this point.

In contemporary bathrooms materials such as glass, cement, steel, and wood are often used—here, a treated wooden sink is a quite unusual and eye-catching feature.

Materials like Corian can be molded and cast into shapes. This runaway for excess water has been designed as an integral part of the sink surround.

Clip-on towel racks fit onto most styles of wall-mounted radiators.

A corkscrew radiator is a fun-looking, useful addition to a bathroom.

Work and play areas

Planning work and
play areas

If you have space to spare in the home, think how to put it to best use. If you work from home, you will require a dedicated work space, or you may want to set an area aside to pursue a hobby. Older children may need a quiet place to study, while younger children need somewhere to play.

Working and playing in the home

The number of computers used in the home is fast catching up with televisions. More home-working is being done on computers by people who are self-employed, or who job-share. Household accounts and mailing lists are also stored on computers, which can be a helpful way to avoid clutter and run a home efficiently. Many schoolchildren also use them on a regular basis to help with their homework, to play games, and to email friends.

Home-working is becoming an increasingly popular alternative to regular office life for domestic and

Left: An attic conversion with glass insets in the roof provides a light-filled and spacious artist's studio.

Opposite: A colorful scheme can be invigorating in a work space, but avoid overfussy wallpapers of distracting patterns.

financial reasons. Financially, it costs a company far less to employ someone who works from their own home, and this is made possible because of the quick and easy interaction offered between home/office and clients by video phones, email, and computer technology.

And just as it is important to have a dedicated work space, so an area dedicated for play can be a great bonus in a family that has children. A playroom or den will be a specific place where toys and games can be kept, which then leaves the main living area pre-dominantly for adult relaxation.

Planning your space

Because of the increase in home-working, more people are seeking out a space from which to conduct their business. Some choose a converted garage, a basement development, attic or loft exten-sion, or separate out-building, while others take over a spare bedroom, or annex part of a large room. Such areas can be made into a playroom.

If you use a basement or attic, you will need to consider three important aspects—access, struc-ture, and headroom.

Access is usually via a stair-case, for which a rectangular

space of 3 x 10ft (0.9 x 3m) will be necessary for standard vertical stairs, while a spiral can squeeze into 5ft sq (1.7m sq). But a spiral staircase, with its triangular-shape steps, can be less easy for very young children and elderly adults to manage.

For a basement development, the floor joists of the room above may need to be strengthened, and in a cramped cellar, part of the floor may have to be excavated to provide sufficient head height and to lay down a vapor retarder. You will require a building permit, as well as structural and architectur-al advice before undertaking such large-scale alterations.

Above: This curving desk gives a student ample work space within her bedroom.

In a basement or cellar you also have to be able to gain access to natural light, overcome moisture, provide adequate ventilation, and, if you want to plumb in an addi-tional toilet and sink, get access to the waste stack and supply pipes. In an attic conversion, you have to watch out for similar things—ventilation is important, as these rooftop rooms can become very hot and stuffy during the summer, and again, if you want to plumb in toilet and wash-ing facilities, you need to find out the proximity of the main stacks and drains.

An attic conversion with skylight or roof windows can make a useful extra space, whether it is used for a play or hobby room where painting, sewing, or photography can be enjoyed, or transformed into a work area. The sloping edges of the roof, which are too low to stand up in, can be utilized for storage, with low cupboards or sliding shelving systems on casters. The shelving system can be constructed so that it is of a triangular shape with decreasing shelf sizes, so that it slides in under the slope of the ceiling, rather than along it. With the limited head height in these areas, recessed spotlights in the ceiling can save valuable inches. In a long, open space, folding doors or partitions can be used to subdivide the room, but you should also try to keep available the option of opening it up again.

Small rooms should be kept light and airy, and decorated

Right: Wire and cable management is a necessity in modern home offices. Here, a specific hole has been provided in the desktop so that cables can be fed out and down to the plug socket, rather than squashed between the back of the desk and the wall.

simply to make the most of the limited amount of space, and, in basement conversions, to make the most of the light available. Don't be tempted to use this additional space as a junk room to store bits of furniture that you don't want elsewhere in the house. Instead, be specific and invest time and money in selecting light-framed, lightweight pieces. You may also find that you need to be careful when buying larger pieces of furniture—you must certainly check that you will be able to get them up or down the staircase into your room.

It is possible that you will have to buy a desk that comes in sections and can be assembled in situ. In small rooms you can save valuable space by having furniture specially designed and built in, although this will probably cost you more.

Where a standard unit may have an overlap or lip that leaves a gap between the wall and the base, you can have a specifically designed table made to butt directly up to the wall. Foldaway furniture can also be useful in rooms where space is limited, as it can then be folded flat when it is

Left: This neat study area has been created out of the space at the bottom of a staircase in the basement. Good electrical lighting is important here, because there is no natural light available.

Right: Adjustable seats allow you to tailor a sitting position to suit your stature—this gives better ergonomic support and helps to relieve physical tension. A seat with wheels can also be useful if you need to turn or move around to collect papers or files.

Making decorative screens

Screening off an area or corner of a room can be done in a number of ways.

There is the standard panel screen made from a wooden frame with infills. There are also curving wooden screens made from small strips of wood, which articulate and undulate like an old-fashioned rolltop desk. These are more flexible than the frame screen, and they can be used in difficult areas and around odd shapes. Alternatively, you could use a bookcase or a row of tall, bushy plants to make a screen.

not in use, but is also very easily opened out when it is needed.

Creating space within a room

Working from home requires discipline, and, where possible, it is best to allocate a separate room entirely to this activity. If you can't afford to dedicate a whole room, then create space within an area of a room that can be used without disturbing others. It is also important to be able to separate work and home life, so that you can concentrate on each part as and when you are involved with it.

If children are using the computer to do homework, they should be free from outside

distractions, so the space should be out of the main thoroughfare of the home or the bustle of the kitchen. This will enable them to concentrate on their task and give it their full attention. If the computer is used for games, then others will also appreciate the fact that the "beep-beeps" and general games activity are isolated from the area where they may be trying to relax or listen to music.

If your work area is part of a larger room, you can create a way of containing it—this can be done with screens, panels, lightweight movable bookcases, or even a series of Venetian or roller shades. These room dividers don't have to be permanent, but can be flexible so that they provide

At-a-glance color guide

Walls in a study should be plain rather than overfussy. Restful colors are good for keeping you calm, but should not be so subtle and restful that they make you sleepy. One possibility is to mix bright and pale colors—paint one wall a vivid and exciting color, such as blue or green, and then paint the other in a much paler tone of the same color. In a dark room, a light or white ceiling will help reflect the available natural light, as will gloss enamel white window frames and surrounds.

privacy and seclusion only when it is needed.

Practical considerations for a work space

There are practical and health implications that should be taken into consideration when planning your work space.

When computers and VDUs (visual display units) are used in a regular office environment, it is the employer's duty to make sure that health and safety regulations are followed, but at home it is up to you. The location of the computer screen should, where possible, be sited near a window and natural light, but the screen must be angled in order to avoid glare that is hard on the eyes and may obliterate parts of the screen.

Don't have the ambient light level in the room too low. The levels of light in the room and the screen should be comparable.

Your desk should be adjacent to shelves or storage where frequently used files or reference materials are stored so that they are easily accessible. If your work involves a lot of paperwork, then you may find it useful to have a desk that has an extra long return, such as an L shape, that provides you with an adjacent surface on which you can arrange papers.

Try to keep the desk free of small items, things that get lodged under books and papers. (See Storage and display, page 380.)

Good ventilation is also essential in a working space, to avoid stress and fatigue. If the room becomes too warm and soporific, you will be in danger of falling asleep. Heat will build up from the VDU and electric lighting, so keep the door open and leave a window slightly ajar.

Machines such as computers, faxes, printers, copiers, and phones always involve a spaghetti of wires and cables. Arrange these wires in order, and keep the cords neatly coiled or wrapped around a cable manager, which will protect the wiring from damage, and prevent people from tripping over them. It will also make it easier to identify a single line should you want to remove it.

Seating is important. At home, one chair tends to be used for all situations but the home office chair should be adjustable so that the height and position can be tailored to suit each individual in the household who will be using it— from child to adult.

To get the correct position, sit on the seat and adjust it until, while still seated, your horizontally outstretched arms are about at the same level as the bottom of

Right: A study area does not have to look like an office—it can fit with the style of the rest of the room. Here, this elegant desk works in a Scandinavian period-style room.

the VDU casing, your eyes are at the same level as the top of the VDU, and your feet are flat on the floor. If you work in a seated position for long periods, you may find that a footrest is comfortable.

When using a keyboard, your hands should not be too bent at the wrist, and the keys should be easy to tap softly. To avoid eye strain and headaches, make sure that the screen is at a comfortable distance from your eyes. This is around 2ft (61cm), but less is acceptable if using a laptop.

Practical considerations for a playroom

A dedicated playroom can be brightly painted, imaginatively decorated, and completely child-friendly, rather than having to be compromised because it is in a space shared with adults.

You should avoid having prominent sharp corners on furniture and fixtures. Where possible, sand or rub the points down until they are more rounded and soft, or stick on adhesive plastic corner caps to prevent small children

banging their heads or limbs against them and being bruised. The same applies to work areas, as adults may bang their legs or hips against a table edge or cupboard corner as they rush about.

Color, light, and atmosphere

Both work and play areas benefit from being light and airy—they are places where the mind and

body need to be alert and active, and the décor and surroundings should help to promote this outlook. The space should be conducive to concentration, but it should not be dull or boring. If you have converted a cellar or attic space, you will need to make the most of any available light—use every trick in the decorator's book to make the space seem spacious.

Above: A work area should be bright and airy. Make the most of all available light by positioning your desk near a window. Make sure, however, that there is no reflected glare on your computer screen.

First, keep the ceiling plain or simply patterned, and decorate the walls and ceiling in a light color. Smooth wall surfaces will also reflect light more efficiently than rough or textured ones. If you do want to introduce a strong or dark color, use it on one wall only, as a special feature panel, and preferably on the wall that has a window set into it, so that the light from the window will counteract any darkness. Dark colors can be oppressive and depressing, and vibrant reds, pinks, and oranges too hot and lively. This could make you feel agitated, and distract you from your work.

Plain colors or light, geometric patterns are best for a work space. If you make it too floral or bedroomy, it will detract from your sense of purpose. For business visitors, fussy floral papers may give the impression that you are less than serious, or not focused on your work. Light, fresh colors such as lemon, green, and blue, or neutrals such as beige or oatmeal, are clean and appropriate.

Striped room dividing shades

Most of us need an area to complete paperwork. If your work area is in the corner of a room used for another purpose, then these shades are ideal for screening a messy desk or hobby area. Making your own allows you to tailor them to fit your space. Most mediumweight fabrics can be made into shades by using a fabric-stiffening solution. Choose a fabric of a sufficient width to avoid joints that would prevent the shade rolling up neatly. If the area that you wish to cover is wider than your fabric, make several shades that will give access to different areas.

Materials

Roller-shade kits
Cotton fabric
Fabric-stiffening spray
(with flame retardant)
Painter's tape
Latex (acrylic) paints
Fabric-painting medium
Thread

Tools

Tape measure
Set square
Scissors
Pencil
Junior hacksaw
Tailor's chalk pencil
Small paintbrushes
Iron
Staple gun
Needle

Preparing the materials

1 Make a drawing of the area to be covered, with accurate width and height measurements. Decide where you will attach the shades, and work out how many kits you will need. Use a tape measure, set square, and scissors to cut the fabric. Mark the lengths of doweling rods, using the width of the fabric as a guide.

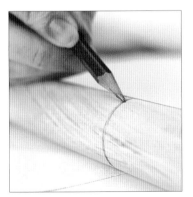

Measure the doweling rods, using the width of the fabric as a guide to fit the size you require.

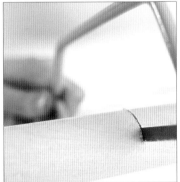

If the doweling rods supplied are too long, use a junior hacksaw to trim them down.

Know your materials

Roller-shade kits can be purchased from most large furnishings stores. They are a good-value choice if you have large windows, and they also allow you to use your own choice of fabric with patterns to suit your room.

The kits supply the winding mechanism, a wooden or metal roller, the brackets to attach the shade to the window, and a string pull. Some kits also include the stiffening spray needed to make your chosen fabric more rigid. If possible, try and get one that also gives the fabric a degree of fire-retardancy.

Cutting to size

2 If necessary, trim the lengths of doweling rods that are supplied in the roller-shade kit, using a junior hacksaw (see picture bottom right, page 375).

3 Spray the material with fabric-stiffening spray for shades. This will also prevent any cut edges from fraying, and make the fabric fire-retardant.

Drawing the stripes

4 Using a pencil, mark out stripes of different widths, and apply strips of painter's tape to the edges.

Adding the colors

5 Use around six latex (acrylic) colors mixed with a fabric-

painting medium, and paint the stripes. Allow the stripes to dry between colors for the recommended time before reapplying strips of painter's tape for the next color.

6 When all the stripes have been painted, iron on the

Spray the material with fabric-stiffening spray for shades to make them fire-retardant.

Use a pencil and a rule to draw stripes of different widths onto the fabric.

With a medium paintbrush, paint the stripes. Use painter's tape to be sure of clean lines.

reverse side, making sure that the instructions on the fabric-painting medium are followed. This is so that you are sure that the paint is colorfast.

Assembling the shade

7 Attach the fabric to the roller mechanism, using the adhesive strip provided. Reinforce this with a staple gun if your shade is long and heavy.

8 Using a needle and a piece of coordinating thread, sew a channel for the rod at the bottom. Feed the rod through the channel, and then slot it in place. Finally, attach the pull cord supplied with the roller-shade kit to the center of the bottom rod.

When the stripes are dry, iron on the reverse side to make sure that the paint is colorfast.

Attach the fabric to the roller mechanism using the adhesive strip provided in the shade kit.

Sew a channel at the bottom of the shade, then feed the rod through, and slot in place.

Alternative

If you want a more permanent, formal way of dividing your room, consider installing a series of doors that can be folded back to create one large room when required. These doors can run on small wheels, which slot into tracks on the floor and ceiling. Alternatively, they can be hung on sets of door hinges and anchored in place with simple bolts that slot into plates on the floor. Ready-made bi-fold doors and tracks can be bought from hardware stores, or search for reclaimed doors. Paneled doors can be customized by removing the top panels and replacing them with fretwork or glass. This allows plenty of light to filter through, while still giving each side of the room a degree of privacy. Fretwork screen panels can be bought in a variety of designs and materials, including MDF, masonite, and pressed metals. Glass panels can be bought from a glazier, who will cut them to fit. You can choose from plain, frosted, or specialized colored or stained-glass panels.

Storage and display

In work and play areas, storage is important. In a work space you will need to have reference books and files to hand, and in a play area different types of toys and games should all be kept in their own containers or drawers, so that they don't get lost or form one hideous jumble.

Work space storage

In a work space, the most important thing is to avoid too much clutter. Keep things that you need to hand, and store items that are seldom used on upper shelves or more distant cupboards and filing cabinets. Avoid a build-up of files, boxes, and paperwork around you, as it can make you feel hemmed in and overpowered by your surroundings. The best way to keep paper under control is to edit it regularly—don't let an In tray build up to a state where it overflows into a second basket.

If your desktop is organized, it also makes it easier to cope with things that pass over it. A good basic stationery kit, such as paper clips, eraser, stapler, and Scotch tape should be kept in a divided or sectioned drawer, as this will help you to know exactly where each thing is, and it will be easy

Above: Box files are extremely useful, and can be labeled so that you can locate items very quickly.

Right: A filing cabinet can be positioned underneath your desk, which will make it easy to reach paperwork and makes good use of space.

to lay your hands on things when you need them.

Small items, such as paperclips and thumbtacks, can be very effectively stored in clear-glass jars with screw-on lids. The lids keep the contents firmly inside, but the glass sides make it simple to identify what is where. Clear plastic containers can be useful, but the lids tend not to stay as firmly in place as the old-fashioned screw type, and in time thin, shiny plastic may become brittle and crack.

But a working space doesn't need to be dull and regimented. In fact, stationery and office accessories compose one area where the use of color, pattern, and design have recently made a huge impact.

Files that were once covered in a standard gray or dull casing are now widely available in bright-colored covers, which can make it easier to identify an individual file at a distance. Instead of buying a dozen files in the same uniform finish, have different-color ones so that you will be able to memorize what color relates to a particular topic. This will also give your work space a more lively appearance. Or you can create your own (see box, page 382).

Another useful piece of apparatus can be a wall grid. This may

be made of wood or metal, and is a panel of bars onto which items can be hung. Wall grids are generally more robust than notice-boards and with small butcher's hooks can be a good place for hanging tools such as scissors, hammers, and wrenches.

Larger sections of wall grid can support small shelves, and may be used in the area of wall in front of a work station. The various hooks and attachments can then be used to display stationery elements, such as Scotch tape, sticky labels, a clock, scalpel, or cutting knife, rules, etc, putting everything on display and immediately to hand. This type of

Above: Storage specifically designed to hold certain items, such as tapes and CDs, not only contains them, but also makes them easier to view and select.

arrangement is better for a wall by a desk or secondary workstation, rather than the primary one, as the equipment hanging in front of a person trying to work may become distracting and make the space feel reduced and cluttered.

If a lot of storage and shelves are necessary in your work space, you can make it seem less dominant by painting it the same color as the wall. This will make the shelves appear to be an integral

Decorative labels for storage boxes

Labeling and identifying the contents of boxes and files is important so that they can be easily noted. For business files, use clear white labels with bold black printed letters. If files or boxes are used in a moist environment, or will be lifted with wet hands, then cover the labels with a strip of clear adhesive plastic. For young children of pre-reading age, color-coding can be helpful, so you can put dolls' clothes in a pink box, toy soldiers in a red one, and books in green, etc, or you can cut out appropriate pictures to make it easy for them to see what belongs where.

Right: In a small study, tempered glass or acrylic shelves are useful because they provide ample storage, but don't appear too heavy or block out light.

Top right: Magazine holders come in a variety of materials, colors, and finishes so they can coordinate with your decorative scheme.

part of the wall, rather than a feature set against it.

Useful work-space furniture

If your work requires you to gather information, swatches, or reference material from elsewhere and bring it back to your desk, then a trolley may be a useful addition to your furniture. The trolley can be used to move material from one area to another in one move, rather than you staggering backward and forward several times with armfuls of files. The trolley can also be pulled right up to your desk, where you can then easily access the documents, using the upper levels of the trolley as an extension to your desk.

As well as modern office equipment, old or antique pieces can be

useful, as well as interesting and attractive. Old wooden store-display systems with glass-fronted drawers can make a pleasant change in a home office, and will blend in easily with traditional furnishings and fabrics. Plan chests, with their rows of large, flat drawers, not only provide ample storage, but are usually of such a size and construction that the top can be used as an additional work surface, a partial room divider, or even a place to put a kettle or coffee machine.

Just as the plan chest can be used to create a low or partial divider, a small bookcase can be used in the same way. These low barriers help to divide work from home space, but don't cut off the flow of light or line of vision. A three-shelf bookcase, up to 3ft (92cm) high can be secured to the floor and an adjacent wall to make sure that it is stable. The side facing the work space will display the shelves and provide storage, while the back will face into the other half of the room, and may be concealed by the back of a sofa or painted to match the wall in that area.

Display in work spaces

Although the primary function of your work space should be practical, there is no reason why you should not create a display of a few ornaments on top of a set of box files to create a comfortable, welcoming environment. If you have a pinboard beside your desk,

you will also be able to place things such as a calendar, family photos, and useful phone numbers on it. This can be livened up with posters, too. Be careful not to let your work space become too cluttered, though.

Storage in play areas

If a child's bedroom doubles as a play area, by putting toys away in boxes out of sight at the end of the day, you are removing the temptation for a small person to get out of bed once the door is closed and continue playing. Good toy storage can help young

Making your own hanging storage

Cut a long rectangle out of your chosen material. If you are thinking about hanging it behind a door, then take the dimensions of the door and reduce it so that the back sheet is about 2ft (61cm) shorter than the door measurement from top to bottom, and about 9in (23cm) narrower at both sides.

Hem the back panel, and make a casing top and bottom to hold a length of dowel the same width as the material. Slide the dowel into the casing, and sew over the ends of the fabric to keep it in place. Measure the items you plan to put in the pockets, and cut the material to the same size with an additional generous hem allowance. Hem the top edge, turn in the sides and bottom of the pocket, and sew onto the back panel.

Left: This storage system has a variety of sizes of shelves and forms an efficient office space along just one wall.

Above: This tall system of shelves in a child's bedroom not only stores toys and books efficiently, but also displays them in an attractive way.

children as they learn about discipline and tidiness, too. It also helps to keep the floor area clear when games time is over, so that if there is a change from day- to night-time activity, the space will quickly and easily adapt. Adults also need to be able to check on sleeping children without falling over in-line skates or toy trains, or treading on a favorite toy.

Plastic crates with lids that stack neatly one on top of another work well in a child's room. These can be arranged along a wall and labeled so that the contents are easily identified without having to open each and every box. Drawers on wheels or casters can be slotted under a bed or bunks, and narrow shelves are ideal for books and small toys, such as soldiers, small cars, or dolls.

If a small child learns that his or her toys are always returned to the same box or bag, then they quickly learn the routine. This will also save the parent or helper the thankless task of searching endlessly for a specific item.

Having easy-access storage should stop smaller items or play things getting separated or lost. For a slightly older child's bedroom, you could store smaller items, such as paintbrushes and crayons, or favorite soft toys, in a wall or door hanging with

pockets. This is simply made from a strong cotton such as calico or canvas, or even a more interesting material such as denim (see box, page 383). The panel can be fixed to the wall or the back of the door by hooks and eyelets, or with a stout piece of cord attached to either end of the top piece of dowel and looped over a couple of strong hooks. The pockets can be made in contrasting colors to the back panel, or decorated with felt letters, cut-outs of the things that are stored in them, or buttons to add interest.

Display in play areas

In a child's room, storage can also double as a display area. For example, a troop of cowboys can look fun if they trot across a shelf. If Barbie is the dream doll of the moment and the bedroom is painted pink in her honor, then the doll herself should be on show to be a part of the overall scheme.

Display areas can also be informative. A pinboard for school certificates or good reports, as well as homework and activity timetables, will be useful. Pictures may also need to be tacked—by using a cork noticeboard you can protect the wall surface from new tack holes when the current fashion changes.

Tongue-and-groove display panel

Lightweight, slatted panels are ideal in a home office or a study with changing storage needs. We made the panels using tongue-and-groove floorboards, with the tongues removed. The ingenious part is that the grooves provide an anchor for shelves and pictures, which can be hung at varying heights. Simply unhook and rearrange to change the layout. The panels can be fastened directly to the wall or to vertical furring strips.

Materials

Wooden furring strips
Tongue-and-groove floorboards
Wood screws
Knot sealer
Acrylic primer
White acrylic satinwood paint
Wood glue
Metal trim

Tools

Handsaw
Workbench
Tape measure
Sharp plane or jigsaw
Abrasive paper
Electric drill
Countersink bit
Paintbrush
Hacksaw
Screwdriver

Measuring the area

1 Decide on the height and width of the screen. Using a handsaw, cut the furring strips and floorboards to the required size.

2 Secure each floorboard in turn on a workbench and, with a sharp plane or a jigsaw, remove the tongue.

Securing the floorboards

3 Lay out the cut floorboard lengths, allowing ½in (1cm) spacing between each one.

Using a handsaw, cut the strips and tongue-and-groove floorboards to the required size.

Secure each floorboard to the workbench, and remove the tongue with a jigsaw.

Know your materials

We used tongue-and-groove floorboards here because they are stronger than tongue-and-groove wall paneling, and the deeper groove along their length was perfect for hanging picture hooks and shelves from. Use picture hooks made to hang over a picture rail to suspend the pictures from the grooved boards.

It is important to treat the knots in the wood (the rounded marks where branches were) with knot sealer. This is a shellac-based product that seals the knots and prevents resinous sap bleeding through the paint.

Place the furring strips in position at each end. If you are making a wall over 13ft (4m) wide, you should add another central furring strip for stability.

4 Drill and screw through the back of the strip into each floorboard using a countersink

bit, making sure that the screw head sits beneath the surface.

5 When all the floorboards are secured on the strips, turn the panel the right way up and sand thoroughly with a piece of abrasive paper. Using an old paintbrush, apply knot sealer to any resinous knots (this will prevent resin bleeding through the paintwork and spoiling the finish). Fasten the strips securely to the wall with fastenings suitable for the wall type.

Painting the floorboards

6 Apply a coat of acrylic primer followed by two coats of white acrylic satinwood paint, and allow to dry.

Use a countersink bit to screw through the back of the strip into each floorboard.

With a paintbrush, apply knot sealer to any resinous knots to prevent resin bleeding.

Apply a coat of acrylic primer and then two coats of acrylic satinwood paint to the boards.

Making the shelf

7 Use another floorboard (with the tongue removed) to make the shelf. Cut two pieces of the same length and butt together to form the back and base. Cut two identical squares with the corners cut off to form the sides. Glue and screw together. Treat with knot sealer, prime, and paint with white acrylic paint.

8 Use a hacksaw to cut a length of L-shape metal trim to fit the top of the shelf.

9 Drill, countersink, then screw the longest edge of the metal trim in position on top of the shelf. This will slot neatly over the floorboard lengths and anchor itself in the groove.

Use another floorboard to make the shelf, then treat with knot sealer, prime, and paint.

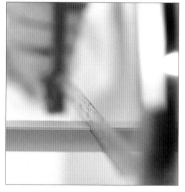

Use a hacksaw to make an L-shape metal trim to fit the top of the shelf.

Drill, countersink, and screw the longest edge of the metal trim in place on top of the shelf.

Alternative

One of the most attractive methods of storing CDs is to slip them horizontally into a grooved panel of wood. Hardwoods with an attractive grain look best, but if you want to make one you will need a router with a groove-cutting bit. You can adapt this idea, making a simpler version by adding pieces of doweling to the front of a flat panel.

Sketch out the rough dimensions to plan the amount of materials you will need. Get a panel of wood or MDF cut to fit your space, and sufficient square-section dowels cut to the same width, making sure that the dowels are deep enough to hold the CDs firmly in place. Use a soft pencil and set square to lightly mark the position of the dowels on the back and front of the panel, making sure that each is a CD-width apart. Spread a thin layer of wood glue over one side of each dowel, and position them all. Tap a row of thin brad nails through from the back of the panel to hold the dowels in place. Attach the panel to the wall.

Lighting for
work and play

The type and arrangement of lighting that you choose for work and play areas are important—work areas should be bright and airy, conducive to concentrating on the task in hand. In children's rooms, safety is a priority, but light shades can still be a fun part of the decorative scheme.

Creating your own decorative shade

Customize a lampshade for a child's playroom by painting the outer surface or sticking on cutout shapes. You could try cutting out motifs from extra curtain or bedding material and applying these to the shade. If you are using a floral motif, leave a little of the edge of the petal hanging over the lower edge of the shade for a decorative finish. Always buy a safety-approved shade, and only decorate the outside surface.

Work-space lighting

The computer screen should, where possible, be sited near a window and natural light, but the screen must be angled to avoid glare that is hard on the eyes and may obliterate parts of the screen. Don't have the ambient light level in the room too low. The levels of light in the room and the screen should be comparable.

A specific, adjustable work light is essential to supplement fading

Right: A desk is best positioned near a source of natural light. Here, mirrors are used to reflect and make the most of the light.

Left: A movable task light that will focus light directly on paperwork or a screen is a basic necessity in a working or study environment.

Right: Task lights should provide a good, even level of light, but should not be too strong or create glare.

daylight. A standard domestic table lamp with shade or central room light is not good enough, as it may cast shadows on the screen, making it difficult to see. Desktop or task lights, such as recessed and directional spotlights, will also be needed to light up the rest of the desk surface.

Playroom lighting

It is best to provide high-level ambient light for a play area so that the lower levels of the room are as cord- and cable-free as possible. Fit childproof safety covers in the wall sockets to deter small fingers, and equip light fixtures with safety plugs that have part-covered prongs.

It is best to avoid small, china-base table lamps or anything that is easily broken—choose robust light fixtures. There are many specially designed for children's rooms, available in large furnishings stores. Lights can also be a fun part of the scheme, particularly in a play area.

If the children using the play room spend most of their time at floor level, then you will need to have a good, broad-beam overhead light, such as recessed spots, in conjunction with wall lights. The wall lights can be contained in an enclosed shade, so that there is no direct access to the bulb, and so that the bulb is contained should it fail.

If the play area doubles up as a work room for an older child or adult, adjustable task lights could be attached to the wall so that they can be positioned over a desk or work area without being in the way of the play area. This type of work light should be angled so that the beam shines diagonally across the papers on the table, to focus on the work.

Using natural light

It is best to keep window dressings simple to make the most of natural light. In a work area, an adjustable roller or Venetian shade is ideal because it can be

used to shield bright, direct sunlight, yet can be rolled or pulled up out of the way on darker days.

In a play room, choose simple curtains, shades, or something like a folded Roman shade that can be effective and attractive. The latter should be placed at a level out of the way of sticky fingers. If the play area is more of an adult recreation room, you may need to tailor the lighting treatments to suit the hobby. For example, if photography or making family videos is an abiding hobby, blackout shades may be needed.

Workplace accessories

Work areas within the home should be softer and more comfortable than a commercial or business space, yet they do need to function efficiently. Storage and good planning are the keys to success, and a built-in desk can convert a wasted space under a staircase or at the end of a corridor into a useful additional room. Because these are domestic environments, you can have fun with accessories such as files and pencil holders, and can indulge in bright colors and fun schemes. However, they shouldn't be too wild, as they might distract you. Once the desk and storage spaces have been allocated, the next most important items to target are ventilation, lighting, and seating. Ventilation is important if you are using electrical machines, as they generate heat and may make a room stuffy and dry. Target lighting, provided by an adjustable spot or desk lamp, will be vital for good viewing, and also for the care of your eyesight. Finally, an ergonomic-design, adjustable chair is another must for good posture and back support.

Clockwise from top left:

An old pewter tankard doubles as a pencil holder—this is a practical, yet quirky storage solution.

Smooth edges, such as those on the arm of this chair and the desk edge, make a more pleasant and safer working environment.

Good storage is essential to keep things in order and easily accessible, especially in small spaces.

The shelves of bookcases can be arranged so that they accommodate specific sizes and types of books.

Transparent shelves don't appear as heavy or dense as solid wood or MDF, and in a small room can make it appear more spacious. However, you should use only tempered laminated glass or acrylic sheet for this type of shelf construction for safety reasons.

Small filing cabinets can be used as a desk base. This also means that frequently used files and papers can be kept close at hand.

Clear labeling will make it much more easy to identify the contents of your files and drawers.

Glare on a computer screen can make it difficult to focus, so have an adjustable side light and shades at the window so you have the right level and direction of light.

Bright, light colors can be invigorating when used in a study or workroom.

If you do a lot of paperwork, be sure that you have plenty of tabletop or desk surface in order to lay the material out.

Coordinating stationery can make a desk area visually pleasing and inviting.

This neat study area has been built in at the end of a corridor, but still provides adequate working space.

Work lights need not be dull—this one has an adjustable head that slides up and down the main steel support.

Old cabinets can be used as storage for paperwork or toys. The solid front panels can be removed and replaced with fine wire, or fabric.

Connecting
areas

Planning connecting
areas

Passages and hallways are an often overlooked part of the home, yet they are important not only because they link one room to another, but also because, if they are decorated in an attractive, clutter-free way, they can make the experience of passing through them more enjoyable.

Above: Hallways need to be practical, so a unit that can hold coats, shoes, and other items is a great addition.

Opposite: Staircases can be sculptural, as this dramatic example shows.

Halls, landings, staircases, and passageways link rooms and various levels in a home, but are often narrow, dark, and difficult to make the most of. If you have a long corridor, try to subdivide it into three parts, such as the entrance hall, the inner passageway or corridor, and the end, so that in each section there is a focus.

Halls

The area immediately inside the front door is a busy place where people arrive and depart, where mail is received, and coats, boots, hats, and gloves are usually kept. It is also an area that forms a barrier between the outside world, a place of transition between the reality of urban living and work and the cosy, domestic interior.

To accommodate the transition and these functions, you should create a space that is tranquil and organized. To deal with the comings and goings in this area, there should be a variety of storage, and a place to sit while putting on and taking off shoes. It should also be decorated so that it appears bright and inviting.

Accessories

The first accessory in this entrance area is usually a rough-texture mat on the floor, immediately inside or just outside the door. The inner floor in this area should be covered with a practical finish—something that can be easily cleaned. Stone, wood, flagstones, or tiles are good and can be softened or brightened with a runner, which must be backed with a good, nonslip fastening.

The floor covering should be strong and resilient, as there will be a lot of wear and tear. As nice as a pure-wool carpet would be, it may mark quickly. You can choose a laid carpet, but put a rug or mat over the area immediately inside the door, or a runner that covers

the central track from the doorway, thus protecting the carpet that is underneath.

Passageways

Corridors and passageways are in the center of the home, and will invariably have doorways that open into and out of this space, which is less frenetic and busy than the front door area.

The corridor or passageway is not often filled with people—if it is busy, people are usually just passing through, so it can be an area where some privacy can be had while making or receiving a call. To accommodate this, another table and chair would be useful. The table may be needed for telephone directories, a phone book, a pad, and a pen. A table lamp may also be helpful. If you do not have enough room for a table, then a couple of shelves could be fastened to the wall instead.

Depending on the size of your passageways and corridors, you may find it useful to have pieces of furniture arranged as drop-off or staging points. For example, if

Left: Glass panels above the two main doors off this passageway allow natural light from the rooms on the other side to penetrate this windowless, inside area.

you have a kitchen on one side of a passageway and a living/dining room on the other side, a low table or a small chest by the living/dining room door could be very useful for resting a tray of plates or a hot dish while you open the door.

In a long passageway, a resting point outside a bedroom door may also be handy for putting things on while distributing clean linen, light bulbs, books, or other items along the way.

A chest of drawers can also be a worthwhile addition in a corridor or passageway linking bedrooms. The linen for the various rooms can be stored here. After laundering, all the sheets can be returned to the same central container. As a general rule, all the furniture in passageways should be light, narrow, and well-spaced so that the corridor is not an obstacle course.

The end point

The third zone is the end of the corridor or passageway—this should be made a focal point, rather than dismissed as a dark or dreary place. If you come in through the main door and look down the corridor, the eye should be greeted by an appealing sight.

This area should be well-lit so it is easy to see and the length of distance can be assessed.

Top: Folding doors that slide back on themselves are useful to divide areas where space is limited.

Above: A curving wall makes an interesting architectural feature in this connecting area.

Knowing where the corridor or passageway ends gives a psychologically comforting idea of where you are, and what lies between you and the end wall.

Landings

If the hall or passageway passes through a landing area, around a corner, or past a bay window, there may be additional space or width at this point. In this case, the area may be used to create a cameo setting. This can be a simple easy chair and occasional table with books and magazines, or a large piece of sculpture. If the area is big enough to accommodate a good-size table, wall mounted bookcases, and a chair, it could also be used as a study or casual working space.

Staircases

Staircases often lead to and from hallways, and connect one level to another. Stairs need to be well-lit and should have a handrail or structure that encloses the steps, providing a safe support should anyone accidentally trip or slip. In some homes, a skylight or a few windows on an upper level may provide natural light for the stairs.

By setting light wells and skylight windows into the roof, you can provide an invaluable source of daylight. The window need not open—it can be a rigid panel, and if it is not overlooked, does not need to be screened. In a period home, these roof lights were known as lanterns, and were often interesting shapes, such as ovals divided into triangular segments, like an orange. This type of skylight created a feature in an otherwise bland area.

The sides of the staircase can be filled in with tempered glass panels, with fine balusters of metal or wood, or traditional turned rails to let light circulate.

Carpets, runners, and floor coverings used on stairs must be

Above: An oblong window has been set into the top of a long wall that covers two levels of stairs. The window is a feature on the otherwise blank wall, and it gives a vista out onto the upper level.

Right: A wall-mounted table forms a decorative feature in this landing.

Left: Shield-like lights and stenciled, gilded wallpaper add interest to a long hallway.

will have to rely on decorating tricks and techniques to make the place seem light and airy.

A traditional, but practical form of decoration in hallways and stairwells is the use of the chair rail. This is a narrow, raised wooden strip or molding, often with a rounded or simple decorative finish. Below the chair rail the wall can be papered with a thick, protective finish and painted in a dark, even gloss enamel paint that will withstand inadvertent kicks and scuffs. The upper level can be painted in a light, bright color, giving the upper part of the hallway a lift and a feeling of spaciousness.

This type of scheme can be given an unusual oriental twist by painting the lower level of the wall in black and the upper levels and baseboard in red. This chinoiserie style reflects the lacquerware favored in China, and can be lit with ceiling-recessed downlighters for a dramatic effect. In addition, any gilt- or silver-framed pictures or mirrors put on the walls will stand out and sparkle against the background.

The print room, another technique that can be used to

firmly held in place. Stair rods can be used to keep the runners quite secure.

A bookcase could also be tailor-made to fit under a staircase. This is another awkward space that needs to be used carefully. Another choice, depending on the size, is to close it in to provide a separate toilet or cloakroom, or even a general store for vacuum

cleaners and cleaning products. Otherwise, it can be left open and shelved or dressed with a table and chair, or filled with a good-size wine rack.

Decoration and style

As corridors tend to be in the inner part of a home, they are often windowless and dark, so you

framed with borders to look as though they were actual paintings. This technique can easily be adapted, and photocopies or black-and-white photographs could be used in a similar way.

A mirror is also an attractive feature at the end of a passageway, but avoid a single, full-length mirror, as it can be unnerving to watch yourself advancing. An oval mirror, or a collection of different shapes and sizes of mirror can be arranged in an unusual and interesting way.

Linking spaces

Because a corridor is a link between rooms, keep its decoration simple. A fussy, ornate, or floral paper may make the space seem smaller, and may also be overpowering. However, plain walls need not be dull—they can be easily decorated with pictures and mirrors, or real or imitation wood paneling.

Long passageways or connecting areas are a great place to hang a coordinating series of pictures, prints, or paintings. A set of black-and-white photographs, a series of prints or characters, or even a collection of plates or framed scarves can create interest, as well as forming a link from one end of the space to the other. Even if the pictures aren't from

Above: The interior wall that once formed a corridor between the kitchen and the adjacent room has been knocked down to hip height, creating an open passageway.

Opposite: Safety is an important factor on stairways. Here fine, high-tension steel cables take the place of traditional rows of balusters, providing a secure barrier.

decorate the hallway, is an 18th-century device that can be given a modern twist. To create a traditional print room, the walls of a small room or vestibule were painted in a mid-tone to strong color, and black-and-white prints of scenic views, portraits, or landmarks were pasted over the dry paint. The prints were then

Above: Lighting is extremely important within a hallway. Here, low lighting that is situated just above the baseboards illuminates the passageway.

the same series, they can be linked by subject matter, for example flowers and butterflies.

Another way of linking a space is by using a frieze, or by painting the baseboard in a bright or dominant color so that your eye follows it around a corner or up to another level. A carpet, runner, or floor covering of the same color and pattern will also help to give an area unity, but in long passageways this can exaggerate the length and make it feel longer. In cases like this, it is best to have a series of mats or rugs that create pools of interest.

Right: Open tread stairs allow light to pass from one floor to another and also appear less solid and bulky than enclosed treads.

Connecting areas
storage

Connecting areas, such as hallways and passageways, are usually busy places where much of the day-to-day activity of a household will take place. As such, storage here must be space-efficient and flexible to the needs and requirements of all the family.

Storing coats and shoes

You will need a variety of different storage options in your connecting areas. A coat rack is a common feature here. The traditional way to cope with this is to put a strong wooden strip on the wall and fasten a row of hooks to it. This serves the purpose, but is not very inspiring or attractive. To liven it up, the wood could be painted and the hooks made of brass. For a more modern design, the backing could be steel or plastic and the hooks an unusual material, such as wood or chrome. The levels of hanging could also be varied, so that short items can be hung halfway down the wall, and longer ones above.

Two-level hanging arrangements are good for families, so that the children's clothes can be kept at a height they can reach, while the adult clothes are at an upper level. This configuration also gives

Storing books

Hallways and landings are ideal places for storing books, as they require only a narrow shelf, which can be tailored to fit into confined or difficult spaces. Even larger books can be accommodated—if they are too tall for the shelf, they can be laid down on their side or stacked horizontally.

Left: For hall storage, a narrow enclosure with a decorated opaque-glass panel provides perfect conceal-ment for coats and hats.

Above: Mirrored insets in these cupboard doors reflect the light, making the room appear more spacious.

Installing a radiator screen

The easiest way to make a screen is to use a box made out of MDF, chipboard, or wood to fit around your radiator and fasten to the wall—you could employ a carpenter to make this for you. Once the frame is in place, you can fill the front panel to hide the main expanse of the radiator with a number of different materials. Expandable, wooden garden trellis or metal grilles are both choices.

you double the hanging capacity in the same space. The most effective arrangement is to stagger the hooks by placing the lower hooks halfway between the upper hooks. This also stops the garments from hanging directly over one another.

Smaller items, such as gloves, hats, and scarves, are better kept in a drawer or on a shelf so that they don't become entangled in larger pieces of clothing. For hats and bicycle or motorbike helmets, a shelf above the coat hooks is a practical solution. Umbrellas are best in a stand—an old chimney pot or a tall, cylindrical container is ideal.

Shoes and boots are more difficult to accommodate. They should be stacked in pairs and contained in a low, box-style construction, subdivided into compartments. Each pair of shoes can fit into its own niche, but boots may have to be rolled or folded. If the box is on the floor, fastened to the wall, the top may be softened with long cushions and used as a seat.

A straight-backed chair or stool is another alternative. Any seat in this area should be functional—it only needs to be comfortable enough as a temporary rest. If you have a porch or bay window, you may also consider building in a window seat that is hinged so that

the base could be used as a storage place for shoes.

An alternative is a low, two-shelf system along which shoes can be arranged in lines. This can be made with planks of wood or rods. The rods at the back can be slightly raised so that the heels of the shoes rest over them.

Shelves

A table or shelf will also be practical and provide a place to put mail. The table should be of a narrow, console style that lies flat against the wall. Hall tables often become a focus for clutter, junk mail, and debris, so you need to be disciplined and keep them tidy.

A shelf can be small, neat, and fastened directly to the wall above a radiator in a hallway. The shelf may help to guard people from direct contact with the heat of the radiator, and it will help stop small objects from falling down behind it.

Keys are another item you will need in this area, where you keep the car keys, as well as those for the house and office. A small, wall-mounted key rack can keep everything in place and to hand.

A key rack can be simple—cork backing with rows of small cup hooks—or more elaborate, such as a little cupboard with a door that closes to hide the keys.

Leaf and vine design

Inspired by the flowing shapes of plaster and wrought ironwork used throughout history, this design is perfect for adding interest to a dull hallway. We have used traditional stenciling techniques to repeat the motif, but both the size of the pattern and the muted colorway give a contemporary feel. Using subtle shading, and highlighting techniques to mimic the way that light falls, gives a three-dimensional illusion. The pattern is cut out of two large pieces of stencil card, and designed so that the pattern repeats itself when the card is repositioned.

Materials

Painter's tape
Base color—green latex (acrylic)
Large sheets of stencil card
Darker green latex (acrylic) for the vine
White latex (acrylic)
Gray/green latex (acrylic)
Flat acrylic varnish

Tools

Roller and tray
Thumbtacks
String
Pencil
Scalpel
Stencil brushes
Artist's brushes
French curves

Preparing the surface

1 Mask off the area above the effect, then apply the base coat. Allow this to dry. Lay two sheets of stencil card on a flat surface, and use a thumbtack and string to make a compass placed between the two sheets.

2 Draw the first circle with a diameter half the width of the card. Reposition the thumbtack

Using a thumbtack and a piece of string, make a compass positioned between the card sheets.

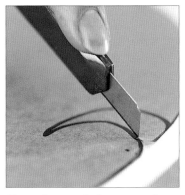

Use a sharp scalpel to cut out the design, making sure there are bridges where necessary.

and draw two more circles either side of the first, just touching it.

Making your design

3 Join up the circles with a pencil to form an undulating pattern, which will form the stem of the vine. Use French curves to follow the pattern, giving the vine its width.

4 Use curve templates to form the curling ends of the vine, and to add in random leaf shapes.

5 Use a scalpel to cut out the design, making sure that you leave bridges where necessary (see picture bottom right, page 407).

Applying color

6 With painter's tape, position the stencil on the wall, and apply the vine color with a dry stencil brush, using a stippling action. Position the second sheet of stencil card so that it joins up with the first pattern and stencil. Repeat this process until the whole wall is stenciled.

7 In order to paint the shadow, decide which direction the light is coming from, and use a small artist's brush to apply a thin, dark gray/green line along the areas of the vine that would naturally be in shadow.

8 To add the highlights, use a small artist's brush to apply an off-white shade along the areas of the vine where the light would fall. If you have a natural light source in your room, such as a window, work with it rather than against it. This will mean that the painted highlights and shadows on the stenciled vine will fall in the same way as they would naturally when the light falls on real three-dimensional objects.

9 When the surface is dry, varnish it with several coats of flat acrylic varnish.

Apply the vine color carefully with a small dry stencil brush, using a stippling action.

Montage of photographs

Materials

Sufficient paper images to
cover your chosen area
White glue or artist's
fixative spray
Wallpaper paste
Acrylic varnish

Tools

Guillotine or utility knife
Metal rule
Paintbrush
Set square
Pencil
Adhesive brush
Bucket for mixing
Soft cloth

Rather than leave treasured photographs languishing in a drawer or photo album, why not use them to transform a wall? We used a computer, scanner, and printer to enlarge and tint our black-and-white coastal images. If you do not have access to a computer, many photo labs can produce poster-size prints from original negatives or you could enlarge images on a photocopier. The paper images can be applied directly to a wall using wallpaper adhesive, or you can stick them to primed masonite.

Cutting the images

1 Use the guillotine or utility knife and metal rule to carefully cut out the images. Make sure that all the photographs are square and that all are an identical size.

Setting the ink

2 To set the ink, test an area of the image by brushing with white glue diluted with water (one part glue to two parts water). If the ink starts to run use artist's fixative spray instead.

Use a guillotine to cut the images so that they are all square and the same size.

Brush the images with a little white glue to set the ink or use an artist's fixative spray.

Know your materials

Artist's fixative spray is used to fix artist's chalky pastel and charcoal drawings. However, it also works well on computer printouts and photocopies that could run if stuck with paste. The spray is available from art and craft stores, and should be applied evenly in a well-ventilated room. To avoid breathing fumes, wear a mask. If you prefer, you could use a two parts to one part solution of water and white glue.

3 Using a set square and pencil, divide up the wall into square sections of around 10sq ft (1m sq)—the precise size will vary according to the dimensions of your images. Dividing the wall will allow you to work on one section at a time.

Fixing the images to the wall

4 Take the required number of images to fill one square on your wall, making sure that the images are varied in terms of color, subject, and tone. Apply paste to the back of the images using standard wallpaper paste and a soft adhesive brush. Allow to soak for at least five minutes (this allows the paste to be absorbed into the fibers of the paper, which will then swell) before applying the photographs to the wall, using the pencil lines as a guide.

With a set square and pencil, mark out the area on the wall where the images will be fixed.

Using an adhesive brush, paste the back of the images with standard wallpaper paste.

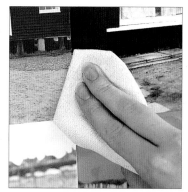

To remove any wrinkles or air bubbles, rub the images gently with a soft cloth.

5 Smooth any wrinkles or bubbles of paste by gently rubbing the image with a soft cloth, making sure that you work out from the center of the image. Allow the montage to dry thoroughly overnight. If any of the edges have lifted during this time, you can simply apply some extra paste with a small brush and then smooth over the surface once again, this time using a steam roller or cloth.

6 Once the image is finished, protect the images by varnishing them with a matte or satin acrylic spray adhesive (to avoid brushmarks). Alternatively, you can apply a conventional varnish to them using a clean, good-quality paintbrush.

Once finished, use a matte or satin acrylic spray adhesive to protect the images.

Alternative

If you do not want to stick images direct onto your wall, it is still possible to create a striking graphic display by mounting and framing your photographs. This works most successfully if all the images are black and white and of a similar size. Simple black lacquer frames make a strong statement without detracting from the images themselves. Special non-reflective acrylic sheet can be used in rooms with strong natural light, as this stops glare on the images, and it is a safer choice than glass, particularly in the bathroom, although it is more prone to being scratched.

Arrange the images on the floor to decide on their positioning. To align the frames perfectly, use a tape measure and level, and lightly mark the position of the nails on the wall in pencil . Make sure you use the correct picture nails and hooks for the type of wall you are hanging on (different varieties are available for solid and stud walls). Check that the hanging wire is at the same point on each frame.

Floor storage unit with slots

This unit is ideal for keeping a busy household in order. Give each member of the family a number, or swap the numbers for initials. It is ideal in the hallway, providing ample storage for shoes and bags. The construction is fairly simple but requires accurate cutting with a jigsaw. We used a method called reverse stenciling for the numbers, and then varnished the whole unit.

Materials

Three 1 ft 4in (40cm) lengths of ¾in (18mm) MDF
Screws
Wood filler
Quick-drying primer
Coffee and cream latex (acrylic) paint
Spray adhesive
Satin acrylic varnish

Tools

Pencil
Jigsaw
Abrasive paper
Sanding block
Electric drill
Countersink bit
Scissors
Stencil brush
Paintbrush

Making a template

1 Make a paper template of the curved upright part of the unit. The height and the depth should be about 1 x 1ft (30 x 30cm). Use the template as a guide to draw around. You should be able to fit five upright pieces on one length of MDF.

2 Cut the design out carefully with a jigsaw, then sand all the rough edges with abrasive paper on a sanding block.

3 Using a pencil, mark the position of a slot running from the back to the middle of the three dividing uprights, 1in

Make a template of the curved, upright part of the unit, and use it as a guide to draw around.

Cut the shapes out carefully with a jigsaw. Remember to wear a mask when doing this.

Know your tools

For this project we used a flexible sanding block. Because of its spongy texture, it can be pushed into awkward corners and crevices. If you have a large area to sand, you could use an electric sander, which does the job quickly and efficiently. For a really professional finish you should always complete the sanding by hand, with fine-grit abrasive paper.

For a super-smooth paint finish, sand lightly between coats with silicon carbide paper. This will leave your paintwork completely free from brush or roller marks, and will also get rid of any accidental runs or drips.

(2.5cm) up from the bottom. Use the MDF base as a width guide for the slot. Mark a corresponding slot on the MDF base, running from the front of the base to the middle.

4 Cut out all the slots, and then sand all the rough edges with a sanding block.

Assembling the unit

5 Slot the uprights and the base together. They should fit snugly without moving.

6 Hold the back of the unit in place and mark the position of the uprights with a pencil line. Drill, countersink, and then screw each upright firmly in place. Fasten the side uprights in place in the same way. Fill all the screw holes with some wood filler, then sand the entire unit using a flexible sanding block.

Priming the unit

7 Prime the entire unit with a quick-drying primer (see the picture bottom left, page 418), then sand lightly with a piece of coarse-grit abrasive paper.

Adding the numbering

8 Paint the back of each slot with some cream latex

Using a pencil, mark out carefully the position of the slots to be cut out with a jigsaw.

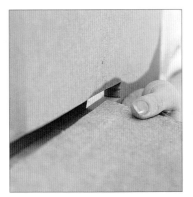

Slot the upright parts into the base, and make sure that they fit snugly without moving.

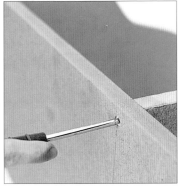

Screw each upright firmly in position, and then fill all the screw holes with wood filler.

(acrylic) paint, and then make sure you allow this to dry for the recommended time.

9 Use a computer and printer, or a photocopier to enlarge the figures 1 to 4. Use scissors to cut them out to form a mask, then use a little spray adhesive to attach the numbers to the back of each of the slots.

10 Use coffee-color latex (acrylic) and a stencil brush for the edge of each number, then finish with a larger brush.

11 Before the paint has dried, peel off each number to expose the base color. Varnish the numbers with two coats of satin acrylic varnish.

Using a large paintbrush, paint the whole unit with quick-drying primer before sanding lightly.

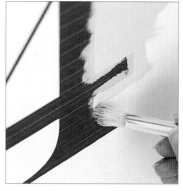

Use coffee-color latex (acrylic) paint and a stencil brush to carefully cover the edge of each number.

Before the paint has dried, peel off the numbers to expose the base color underneath.

Alternative

If you prefer minimal, uncluttered storage, consider turning an alcove into a fitted storage unit. This streamlined unit incorporates shallow shelves for storing shoes. Below is a deep shelf that doubles as a place to sit, beneath which is a deep cupboard for larger items.

The simplest way to create this type of storage is to customize kitchen or other built-in cupboards. If you prefer to start from scratch, plan your design on paper, measuring the height and depth of the items you wish to store. Fasten brackets or wood strips on the wall to hold the shelves, and fasten them in place, adding a larger shelf to form the seat. Attach vertical strips along each side wall in front of the shelves for the doors. Use kitchen cabinet-style concealed hinges to fit the doors level with the wall. Mark the positions of the hinges, and use a special cutting attachment on an electric drill to cut the holes for them. Make the doors from sheets of furniture board or MDF.

Lighting connecting
areas

Connecting areas and hallways are best lit by wall or ceiling lights, which will reduce the amount of restrictions at floor level. Uplighters reflecting off a white ceiling will also double the impact of the light source. Decorative shades can be used to add interest and decoration.

Using wall lights as a decorative feature

Wall lights can be used decoratively by creating a frame to surround the light so that it looks like a picture. Taking the light fixture as the center point, create a frame around it using molding or flat-backed beveled wood, and paint the frame in a stronger shade of the wall color, a contrasting tone, or a metallic finish, such as bronze. Inside the frame put a mount or a panel of another color, or if the rest of the wall is plain, a piece of decorative wallpaper. This will build up an eye-catching surround to the light, and make it more than just a source of illumination.

Above right: A band of decorative mirrors, close to the top of the walls, reflects the light given out by the ceiling fixture, and amplifies it several times over.

When entertaining or holding a party, the vestibule or initial section of the hall is the first part of your home that guests and visitors see and experience, so it should have a warm and welcoming appearance. To achieve this, the lighting should be adequate, but not overbright.

Ambient lighting

In the evenings, guests arriving for a dinner party could be greeted by a low, ambient light augmented by a large church candle or an arrangement of candles. However, candles should always be placed in safe, sturdy containers. At night you can place candles in front of mirrors, so that the flames are reflected and create twice the impact.

Faux skylights

Lighting is important in a corridor because there is seldom much, if any, daylight. In a modern home, you can use large panel lights on the ceiling that look like skylights.

When the light or lights are turned on they will provide a bright but diffuse light, which will illuminate an ample area beneath and create the impression of a window above. The light could be put on a dimmer so that during daylight hours the strength of light is equivalent to natural light outside, but dimmed to a subtle glow in the evening.

Wall lights

Wall lights are another possibility for lighting linking areas. In a long corridor you will need a combination of wall lights to create an ambient atmosphere, and ceiling lights or lamps to be sure that the floor and lower levels of the passageway are lit.

There are also torch-like wall lights that resemble a handheld flare, and simple, semicircular plaster bowls that can be painted to blend in with the main wall color in the hallway.

In a rustic setting, curved, terra-cotta roof tiles, like those seen on Italian villas, can be hung on the wall with the underside facing forward. In this curved area a small dish or candle holder can be attached and a taper, tealight, or pillar candle set and lit. Alternatively, the tiles could be drilled and wired to take a small incandescent bulb. There are also candle-style bulbs that have a built-in flicker and are hard to distinguish from the real thing.

Recessed lighting

Another possibility for decorative lighting, which can be used in an older home, is to put a long, narrow tubular bulb behind the cove or in a picture-rail recess to direct light upwards.

Spotlights

A line of recessed spotlights is an effective way of lighting a corridor. They can also be set on dimmer

switches so that the level of light can be varied.

You may like to put them on separate circuits so that a pool of light can be directed onto an object or arrangement at the end of the hall, while the front and middle parts are in darkness or more subdued illumination. However, make sure the beam of a spotlight does not shine directly into the face of a visitor.

Picture lights

Picture lights add to the overall level of ambient light in a corridor, as well as highlighting the pictures on the wall. The effect can be of a miniature gallery.

Top: Recessed ceiling lights supplement the natural light source from the windows in the dining area.

Above: Spotlights are recessed into the floor along this passageway.

Acknowledgments

To AWJ – absolutely essential

Many, many thanks to the owners and designers of the properties featured in this book, and to the following who helped with our additional styling and location hunting: Jane Taylor and Corrine Day at Heals; Jo Leyland at Purves and Purves; Di and Eva at Sheila Fitzjones; Sam and Kate at Parker Hobart; Melissa at Halpern; LK Bennett, Kings Road, London SW3; Karen and Jennifer at Damask; and Liberty Parker at Habitat. And extra special thanks for Jean Johnston's invaluable help in cross-checking pictures, for Ray's polishing abilities in the kitchen and for Charlie's cheerfulness and clothes folding – what a team!

LOCATION CREDITS (Key: R = Right, L = Left, B = Below, T = Top, D = Detail, M = Middle)

Tara Bernerd (interior design/development) 2 Bentick Street, London W1U 2JX, 020 7009 0101 **and John Hitchcox** (architectural design/development) Yoo The Banking Hall, 20–28 Maida Vale, London W9, 020 7266 2244: pp7, 106 (B), 107, 125, 296 (B)

Bulthaup Kitchens 1 North Terrace, Alexander Square, London SW3B, 020 7317 6000 and 37 Wigmore Street, London W1, 020 7495 3663 (architectural design by John Pawson): pp2–3, 208–9, 214, 219 (T), 231 (B)

Chesneys 194–101 Battersea Park Road, London SW11 4ND, 020 7627 1410, www.antiquefireplace.co.uk: pp86 (L), 87 (BR), 90–1, 93

Damask Broxholme House, New Kings Road, London SW6 4AA, 020 7731 3553, www.damask.

co.uk: pp140 (L), 142 (TL), 150 (T), 167 (TR), 263 (R)

Diligence Providence House, High Street, Stockbridge, Hampshire SO20 6HP, 01264 811 660: fireplaces on pp86 (T) and 110

Lisa Dodds (artist's own home): pp15, 110, 130, 131, 135 (T), 244 (B), 269 (T), 277, 285, 293 (L), 310 (L)

Stephen Featherstone architectural designer and design director of Llewelyn-Davies Architects 020 7612 9435: pp67, 77 (T), 100–1, 121, 131 (D), 172–3, 290–1, 294 (T), 310 (R)

Christopher Healey Furniture 27–29 Union Street, London SE1 1SD, 020 7639 4645, also available through Concord Designs, 01524 412 374, www.concorddesigns.co.uk: pp14 (T), 117, 143 (T), 195, 212 (B), 216 (B), 243 (B), 280

Karen Howes at TMH Designs Ltd 208 The Chambers, Chelsea Harbour, London SW10 0XF, 020 7349 9017, tmh@dircon.co.uk: pp20 (T), 61 (T), 76, 80 (T), 86 (R),

109 (D), 122 (T), 132–3, 150 (B), 159, 167 (T), 175, 196, 211, 219 (L), 231 (T), 247 (T&B), 292 (B), 296 (T)

Interior Design House The Coach House, 8 Avenue Crescent, London W3 8EW, 020 8752 8648 (interior designer Fleur Rossdale and architect Peter Wadley, 020 8752 8642, wadley@dircon.co.uk): pp26, 108 (B), 111, 166 (B), 215 (T), 261 (B), 266–7, 270 (T), 297 (L)

Hunter Johnston (architect) 020 7976 5000: pp11 (T), 60, 95 (T), 109 (main picture), 130 (T), 213 (T), 287 (T), 292 (R)

Ivan and Shelia Levy 277 Kings Road, London SW3, 020 7376 7767: pp12, 75, 87 (T), 89, 94, 99, 104 (R), 105, 123, 130 (B), 131, 164 (T&L), 165, 166 (T) ,167 (B), 176 (R), 269 (B), 293 (L), 298

California Closets (storage specialists) Unit 8, Staples Corner Business Park, 1000 North Circular Road, London, 020 8208 4544, www.calcloset.com: pp164 (T), 165, 166 (T), 298

Gordana Mandic at buildburo Unit 4 Iliffe Yard, Crampton Street, London SE16 3QA, 020 7708 3911, www.buildburo.co.uk: pp10 (B), 27, 176–7, 199, 216 (T), 219 (R), 225, 268, 279 (B&L), 309, 311 (R)

John Minshaw Designs Ltd (interior designer) 119 George Street, London W1H 5TB, 020 7258 0627: pp73, 77 (B), 79 (B), 97 (L), 144 (B) 146 (R), 168 (R), 174 (L), 198, 205 (B), 210 (T), 212 (T), 247 (L), 260 (R), 263 (L), 279 (R), 293 (R), 299

Claire Nelson at Nelson Designs (interior designer) 169 St John's Hill, London SW11 1TQ, 020 7924 4542: pp169 (L), 174 (R), 210 (B), 215 (T&R), 242, 245, 262 (B), 271

Original Bathrooms 143–145 Kew Road, Richmond, Surrey, 020 8940 7554: pp54, 240 (T), 243 (TL), 246 (T), 260 (T), 262 (T&M), 264 (all pictures)

Gregory Phillips Architects 66 Great Cumberland Place, London W1H 7FD, 020 7724 3040: pp20, 21, 37, 76, 88, 102 (main picture), 122 (B),134 (B), 138–9, 141, 169 (R), 213 (B), 240 (B), 241, 260 (L), 297 (R), 311 (L)

Camilla Ridley (fashion designer) 339 Fulham Road, London SW10 9TW, 020 7351 7259, www.camillaridley.com: pp17 (BR), 148 (T), 168 (T&B)

Stephen Ryan (design and decoration) 7 Clarendon Cross, Holland Park, London W11 4AP, 020 7243 0864: pp8–9, 78, 95 (B), 104 (L), 142 (R), 145, 149 (B), 179, 198 (T), 203, 204 (R), 259, 294 (L), 295

Andrea Sedgwick at Interiors Bis 60 Sloane Avenue, London SW3, 020 7838 1104: pp14 (B), 85, 108 (T), 140 (D), 143 (B), 164 (B&R), 251, 261 (T), 273, 281, 294 (R)

Victoria Stapleton at Brora 344 Kings Road, London SW3, 020 7352 3697, www.brora.uk: pp46, 55, 103 (T), 146 (L), 148, 151 (R), 176 (L), 192, 305

Emily Todhunter at Todhunter Earle Chelsea Reach, 79 Lots Road, London SW10, 020 7349 9999: pp79 (R), 106 (T), 133 (B), 134 (T), 140 (R), 147, 150 (T), 163, 193, 204 (L), 215 (B)

Sasha Waddell (Swedish furniture shop and interior design service) 269 Wandworth Bridge Road, London SW6 7LT, 020 7736 0766: pp102 (D), 103 (B), 125 (B), 149 (T), 178 (R), 197, 217, 244 (T), 272

Helen Wilson at FK&F (kitchen specialists) 19 Carnwath Road, London SW6 3HR, 020 7736 6458: pp6, 16 (BR), 35–6, 135 (B), 144 (T), 194, 230, 246 (B), 270 (B)

Worlds End Tiles Railways Gds, Silverthorne Road, London SW8, 020 7819 2100: pp54 (T), 55, 193 (B), 243 (T&R)

ACCESSORIES AND PROPS

The following companies kindly lent products for photography.

Aero 347 Kings Road, London SW3, 020 7351 0511

Alessi showroom 22 Brook Street, London W1K 5DF, 020 74912428

The Chair Company 82 Parsons Green Lane, London SW6, 020 7736 5478, www.thechair.co.uk

Channels 3 Kings Road, London SW6 4SB, 020 7371 0301

Cucina Direct 0870 727 4300 for catalogue or order via www.cucinadirect.co.uk

Habitat 196 Tottenham Court Road and various branches, 0845 601 0740, www.habitat.net

Heals 234 Kings Road, London SW3, 020 7349 8411 and 196 Tottenham Court Road, London W1, 020 7636 1666, www.heals.co.uk

Ligne Roset 23–25 Mortimer Street, London W1T 3JE, 020 7323 1248, www.lrwestend.co.uk

Parma Lilac 020 8960 9239

The Pier 200 Tottenham Court Road, London W1P 0AD, 020 7814 5042, mail order 020 7814 5020, www.pier.co.uk

Purves & Purves 80–83 Tottenham Court Road, London W1, 020 7580 8223, www.purves.co.uk

Russell Hobbs 0161 947 3170

Index

First published in 2004 by Bay Books®, an imprint of Murdoch Magazines Pty Ltd
Copyright © 2004 Murdoch Books®

ISBN 1 74045 280 1

Commissioning Editor: **Natasha Martyn-Johns**
Editor: **Claire Musters**
Managing Editor: **Anna Osborn**
Design Manager: **Helen Taylor**
Photo Librarian: **Bobbie Leah**
Photography: **Ray Main and Graeme Ainscough**
Stylist: **Charlotte Cave**
Photographic Assistant: **Sophie Munro**
Design concept: **Tracy Loughlin**

Material in this book was originally published in *The Essential Guide to Decorating*

Murdoch Books® is a trademark of Murdoch Magazines Pty Ltd

Colour separation by Colourscan, Singapore
Printed by Sing Cheong Printing Co. Ltd.
PRINTED IN HONG KONG